FUNDAMENTALS OF COST AND MANAGEMENT ACCOUNTING

IAN MEARNS ACMA

Pitman

Pitman Publishing
128 Long Acre, London WC2E 9AN

A Division of Longman Group UK Limited

© Longman Group UK Limited 1981

First published in Great Britain 1981
Reprinted 1983, 1984, 1985, 1987, 1988, 1990, 1991

ISBN 0 273 02751 4

Produced by Longman Group (FE) Ltd
Printed in Hong Kong

Contents

Editor's preface

The nature of accountancy education and the content of accountancy examinations has been gradually changing during the last decade. The traditional emphasis was on accounting techniques and procedures. This has now widened and the accountancy student is expected to know some thing about accounting theory, quantitative methods, electronic data processing and the behavioural sciences. Moreover, examination questions are becoming increasingly concerned with concepts rather than techniques. Previously a student could pass accounting examinations by just fast 'number crunching'. But modern examinations require students to analyse, interpret and even critically appraise the results of their calculations. Thus students not only need to learn techniques by rote they also have to understand them.

The majority of accountancy text books provide fairly good instruction for learning accounting techniques by rote, but are not sufficiently thorough in their subject treatment to give the student the necessary understanding. This is because, generally just a single chapter is given for a vast subject area. Accordingly many accounting text books are inadequate for accountancy students' needs. The purpose of the Professional Education Series is to provide text books covering specific subject areas in sufficient depth and breadth to meet accountancy students' needs. The current series contains five books:—

Accountancy control systems that examines in great detail the principles, practice and problems of planning and control systems with a special emphasis on the behavioural implications of accountancy controls.

Decision making that integrates accounting and mathematical decision making techniques from basic through to very advanced levels.

Accounting standards that provides all the detail necessary for professional accountants plus explanations of the background to each accounting standard and the problems of implementation.

Inflation accounting that provides an authorative reference source and clear descriptions of the principles, techniques and problems of this controversial subject.

Every book in the series is written to help students pass their examinations and each chapter is followed up with examination practice questions. Detailed answers for all the questions are provided in the model answers section of each book.

About this book

The author has made a detailed study of the examination requirements of the accountancy bodies during the past five years to determine the appropriate content for this book. The book is intended to help the student who has to sit introductory or intermediate level accountancy examinations that will contain questions on basic costing and management accounting. The book clearly explains the detail of basic costing for materials, labour and overheads, paying special attention to subject areas that frequently appear in examination questions. After this detailed introduction to costing principles and techniques the mysteries of cost accounts and double entry are explained. The remaining chapters deal with the principles and techniques of different costing methods including marginal and absorption costing, standard costing and budgetary control. All of these topics are given detailed coverage with relevant past examination questions included at the end of each chapter. Model answers for the practice examination questions are given at the end of the book.

Acknowledgements

Acknowledgements are due to the professional accountancy bodies for their kind permission to reproduce past examination questions and also for the use of 'Terminology of Management and Financial Accounting' published by the Institute of Cost and Management Accountants. The relevant acknowledgement is made for each examination practice question where appropriate.

February 1981   PAUL NORKETT

1
General principles of cost accounting

Definition of Cost Accounting

The Terminology of Management and Financial Accountancy published by the Institute of Cost and Management Accountants defines Cost Accounting as:

> 'The application of accounting and costing principles, methods and techniques in the ascertainment of costs and the analysis of savings and/or excesses as compared with previous experience or with standards.'

The key phrase in this definition is 'the ascertainment of costs',for comparisons cannot be made and savings and excesses cannot be analysed until costs have first been ascertained. To determine the costs, it is necessary to apply certain principles, methods and techniques.

Finding out the costs, then, is the central activity in cost accounting and this is emphasised by the definition given to the term Costing in the Terminology of Management and Financial Accountancy. It is defined simply as 'the ascertainment of costs'.

Purpose of Cost Accounting

The purpose of cost accounting is to provide executives and managers with information to assist them to manage effectively.

Why does a manager need information? How does it assist him in the performance of his duties? In order to give an answer, it is necessary to consider briefly the nature of a manager's job.

Although the nature of his job depends on his functional responsibility and on the level in the management hierarchy at which he operates, it is possible to generalise about certain aspects of the manager's work. There are three activities carried out by managers at all levels, namely, Planning, Decision-making and Control, and although they are not the only constituents of a manager's job, they represent three of the most important.

Planning. Planning is a necessary ingredient of a manager's job, but before he can create any plans, the manager must have clearly defined objectives. He must be aware of the results he is expected to achieve. Put simply, he cannot plan how to get somewhere unless he first knows where he is supposed to be going. Once objectives have been specified, plans can be drawn up to ensure that the desired objectives are accomplished.

The objectives, or goals, of an individual manager will derive their existence from the primary objectives of the company. These corporate objectives will embrace both long-term and short-term aims. They should,wherever possible, be expressed in financial terms so that, at some future date, it is possible to measure actual performance against predetermined objectives.

One of the primary objectives, possibly the top short-term objective, will consist of a profit target for the ensuing year. To meet the profit objective it is essential to plan. All the skill and endeavour of the company's employees will be in vain if they are not directed systematically towards the desired ends. One cannot just hope that the required profit will be forthcoming; a plan must be conceived and put into operation to ensure that it is achieved.

For example, a marketing plan must be devised so that the profit objective can be translated into a sales budget. It is at this moment that cost information can be provided. It should be possible to ascertain the cost of producing individual products, and the size of the profit margin made by each. Consequently, the marketing plan can include the combination of products which will most likely generate the required profit. Furthermore, by identifying the cost of individual products, one is able to see the effect on profit of changes in the volume of sales and in the type of product sold. An increase in the sales of one product would make a higher contribution to profit than a rise in the sales of another.

It is essential that these facts are made available at the planning stage so that the business can concentrate on those products with the highest profit potential and devote less attention to those with low profit margins. A comparison of previous plans with actual results would indicate whether current proposals are realistic.

In addition, estimates of future cost levels can be supplied to assist the marketing function to determine selling prices. Cost estimates can also be used as a basis for negotiating future contracts.

But planning does not stop here. The marketing executive will need to analyse the sales budget by geographical area, by salesman and by major customer. This analysis will be phased by weeks or months over the financial year. Actual performance will be monitored and if the original plan is not being achieved, some revision will be necessary. Distribution costs may be higher than predicted; an experienced salesman might resign; a new product may be selling more slowly than expected. If these setbacks are reflected in lower profits the marketing executive will have to amend his original plan. As actual achievement is rarely identical with initial intentions, planning becomes therefore a continuous process. The area sales managers who report to the marketing executive will also be involved in this constant process of planning.

The marketing function has been chosen in order to illustrate the part that planning plays in a manager's job. But planning is also an integral part of the jobs of other functional executives and cost information is required to enable them to fulfil their responsibilities adequately.

Decision-making. The time when a sudden whim of the boss gave rise to important decisions should now be a thing of the past. The size and complexity of modern business demands that the decisions of today's professional manager are based on facts and it is essential, therefore, that he is supplied with adequate information. The result of making the wrong decision can be extremely costly especially in times of intense competition. Cost information, properly presented, will significantly reduce errors in decision-making.

Decisions involve choice, selecting the best course of action from a number of alternatives. The manager therefore must assess the advantages and disadvantages of adopting a particular course of action. Each alternative should be evaluated in financial terms. What are the consequences of selecting each available option? What is the effect on costs and profit of making a certain decision? There is a danger that a manager will be influenced by his emotions when making a choice, that he will unwittingly engage in a degree of self-deception. Some managers are excessively optimistic about the outcome of a decision they propose to make. Unless they are in possession of facts their decisions will be purely subjective.

Cost information will also help to reduce the uncertainty surrounding many business decisions so that it should be possible to make informed predictions about the outcome of each alternative examined.

Management is faced with a number of varied decisions. Should the company continue to perform a certain operation or would it be less costly to sub-contract it? This is often referred to as a 'make or buy' decision.

Is it better to buy machine A or machine B? Would it be more economical to rent rather than purchase? Should an increased demand for the company's goods be met by more efficient machinery or by increasing the labour force?

These are all decisions that cannot satisfactorily be made without a knowledge of the costs and benefits of the various alternatives.

Decisions have to be taken in every area of the business. A production manager may need to decide how best to cope with a sudden demand for increased output. He will need to know the cost of overtime working. Alternatively, he may sub-contract a proportion of his load. Again, he may consider satisfying peak demand by hiring temporary labour. These alternatives must be studied in the light of the cost information available, for cost will be a determining factor.

Control. Information is required by management to ensure that resources are used properly. A manager cannot hope to control effectively the area for which he is responsible unless actual performance is measured against plans. It is essential that he knows whether he is achieving his objectives. Cost reports, either routine or ad hoc, promptly issued, are invaluable in assisting a manager to direct operations so that plans can be achieved.

The cost information must be in sufficient detail to enable management to isolate areas of weakness. A detailed analysis of costs by product, job, function, geographical area, department and nature of expense should be available if inefficiencies are to be minimised and waste reduced. Moreover, the costs should be related to individual responsibility so that the performance of the manager responsible for the control of an item of expenditure can be measured against target.

Sometimes it is not easy to determine who is responsible for excessive costs. High material costs could be due to spoiled work and be the responsibility of the production manager or foreman. However, the cause might be the result of inefficient buying by a centralised purchasing department which paid higher prices for materials than necessary or bought materials of poor quality.

Excessive labour costs can be due to a variety of causes. For example, there are occasions when production workers cannot proceed with their normal work and there are a number of reasons why this idle time occurs. It could be caused by bad planning in the production department, or the fault could rest with the storekeeper because of a failure on his part to requisition further supplies at the right time. The idle time could be due to a buyer who did not follow up a purchase order, with the consequence that the supplier was late with the delivery.

Again, men could be idle because of the breakdown of a machine which had not been properly maintained by the maintenance department. It is important to investigate the costs thoroughly and to relate them to individual responsibility wherever possible.

It was stated earlier in the chapter that cost accounting not only involves ascertaining costs, but also includes making comparisons and analysing savings and excesses. A comparison of each item of expenditure with a predetermined standard or budget will enable management to concentrate attention on those costs which reveal adverse variances. Cost reports could include an analysis of variances by cause and suggestions for management action. Items where action by management would produce the greatest benefits could be highlighted. There should therefore be a continuous flow of information to enable management to control the day to day activities of the business and to take prompt corrective action where necessary.

Comparisons can also be made with the results of a previous month or with the same month in a previous year. It might be possible also to contrast the results of similar departments within the organisation.

Factors other than cost. The communication of cost information will assist executives and managers in their planning and control activities and in decision making and this support will help them to discharge their responsibilities more effectively.

However, cost information is only a part of the total information requirements of managers. For example, there are factors other than cost to consider in the preparation of a marketing plan.to concentrate on those with the highest potential profit margins would be unwise if consumer needs were not taken into account.the marketing executive will need to study the results of market research and will require details of competitors' prices. He will need to take into account trends in fashion, probable technological changes and the long-term prospects of a new product. The presence of 'loss-leaders' on the shelves of supermarkets is evidence that selling prices are not based solely on cost information.

The decision-maker also uses criteria not related to cost.a reduction in costs might accrue from a decision to sub-contract a particular process, but if trade union support is not forthcoming management would probably decide that the maintenance of good labour relations and not cost reduction is the criterion on which the decision should be based.

A decision on the acquisition of a new machine may not be based entirely on cost. It may be cheaper in the long term to rent rather than buy, but lack of cash might be the key factor. In order to preserve the liquidity position of the business, expenditure of a capital nature might be delayed for the time being. The only alternative therefore would be to rent and incur higher revenue costs.

A manager cannot effectively control his department by merely consulting cost data. Any corrective action invariably involves people, and their needs and aspirations must be considered. A manager therefore requires information on those things that motivate them and that is not something that can be found on a cost statement. He must listen to what his subordinates have to say and be prepared to be guided by what he hears.

He must also consider the requirements of other managers, how he can help them to achieve their objectives.

The purpose of cost accounting is to assist managers, not dominate them. Cost information is for their guidance and they must be free to disregard it if they choose, for other factors have a bearing on planning, decision-making and control.

Cost Accounting and Financial Accounting compared.

Below, seven statements are made about Financial Accounting and seven about Cost Accounting. A comparison can be made by referring to the same number for both the former and the latter. In the first statement the subject matter is 'transactions'; the second statement concerns the manner in which expenditure is classified; and so on.

Financial Accounting

1. This is defined by the I.C.M.A. Terminology as 'the analysis, classification and recording of financial transactions, and the ascertainment of how such transactions affect the performance and financial position of a business'. The transactions mentioned in this definition are external transactions; dealings with customers, suppliers and shareholders. For example, financial accounting is concerned with the recording of purchases, and accounts are opened for individual suppliers when items are bought on credit.

2. The analysis of cost is usually by nature of expense only, for example, stationery, electricity, advertising.

3. Profit is calculated for the business as a whole.

4. The year-end accounts are used mainly by people outside the company, for instance, the Inland Revenue, creditors and prospective shareholders.

5. Accounts are normally published yearly or, in some cases, half-yearly.

6. For limited companies, financial accounting is a legal requirement. Section 147(1) of the Companies Act 1948 states that 'every company shall cause to be kept proper books of account with respect to -

> (a) all sums of money received and expended by the company and the matters in respect of which the receipt and expenditure takes place;
>
> (b) all sales and purchases of goods by the company;
>
> (c) the assets and liabilities of the company.'

It is compulsory, therefore, for a limited company to keep a cash book, day books, personal accounts, a plant register, or similar records. Even partnerships and sole traders, though not covered by the Act, are more or less bound to record financial transactions in order to satisfy the Inland Revenue.

7. Financial accounting is mainly concerned with historical information, recording what something *has* cost.

Cost Accounting

1. Internal transfers are recorded in the cost accounts as well as external transactions. For example, the cost books will record the movement of materials from stores to the factory floor and also the transfer of partly completed products from one department to another.

2. The emphasis is on a more detailed analysis of costs, for example, by function, department, product, job, and so on.

3. Because of this detailed analysis of costs it is possible to calculate the net profit of divisions, departments and products. These results can be related to individual responsibility, thus measuring the perfor-

mance of divisional and product managers. In some organisations it is considered worthwhile to go one step further and calculate the net assets employed in a department or by a product. The performance of each manager can then be measured in terms of 'Return on Capital Employed'.

4. Cost accounts are produced for the benefits of personnel inside the organisation, namely, the executives and managers.

5. Departmental or product profit and loss accounts are generally prepared monthly.

6. Cost accounting is optional. An organisation is free to reject any suggestion that it introduce a costing system. For some businesses the cost of introducing and operating the system might outweigh the benefits received.

7. Cost accounting is also concerned with historical information but, in addition, estimates of future costs are made. Many of the techniques of cost accounting, for example Standard Costing and Budgetary Control, are used to provide standards and forecasts, to find out what something *ought* to cost.

Meaning of 'Cost'

According to I.C.M.A. Terminology, Cost is 'the amount of expenditure incurred on, or attributable to, a specified thing or activity.'
Note the use of the word 'expenditure'. Consequently items such as ordinary dividend and taxation are not included in the meaning of the word 'cost'. They are appropriations of profit. They relate to the manner in which the profit is divided.

The term 'cost' refers to the cost that appears in the equation, Sales-Cost = Profit (or Loss).

However there are some items of expenditure which, although falling within the meaning of 'cost' are omitted from cost statements and reports. This is because they are :

(a) purely financial in nature, e.g. debenture interest;

(b) considered abnormal, e.g. costs associated with fire, flood damage, strikes, etc.

As the purpose of cost accounting is to provide management with meaningful information, reports which include exceptional items which occurred during one period only would probably mislead.

It is unwise to use the word 'cost' by itself and it should,wherever possible, be qualified in some way, for example, opportunity cost, marginal cost, fixed cost. These terms are examined later in the book.

'Cost' provides a common denominator so that items which are different, such as material and labour, can be converted to monetary values.

It is therefore possible to make comparisons between departments which use different materials and which use materials and labour in different proportions.

Cost Units

A cost unit, as defined by the I.C.M.A. is 'a quantitative unit of product or service in relation to which costs are ascertained'.

Costs are expressed as an amount of money per unit. The choice of unit will depend on what is being produced or what service is being provided. The cost unit for a baker would be a loaf of bread.Having ascertained his costs, he then relates them to his product. He would then express his costs as, say 25 pence per unit, that is 25p per loaf of bread. But a unit does not have to be a single item. The cost unit for another baker might be 100 loaves. This baker would show his costs, say £25 per unit, i.e. £25 per 100 loaves. The unit is used, therefore, as a basis for measuring costs and making comparisons between one period and the next, or between actual cost and some predetermined standard.

A cost unit for a business producing some form of liquid could be a gallon, a litre, a bottle or a crate. A company which produces more then one type of liquid will have more than one cost unit.

Organisations which provide a service also need to select a cost unit. A bus company might choose 'passenger/miles' whereas 'student/hours' would be appropriate for a school or college. Service costing is discussed in more detail in chapter 5.

A business which undertakes contracts or specific orders would express its costs as 'so much per job' or contract. Thus a job or contr-act can also be a cost unit in which case the cost of each unit would probably be different. One job might cost £1,000, another £20.

Cost Centres

A cost centre is ' a location, person or item of equipment (or group of these) in respect of which costs may be ascertained and related to cost units' - I.C.M.A. Terminology. When a costing system is being devised, it is important to divide the business into various centres so that costs can be accumulated for each centre.

A location can be a cost centre; examples are the machine shop, canteen, purchasing function, Leeds factory and south-west area. All relevant costs are charged to a particular location's cost centre. The canteen, for instance, will be charged with the cost of food purchased, the wages and salaries of the canteen manager, cooks and waiters, a proportion of rates and electricity, the cost of repairs to canteen equipment and so on.

As the definition above states, a person can be a cost centre. All the costs associated with the managing director would be allocated to his cost centre. These would include his salary, entertaining expenses,

telephone rental and calls, secretarial services, motor expenses, and travel and hotel costs.
A cost centre can comprise a single item of equipment, such as a machine. The same process of collecting costs takes place. The mach - ine will be charged with maintenance costs, depreciation, insurance and power consumed.
Cost centres can be divided into smaller centres. For example, an entire factory can be a cost centre and the various departments that make up the factory can also be cost centres. This also applies to personnel and machines within some of the departments.
The number of centres chosen and the size of each will vary from business to business. Too many cost centres will result in a mountain of detail that will be expensive, confusing and unnecessary. On the other hand, if only a few cost centres are established, the degree of information necessary to assist management to plan and control the operation of the business will not be available.
Consideration has to be given to the costs which are to be controlled and who is to control them. The use of cost centres should assist in relating cost to individual responsibility. Each cost centre therefore should be the responsibility of one person only.
Where costs have to be apportioned, only those cost centres which benefit from the cost should be charged. Where the activity of a cost centre consists of providing a service to other cost centres, for example the canteen, all the costs of the service department must be distributed to the departments using the service. Chapter 4 deals with the apportionment of overhead. The sum of the totals of the various cost centres is then ascertained and related to an appropriate cost unit

Cost Elements.

Cost can be divided into three separate and distinct elements, namely, Materials Cost, Wages Cost and Expenses. The I.C.M.A. Terminology defines these terms as follows :

Materials Cost. The cost of commodities, other than fixed assets, introduced into products or consumed in the operation of an organisation.

Wages Cost. 'The cost of employees' remuneration.
Note: for the specific purposes of individual enterprises the term would require more precise definition. Some may prefer to classify salaries of managers and clerical staff as wages, whilst others may not. Some may prefer to treat holiday pay and employers' contributions towards national insurance and pension fund as wages whilst others may not'.

Expenses. 'All costs other than materials and wages'

Each of these three elements can be sub-divided into Direct Costs and Indirect Costs, thus :

Direct materials cost	Indirect materials cost
Direct wages cost	Indirect wages cost
Direct expenses	Indirect expenses

Direct materials cost. The I.C.M.A. Terminology defines this term as 'the cost of materials entering into and becoming constituent elements of a product or saleable service.' Steel plate enters into and becomes part of a motor car, so it can be described as direct material. The food provided by a hotel is direct material because it is a part of the saleable service. The same can be said for the goods bought by a retailer in order to sell to his customers. The baker's dough and the builder's bricks are direct materials, the examples are numerous.

Direct wages cost. The definition given by the I.C.M.A. Terminology is 'the cost of remuneration for employees' efforts and skill applied directly to a product or saleable service.' It includes the wages of workers who transform the raw materials and components into a finished product, for example, the dough into bread and the bricks into a building. Also included are the wages of sales assistants who sell the retailer's goods and waiters who serve the meals at a hotel.

Direct expenses. These are 'costs other than materials or wages, which are incurred for a specific product or saleable service.' An example is the hire of a crane for a specific contract.

The total cost of direct materials, direct wages and direct expenses is known as Prime Cost, and the total cost of indirect materials, indirect wages and indirect expenses is referred to as Overhead.

Direct and Indirect Costs.

Direct costs, therefore, are those costs which can be easily associated with a particular product or saleable service. The costs incurred are charged directly to the product or service concerned. With indirect costs an element of sharing is involved. They cannot be identified with a particular product and there is a need to apportion the costs between two or more products.

Materials of small value. There are some materials which are direct in nature but because their value is small they are treated as overhead. For example, screws, nuts, bolts and washers enter into and become part of the product. However, it is hardly worth the trouble of ascertaining the cost of say, half a dozen screws in order to make an accurate charge to the product. Consequently, materials of small value, although direct, are treated as indirect for costing purposes.

Division of indirect cost by function. The total indirect cost, or overhead, is generally analysed by function. The following table includes examples of overhead incurred within each function.

Function	Indirect materials	Indirect wages	Indirect expenses
Production (including purchasing)	Lubricating oil; consumable tools, e.g. hacksaw blades; stationery,e.g.purchasing orders,material requisitions.	Salaries of foremen,inspectors, storekeepers,and production control staff; idle time	Factory rent and rates; insurance of plant and machinery; power,lighting and heating of plant and machinery and factory buildings.
Marketing	Packing materials; petrol for salesmen's cars and delivery vans.	Salaries and commission paid to salesmen; wages paid to drivers of delivery vans	Advertising; bad debts; depreciation of salesmen's cars and delivery vans; market research.
Administration (including accounting, personnel, legal and secretarial)	Office stationery.	Office salaries, including directors.	Hire of typewriters; bank charges; audit fees; telephone rental and calls; rental of copying machines; electricity used by administration staff.
Research and Development.	Books for technical library.	Salaries of scientists and engineers.	Depreciation of test gear.

Overleaf is a cost statement which shows the various elements of direct cost together with a functional analysis of overhead. Such a statement could be used to summarise the costs of a department or a product, even the costs of an entire company. The statement could also be used to summarise the costs associated with an individual job or contract.

	£
Direct materials cost	20,000
Direct wages cost	10,000
Direct expenses	2,000
Prime cost	32,000
Production overhead	22,000
Cost of production	54,000
Marketing overhead	11,000
Administration overhead	9,000
Research and development overhead	6,000
Total cost	80,000

Other terms are sometime used instead of Cost of Production, such as Factory Cost, Works Cost or Cost of Manufacture.

In some instances, marketing costs are treated as direct. A contract may necessitate exceptionally high delivery costs and it would be unfair to charge such costs to overhead and subsequently apportion them to all contracts. In consequence, it might be more sensible to treat the delivery costs as a direct charge to the contract.

Equally, some research and development costs are direct in nature. A contract might be received which requires research in a certain field, the finished product consisting of a report of the findings.

In a cost statement like the one above, marketing direct costs and research and development direct costs must be shown separately below the 'cost of production' line. Although direct, they are not part of the prime cost which is a term normally restricted to include only direct *production* costs

It is therefore possible to summarise the discussion on direct and indirect costs by using the following equation:

Prime cost + other direct costs + overhead = Total cost.

Example. The following is a summary of the costs incurred during a certain period by a manufacturing company. Draft a statement, similar to the one above, showing the sub-divisions of Total Cost.

	£
Wages traceable to jobs	90,500
Wages paid to men on maintenance work	10,300
Materials used on jobs	113,750
Factory rent and rates	4,900
Salesmen's salaries	12,070
Works salaries	19,100
Directors' fees	6,000
Hire of crane for job number 542	830
Carriage inwards on raw materials	720
Carriage outwards	1,700

Cost of idle time in factory	440
Corporation tax	6,800
Commission to salesmen	1,550
Auditors' fees	2,900
Bad debts	80
Dividents paid	1,850
Lubricating oil	25
Office salaries and expenses	5,000
Insurance on finished goods	2,000
Depreciation of delivery vans	1,200
Depreciation of plant	2,400
Consumable tools	270
Lighting of showroom	700
	285,085

COST STATEMENT

For the period ending ....

Direct materials cost	114,470
Direct wages cost	90,500
Direct expenses	830
Prime cost	205,800
Production overhead	37,435
Cost of production	243,235
Marketing overhead	19,300
Administration overhead	13,900
Total cost	276,435

Explanatory Notes

1. Direct materials cost includes £720 in respect of carriage inwards on raw materials.

2. Production overhead comprises:—

	£
Wages paid to men on maintenance work	10,300
Factory rent and rates	4,900
Works salaries	19,100
Cost of idle time in factory	440
Lubricating oil	25
Depreciation of plant	2,400
Consumable tools	270
	37,435

3. Marketing overhead consists of:—

	£
Salesmen's salaries	12,070
Carriage outwards	1,700
Commission to salesmen	1,550
Bad debts	80
Insurance on finished goods	2,000

Depreciation of delivery vans	1,200
Lighting of showroom	700
	19,300

4. The following items are included in Administration overhead:—

	£
Directors' fees	6,000
Auditors' fees	2,900
Office salaries and expenses	5,000
	13,900

5. Corporation tax of £6,800 and dividends paid of £1,850 have been omitted as they are appropriations of profit and not costs.

Classification of Cost.

It is important to appreciate that there is no one way in which costs can be classified. Costs may be classified by:

(a) function, e.g. production, marketing, administration;
(b) type of expenditure, e.g. salaries, entertaining, advertising;
(c) geographical area, e.g. south-west, south-east;
(d) department, e.g. assembly, stores, machine shop, canteen;
(e) job or contract;
(f) product;
(g) element, i.e. materials, wages, expenses;
(h) direct or indirect;
(i) behaviour, i.e. fixed or variable;
(j) time.

The method of classification will vary and must be related to the purpose for which the information is required. It is necessary to have a flexible system of cost classification to enable costs to be classified in a number of different ways.

The Role of the Cost Accountant.

Ascertaining costs is the responsibility of the cost accountant. It is his task to calculate the costs and make comparisons with budgets, estimates and forecasts and to examine the savings and excesses that arise. He will also compare costs in one accounting period with those of another period and draw the attention of management to areas of inefficiency and waste. The cost accountant must explain to management why actual performance differs from plan, and variances should, where possible, be analysed by cause.

Nevertheless, managers should not be bombarded with a mountain of information. They will not be grateful if they receive cost reports with page after page of minute detail. They are too busy to sift through a thick brochure to try and find what is important. It is the role of the cost accountant to direct the attention of management to important issues, to highlight those areas which require maximum consideration. Cost data needs to be edited and should be appropriate to the interests of the recipient. Information extracted for the managing director will be different from that required by the foreman. The personnel function will call for certain data, whilst the marketing function will demand other data. The cost accountant must appreciate the various information requirements within the organisation. Graphs and charts can be used to make the information clearer and easier to understand. The same information may have to be presented in various forms to a number of different recipients.

The cost accountant must be ready to interpret the information if requested and should speak the language of the manager using the cost report or statement. It is essential that reports are not misunderstood. There is a danger in managers drawing the wrong conclusions and misusing the information in their possession. The cost accountant must be alert to this possibility. Consequently, when information is requested the cost accountant should ask 'For what purpose is the information required?' It may be that the manager is asking for the wrong information. The cost accountant, if he knows the purpose for which the information is required, will be better able to advise management on solutions to its problems. There are occasions when the cost accountant should volunteer information. Because of his special training and experience he is in a position to anticipate the needs of management; he can offer advice and make suggestions that are not immediately apparent to the managers who are much closer to the problems.

The cost accountant should possess a breadth of vision and appreciate that factors other than cost have to be considered. Managers will seek his help on how they can best achieve their objectives.

It is the responsibility of the cost accountant to see that cost reports are issued promptly. At the same time he must decide on the degree of accuracy necessary. There is no merit to devoting a lot of time to the preparation of a report that is accurate to the last penny if a manager receives it too late to take any action. The information should be ready at a time when it is of most value. Also, the cost of providing information has to be taken into account for sometimes the benefits received are not proportionate to the cost incurred. Some requests may therefore have to be refused.

The cost accountant is also concerned with the flow of information to the cost department. Documents such as time sheets and stores requisitions must be scrutinised for accuracy and legibility. Procedures and forms should be periodically reviewed and, if necessary, revised. He must be able to devise and implement new systems and procedures. His duties and responsibilities bring him into contact with almost every aspect of the business and he must have the ability to communicate effectively and to present recommendations succinctly to management.

Finally, the cost accountant must retain adequate records, including stock records so that stock can be valued without the need for frequent stocktakings. Stock valuation is necessary so that monthly profit and loss accounts can be prepared. He is also concerned with directing the annual budgeting exercise.

Principles, Methods and Techniques.

The chapter commenced with a definition of cost accounting in which it was stated that accounting and costing principles are used to ascertain costs.

There is a need, for example, to apply the accounting principle of consistency. In cost accounting, comparisons are often made and it is therefore essential that there is a consistency of treatment within each accounting period and from one period to the next. Direct costs in one period should not be treated as indirect costs in the following period. Consistency is required in the pricing of stores issues and the apportionment of overhead. Inconsistency would result in managers making wrong inferences and they would soon feel unable to rely on the cost accounting information.

Another accounting principle used in cost accounting is the double-entry principle and chapter 6 is devoted to this topic.

Chapter 7 deals with the Marginal Costing principle and chapters 8 and 9 contain a review of the techniques of Budgetary Control and Standard Costing.

Costing Methods are discussed in chapter 5

Cost Accounting and Management Accounting compared.

The terminology of Management anf Financial Accountancy defines management accounting as :

'The application of professional knowledge and skill in the preparation and presentation of accounting information in such a way as to assist management in the formulation of policies and in the planning and control of the operations of the undertaking.'

When contrasting cost accounting and financial accounting, differences were easy to identify. With management accounting this is much more difficult. The demarcation line between the two is more blurred and perhaps it could be said that there is no demarcation line at all. Some avoid the issue completely and talk of Cost and Management Accounting.

If one studies the definitions, it becomes apparent that while cost accounting uses accounting principles, management accounting uses accounting information. The management accountant, then, has a much wider role than the cost accountant. He will provide information other than cost information. He will use the financial records, such as the personal accounts of debtors. He may analyse the outstanding debts by age and by major customer. He will provide ratios that link debts with the volume of sales. This is essentially financial information and the management accountant will present it in such a way as to assist management to formulate future credit control policy.

In management accounting therefore *all* accounting information is used, not just information that arises out of cost accounting.

Consequently, therefore, the status of the management accountant is usually higher than that of a cost accountant. He is often part of the top management team and is in closer contact with top management. He often shares in the corporate management responsibility and is involved in corporate planning, business finance, setting company objectives, laying down policy and procedures, and the appraisal of investment proposals.

EXAMINATION PRACTICE
Students are advised to attempt the questions under simulated examination conditions. Then check their answers with the suggested answers at the back of the book.

Question 1   Costing principles   **Answer page 248**

The classification of costs is important in any cost system.
You are required to state:
(a) what is the main purpose of cost classification;
(b) three typical functions in a business by which costs may be classified;
(c) two methods of cost classification, other than by function.

(Institute of Accounting Staff)

Question 2   Costing principles   **Answer page 248**

(a) List the main groups of items you would expect to find in a functional classification of marketing costs.

(b) How would you expect marketing costs to be analysed for management control purposes? What purposes are served by such analyses?

(Association of Certified Accountants)

2
Materials

Introduction

In the previous chapter it was stated that cost comprises three elements. This chapter is concerned with the first of these elements, namely, Materials.

The importance of an effective system of material control cannot be over-stressed, for in many organisations direct materials cost is the largest single item of expenditure in the trading and profit and loss account. Indeed, in some businesses, the expenditure on direct materials amounts to 90 per cent of the total cost. Nevertheless, many a cost reduction programme begins with the cry 'ten per cent off overheads'. The use of the telephone is restricted and the number of extensions are reduced; typed monthly accounts give way to hand-written copies; and the photographing of documents cannot be carried out unless the approval of top management is obtained. There may be a place for such a cost-cutting exercise, but it should not be forgotten that in many businesses the expenditure on overhead is only a fraction of the expenditure on direct materials.

Where proper control of materials is lacking, losses are likely to result due to waste, production delays, obsolescence and many other causes. Furthermore, capital will be unnecessarily tied up if there are no effective stock control procedures.

There is ample scope for economy, therefore, if consideration is given to the purchase, receipt, inspection, storage, issue and usage of materials and also the procedures necessary to pay for the goods purchased and account for their movement throughout the factory.

Purchasing

The procurement of materials is the responsibility of the purchasing function which is headed by the Buyer or Purchasing Manager. This responsibility includes the purchase of indirect materials and items of a capital nature as well as direct materials. The buyer has it in his power to commit large sums of money on behalf of the company and the consequences of failing to perform his duties effectively are far-reaching.

Although this is not a book about Purchasing, the subject cannot be ignored by the cost accountant who has a responsibility to direct the attention of management to areas where costs can be reduced. It is therefore necessary for him to have a background knowledge of purchasing procedures.

The Purchase Requisition: The purchasing process is not started by the buyer. He does not buy materials for himself, but acts on behalf of others in the organisation who require materials. Consequently the authority of the buyer is limited, for he cannot purchase goods unless he first receives a Purchase Requisition (see *Figure 1*). This is an internal document used by the person requiring the goods and it represents a formal instruction to the buyer to purchase the materials requested.

PURCHASE REQUISITION

Date ....19....   Serial No.P.R. 1234

Quantity	Material code no.	Job/Cost code no.	Description

Delivery required by .... at ....

Signed by .... Approved by ....Department ....

For Purchasing department use
Purchase order no. ....Date of purchase ....

Supplier .... Expected date of delivery ....

Figure 1 - Purchase Requisition

The purchasing department will usually receive requisitions from the following:
(a) the storekeeper, when there is a need to replenish standard items of stock;
(b) the production control department for non-standard items which are required for specific jobs and not usually issued from the stores;
(c) the site services manager (or plant engineer) for items of a capital nature and materials required to carry out maintenance work to buildings, and plant and machinery;
(d) various heads of department for items of indirect materials, e.g.

ledgers for the accountant, food required by the canteen and medical supplies to be used by the nurse.

The materials requested by the production control department will often be listed on a Bill of Materials , which is a schedule of the parts necessary to execute a particular order. This schedule will often contain many items of material, and in order to avoid making out a number of purchase requisitions the bill of materials can be attached to one requisition.

The buyer should have in his possession a list of those persons within the organisation authorised to requisition materials. It must be emphasised that those who initiate purchase requisitions cannot raise purchase orders. Moreover, they can only order materials within the sphere of their authority. Furthermore, their authority may be limited in some way. For example, the site services manager would not be able to request capital equipment without the authority of top manage - ment. Heads of department may only be authorised to requisition materials up to a specific amount, say £100, any larger amount requiring the signature of the managing director. Any purchase requisitions not properly authorised should be rejected by the buyer.

Two copies of the purchase requisition will usually be prepared, the top copy being sent to the buyer and the second copy being retained by the department raising the requisition.

The Purchase Order: On receipt of the purchase requisition the buyer will raise a Purchase Order (see *Figure 2*) except that before he can do this he must select a suitable supplier. Inquiries may have to be made in order to find a source of supply. Various suppliers may be asked for quotations or invited to submit tenders. However, the purchasing department should maintain up-to-date records giving information on suppliers so that inquiries can be kept to a minimum.

Before deciding on a particular supplier consideration must be given to the following:

(a) Price. It is important to ascertain whether discounts are given for large quantities, for the buyer may wish to take advantage of such an offer by placing an order for a significant amount. Also, does the price include delivery or is an extra charge made for transporting the goods to the purchaser's factory? Are containers returnable, and if so, is a credit received for their return? These discounts and additional costs are discussed more fully later in the chapter.

As materials represent a high proportion of total cost, the buyer can make a considerable impact on unit costs by obtaining materials at the lowest possible price. However it is not always wise to force down suppliers too much on prices. The buyer should act responsibly and be

```
                GAMMA AND DELTA LTD
                   PURCHASE ORDER
To .............................    Purchase order No. 13579
   .............................    Date .....................19.....
   .............................    Your ref.No.....................
   .............................    Our ref.No.....................
Please supply, in accordance with the attached conditions,
the following:

Quantity        Description     Code number     Price




Delivery required by ................. at ...........................................
Terms .....................
Please quote our purchase order number on all communications, and
acknowledge this order
Signature of buyer ..................... per Gamma & Delta Ltd.
```

Figure 2 - Purchase Order

Notes:

1. The reference number of Gamma and Delta Ltd. is for the number of the internal purchase requisition.

2. The terms refer to any cash discount terms which were stated on the supplier's quotation.

---

prepared to pay a fair price for materials. If the supplier reduces his prices to an unreasonable level, his profit margin may be eroded and this could cause him to terminate his business. The purchaser would then lose a useful source of supply.

(b) Quality. Price is not the sole criterion; quality is also important. If the buyer purchases materials of poor quality the standard of the finished product could be affected and there is the likelihood that it will not perform as well as expected. A loss of future orders could follow. In addition, sub-standard material often produces waste during the manufacturing process and could also cause the breakdown of expensive plant and machinery.

Nevertheless, there are occasions when it is unwise to pay too much attention to high quality. In some instances lower quality material might serve the same purpose. It very much depends on the nature of the business. If an organisation is dealing in low-priced goods, then a cheap substitute material may be quite adequate. The buyer should consider whether better quality material adds anything of value to the finished product. Will customers be prepared to pay a higher price for a better quality product?

On the other hand, it is possible that materials of a higher quality could result in a reduction in the quantity of material used. The buyer should seek the advice of the production control department on the question of quality standards and liaise with the chief inspector to discover which materials are not passing the test and inspection programme.

(c) Delivery. The buyer is responsible for ensuring that the materials are delivered to the factory on time. It is extremely important therefore that a supplier is selected who can keep to his delivery promises. If he selects an unreliable supplier who delivers late, the consequences could be far-reaching. The delay could bring about a standstill as employees wait for materials. Plant is left idle. Promises made to customers concerning delivery are not kept, causing a considerable loss of goodwill. This, in turn, could affect future orders and a reduction in the volume of sales might follow. Some customers may make a claim on the company if penalty clauses have been included in contracts.

It may make more economic sense to pay a higher price for materials if in paying a higher price the purchaser can be assured of delivery on time. A cheaper price paid to an unreliable supplier may work out more expensive in the long term. The purchasing department should include in its records the previous performances of suppliers with regard to delivery.

(d) Availability. It is sometime not advisable to rely too heavily on one supplier. To put all one's purchasing eggs in one supplier's basket could be disastrous if that supplier goes out of business. The buyer must be continually on the lookout for new sources of supply and must be prepared to listen to salesmen who call from time to time.

(e) Quantity. The quantity of materials to be purchased is normally determined by someone other than the buyer, for the purchase requisition will state the quantity to be ordered. However, if the business is sufficiently large and the purchasing function is centralised, the buyer will be receiving requests from a number of production control departments. It would be uneconomic to place an order for, say, ten items one day and to follow this with a further sales order for another ten the next day.

The buyer should attempt to predict when a shortage of materials is likely to occur, because prices tend to rise in such circumstances. Future price movements and the availability of quantity discount will influence his decision on the quantity of material to be purchased. However, a number of factors influence the quantity of material to be ordered and this will be dealt with more fully later in the chapter under the heading of Stock Control.

(f) Terms of Payment. The business could be going through a period of cash flow difficulties. Perhaps the accountant has advised the buyer to give preference to suppliers offering long-term credit facilities. All other things being equal, the buyer should place orders with those suppliers giving the best terms of payment.

The buyer will need to balance all these considerations. In times of fierce competition it will be important to keep unit costs as low as possible and there will be pressure on the buyer to buy at the lowest possible price and to take advantage of any quantity discount available. At other times the amount of working capital in the business may be limited and in these circumstances there will be a need to restrict the quantity ordered so that capital is not tied up unnecessarily in large quantities of stock. Again, there may be situations when an urgent delivery of materials is required and the need to have goods delivered quickly will take precedence over the price to be paid.

Whe the buyer has selected a supplier, he will raise a purchase order. The routing of the copies will be as follows :

(a) to the supplier;

(b) to the department originating the purchase requisition to inform it that the goods have been ordered;

(c) to the goods inward department to indicate that the goods will be arriving;

(d) to the accounts department which deals with the passing of the supplier's invoice for payment;

(e) retained by the purchasing department.

Processing the Order .The purchasing department must follow up the order so as to be sure that the materials are delivered on time. This will include telephoning the supplier a few days before the promised delivery date. The purpose of this is to obtain advance warning of possible late delivery so that alternative arrangements can be made if necessary.

Long Term Purchase Contracts. When the demand for a certain item of material is known it may be advantageous to the purchaser to place a long term purchase contract with a particular supplier. If the supplier can be assured of future orders, he is going to be more amenable to quoting at a lower price. The buyer will raise purchase orders against the contract when a delivery of materials is required. The advantage to the purchaser of negotiating long term purchase contracts, which arc usually for periods of up to twelve months, is seen in lower unit costs and a reduction in the quantity of stock held.

Receiving

In order to facilitate the delivery of materials the goods inward dep-artment should be located as near to the entrance of the factory as possible. A delivery note or advice note will normally accompany the goods and the details on this document should be compared with the actual goods delivered. The materials should be inspected for damage and, where appropriate, weighed, measured or counted. If everything is in order, the delivery note is signed and returned to the carrier.

The goods should be checked against the purchase order and if there

---

GOODS RECEIVED NOTE

Supplier ....   Serial No G.R.N. 2468
Carrier ....   Date ....19..... ....
Date of delivery ....19...   Purchase order No. ....

Quantity	Material code No.	Job/cost code No.	Description	For office use only Price Value

Goods received by.................   Inspected by ....

Figure 3 - Goods Received Note

is any discrepancy the buyer should be informed. The goods inward department then completes a Goods Received Note (see *Figure 3*), sometimes called a Goods Inward Note. An inspection note should also be completed. This document is often part of the goods received note. The routing of the goods received note is as follows :

(a) to the purchasing department;

(b) to the department which originated the purchase requisition; the goods received note should accompany the actual material;

(c) to the accounts department;

(d) retained by the goods inward department.

Any material damaged or over-supplied and goods received which were not ordered will be the subject of a debit note sent by the buyer to the supplier , a copy of which should be forwarded to the accounts department.

Payment

The supplier having supplied the materials will then forward his invoice to the purchaser. On receipt it is the normal practice to stamp the invoice and give it a reference number. The stamp will also have spaces for a code number and a signature. The details are entered in a purchase register.

Before passing the invoice for payment it is necessary to ascertain that the goods invoiced were actually ordered. This is done by comparing the invoice with a copy of the purchase order. Also one must make sure that the goods have in fact been received. A comparison of the invoice with a copy of the goods received note will provide the answer. A check should be carried out on the invoice prices to ensure that they are in agreement with those stated on the purchase order.

Consideration has to be given to the degree to which extensions and totals are checked. Some companies check every extension and addition whereas others carry out no checks at all. The view of those which adopt the latter procedure is that the cost of checking every extension and total is far greater than the sum of the discrepancies found. However, it is perhaps advisable to undertake at least some checks, say on those invoices over a certain amount.

Once these procedures have been carried out, the invoice can be passed for payment. It is essential that the details of the invoice are entered on the back of the accounts copy of the purchase order so as to avoid the passing or payment of a duplicate invoice. Also where the supplier has only delivered and invoiced part of the order it is an easy matter, when comparing the front of the purchase order with the back, to note that part of the order is still to be delivered and invoiced.

Some invoices are for services rendered, for example, window cleaning. It is apparent that in these circumstances a goods received not will not be made out. However it is necessary to confirm that the work has been undertaken and a list of persons authorised to sign invoices for services should be drawn up.

Material Cost.

Having passed the invoice for payment it is necessary to calculate the materials cost. A supplier's invoice can be a complex document. An explanation of some of the terms used on a supplier's invoice is given below:

(a) Trade discount. This is an allowance made to a purchaser who sells the goods again, for example a wholesaler. It is to compensate him for storage costs, breaking or separating materials, buying in bulk, re-packing and distributing small quantities.

(b) Quantity discount. This is an allowance to those who buy large quantities. The advantage to the supplier of an order for a large quantity is that longer production runs are possible and the cost of continually re-setting machines is minimised. His delivery and packing costs are reduced and all or part of the savings are passed on to the purchaser in the form of a quantity discount. However, although quantity discount represents a welcome price reduction to the purchaser, there are are other considerations before placing orders for large quantities. This will be discussed later in the chapter in the section on Stock Control.

(c) Cash discount. This represents an allowance made for payment of accounts within a stipulated time, e.g. a 2½ per cent reduction if the invoice is paid within seven days.

(d) Charges for carriage and delivery. Sometimes a supplier's invoice will show the cost of transporting the goods as a separate item. In addition other costs are often mentioned, such as import duty, dock charges, insurance and storage.

(e) Containers. A charge is sometimes made for the containers in which the goods are delivered. The containers can either be returnable or non-returnable. Where the supplier requests that the containers be returned, the purchaser is given either credit in full or for part of the original charge for containers.

The problem is which of these items need to be taken into account in arriving at the cost of materials? The amount posted to the cost accounts will include delivery charges and the cost of non-returnable containers and must be reduced by any trade or quantity discount, but no account is taken of cash discount as this is usually treated as a financial item only.

However, if an invoice contains a large number of items and each item is to be charged to a different job or cost centre it would be time consuming to apportion a small delivery charge over the individual items. Therefore in such circumstances it is more convenient to charge delivery costs to production overhead. If credit is given in full for returnable containers then no entry is made in the cost accounts. If only part of the original charge is credited then the difference between the original charge and the credit is entered in the cost accounts.

Example. A supplier's invoice contained the following information:

	£
100 units of material A at 50 pence per unit	50
less trade discount - 10 per cent	5
	45
Delivery charge	10
Non-returnable containers	3
	58

Cash discount - 2½ per cent - 7 days

The materials cost and therefore the amount posted to the cost accounts would be £58. If payment were made within seven days cash discount of £1.45 would be claimed, but this does not affect the cost accounts as cash discount is normally an item which only passes through the financial accounts. If the containers were returnable and full credit was given the materials cost would be £55.

Storekeeping

An organisation wishing to control effectively its materials cost must appreciate the importance of good storekeeping and stock control. In most organisations cash is tightly controlled but often the control of stock leaves much to be desired and yet a glance at the balance sheets of most companies will reveal that the investment in stocks is quite substantial.

Organisation of Stores. It is essential that stores are organised in a way which best suits individual companies. There are basically three ways in which stores can be organised :

(a) a central store;

(b) independent stores;

(c) a combination of both, i.e. a central store with sub-stores.

The advantages of central stores are as follows.

(a) Stocks are kept to a minimum. In order to operate independent stores there needs to be a basic stock of each item of material required by departments using the store. The amount spent on these buffer stocks is less if there is only one store. Lower stocks mean that less capital is tied up, expensive floor space can be more profitably used, less time is spent in checking stock balances, and the likelihood of obsolescence and deterioration of materials is reduced. Also less staff are required to man the stores.

(b) More expertise is likely to result. Where sub-stores are in operation the storekeeping staff often combine the duties of storekeeping with other tasks. In a central store the personnel can devote all their time to storekeeping. Better supervision is possible and absenteeism is less crucial.

(c) Lower stationery costs will occur. Purchase requisitioning takes place in one area and fewer bin cards are needed.

(d) If the central store is located near the goods inward department material handling costs incurred in moving the material to the stores are kept to a minimum.

(e) Better security is achieved.

The disadvantages of central stores are listed below.

(a) A central store is often located a long way from the department using the materials. More time is spent travelling between the stores and the place of operation.

(b) There is a greater risk of loss by fire.

Location and Layout of Stores. The stores should be located near the goods inward department in order to keep material handling costs to a minimum. Access should be restricted to authorised personnel and the stores should be kept secure, clean and tidy to avoid pilferage, deterioration and damage to expensive materials.

Stocks which deteriorate, evaporate or perish may have to be located in a special place. All stocks should be located in such a way as to prevent pilferage and unauthorised issues. In order to make use of expensive floor space, racks should be as high as possible but nevertheless easily accessible so that materials can be issued quickly.

Material Code Numbers. Each individual item of material is given a part number (say prefixed by the letter 'p'). When a number of parts are assembled together to form a sub-assembly this can be identified by another number (say prefixed by 's/a' to denote sub-assembly). The purpose of using material code numbers is to prevent misunderstanding on terminology and to ensure easy identification. They are used on purchase requisitions, material requisitions and other documents. Material code numbers enable items of material to be priced correctly. One code number should be used for each item and size of material. Storing by reference to description only could cause over-stocking especially where a single item can be referred to by using different descriptions. The student should note that material code numbers are not cost code or cost centre numbers.

Stores documents and records.

(a) Material requisitions. Items of stock should only be issued against a properly authorised Material Requisition, sometime referred to as a Stores Requisition (see *Figure 4*). The chief storekeeper should possess a list of those persons authorised to countersign material requisitions. Details of the material requisition are entered on the bin card (see below). The requisition is then sent to the cost department where it is priced and valued and entered in the cost accounts. The student should not confuse material requisitions with purchase requisitions.

(b) Material Returned Notes. This document is used when materials are issued in excess of requirements. The excess materials must be re-

MATERIALS REQUISITION

Job/cost code No...............   Serial No. M.R. 3210
                                        Date ....19 ....

Quantity Material   Description   For office use only
          code No.   Price   Value

Signed by .... Approved by.................. Dept.....................
Material issued by .... Priced by ....
Bin No .... Stores ledger folio ....

Figure 4 - Material Requisition

turned to stores together with a material returned note and not left on
the shop floor. The layout of this document is similiar to a material
requisition but is often coloured red.

(c) Material Transfer Note. On some occasions excess materials
can be used on another job. If this occurs a material transfer note should
be made out transferring the materials from one job to another.
This obviates the need to return the excess materials to stores and
draw them out again.

(d) Bin Cards. These are kept in the bins, racks or other receptacles and a separate card is required for each type of material. The
data on the bin card (see *Figure 5*) should be kept to a minimum so
that storekeeping staff can concentrate on receiving and issuing materials and devote time only to those clerical duties which are essential.

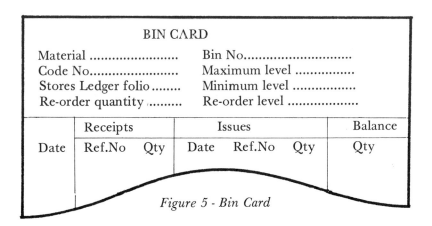

Figure 5 - Bin Card

(e) The Stores Ledger. This is kept in the cost office and is similar to a bin card except that prices and values are included. The receipts and issues columns are part of the cost accounting double-entry system; when materials are received by the stores, the stores ledger is debited; a credit entry will record issues. Like the bin card there is a separate sheet for each item and size of material and the cost accountant should investigate any slow moving or dormant stocks. The stores ledger is illustrated later in the chapter when consideration is given to the valuation of stores issues.

The goods received notes are priced by the costing department from purchase orders in advance of receiving the invoice. An adjustment will be made subsequently if the invoice price is different from the purchase order price, assuming of course that the buyer approves any additional charge. The details are then entered in the stores ledger.

Stock Control.

The objective of any stock control policy must be to ensure that the cost of holding stocks is kept to a minimum, whilst at the same time maintaining the continuous flow of production by ensuring that materials are available when required. This balance is extremely difficult to achieve. The pressure to keep stocks as low as possible arises because of the following factors:

(a) The holding of stocks involves the employment of capital and, while this cannot be avoided, one must try to keep the investment in stocks to the minimum necessary for the efficient running of the business. The employment of capital in unnecessary stocks means that capital is tied up which could otherwise be available for more profitable use; either by investing in additional and more up-to-date plant and machinery which could provide an adequate return by way of increased profits, or by investing the capital outside the business where a reasonable rate of interest might be earned.

(b) The availability of storage space might be limited. The more space that is used for storage, the less there is available for producing the goods that must be sold in order to remain in business.

(c) The costs associated with storage are significant,for example, rent, heating, lighting, material handling, stocktaking, insurance, pilferage, security arrangements, equipment such as bins, racks and steps, and the cost of staffing. The higher the level of stocks, the greater the amount spent on items such as these.

(d) The risk of deterioration, evaporation or obsolescence increases with the level of stocks held.

However some advantages can accrue from buying large quantities. There is the possibility that the supplier will offer a discount if the order is for a sufficient number of items. Furthermore if a number of items are purchased at one time rather than small amounts at frequent intervals there will be a saving in administration costs, for example, the cost of stationery such as purchase orders and goods received notes; there will be a lower number of suppliers' invoices to process and less work for the bought ledger department.

Economic Order Quantity. This is the size of order which produces the lowest cost of the material ordered. It is calculated by taking into account: the price charged by the supplier; the cost of storage; the loss of interest due to cash being tied up in stocks; the cost of transporting the goods to the factory; the likelihood of deterioration and obsolescence; the extra costs which are incurred to avoid deterioration where materials are held in stock for long periods; the administra – tion cost per purchase order; and so on. An attempt is sometimes made to quantify the costs of the various factors for different order quantities in order to ascertain which results in the lowest cost.

Example. The management of your company wishes to decide on the quantity of a certain material to be purchased when replenishing stock. The following information is available :

(a) the supplier's price is £0.50 per unit, but he will offer a quantity discount of 5 per cent if he receives an order for 250 or more and a discount of 10 per cent for an order of 500 or above;

(b) the storage costs have been calculated at £0.20 per unit of average stock;

(c) the administration cost of placing an order is £2;

(d) the rate of usage is 1,200 for a 3-month period.

You are required to evaluate the following alternatives:

(a) the purchase of 1,200 units at the beginning of each quarter;

(b) the purchase of 600 units at the beginning of each quarter and a further 600 half way through;

(c) the purchase of 400 units at the beginning of each month;

(d) the purchase of 200 units at the beginning and half way through each month.

Ignore interest on capital tied up in stocks.

Size of order	Number of orders	Supplier's charge	Storage costs	Admin. costs	Total cost.
		£	£	£	£
1,200	1	540	120	2	662
600	2	540	60	4	604
400	3	570	40	6	616
200	6	600	20	12	632

The optimum size of order is 600 units and the management would therefore be advised to purchase 600 units every 6½ weeks.

Stock levels. Each bin card should state the re-order level, i.e. the level at which the material must be re-ordered, and maximum and minimum stock levels. In order to establish these stock levels it is necessary to ascertain the following :

(a) the rate of consumption of the material;

(b) the re-order period, i.e. the length of time taken to obtain replacement stocks. More precisely this is the period of time which elapses between the raising of a purchase requisition and the receipt of the goods in the stores.

(c) the re-order quantity, i.e the economic order quantity.

The re-order level is the level at which it is necessary to raise a purchase requisition for additional supplies of the material in question. It is calculated thus:

Maximum consumption x maximum re-order period

The maximum stock level is the level above which stocks should not be allowed to rise and can be calculated by using the formula :

Re-order level + re-order quantity - (minimum consumption x minimum re-order period).

The minimum stock level is the level below which stocks should not be allowed to fall. A buffer stock is therefore created as a safeguard against unexpected delays and consumption above what was previously thought to be the maximum during the re-order period. The minimum level can be calculated as follows :

Re-order level - (normal consumption x average re-order period)

The suggested average stock level can be computed as follows :

$$\frac{\text{Maximum stock level} + \text{minimum stock level}}{2}$$

Example. You are required to compute the stock levels for an item of material given the following information :

    (a) normal rate of usage - 200 units per day ;

    (b) maximum usage   - 250 units per day;

    (c) minimum usage   - 120 units per day;

    (d) re-order period   - 5 - 15 days;

    (e) re-order quantity   - 4,000 units

Using the formulae given above:

re-order level = 250 x 15   = 3,750 units

maximum stock level = 3,750 + 4,000 - (120x5) = 7,150 units

minimum stock level = 3,750 - (200x10)   = 1,750 units

average stock level $= \dfrac{7,150 + 1,750}{2}$ = 4,450

    The repeated use of these formulae could bring about the storage of large quantities of stocks. Before using them for every item of stock consideration should be given to the possibility of a number of adverse conditions occurring together, such as the high usage of material occurring at the same time as a failure on the part of a supplier to deliver on time.

    The levels should be reviewed periodically for circumstances are quick to change. The availability of capital may be a major consideration one month but six months later the keeping of customer delivery dates might be the determining factor in fixing stock levels.

    Some would advocate the use of buffer stocks in order to be certain that a 'stock-out' does not occur. However buffer stocks consume a lot of capital especially if many different items of material are held in stock. It should be noted that the frequent use of these formulae is tantamount to avoiding all risks and it is not wise to use these methods right across the board. A certain amount of risk-taking and uncertainty is inherent in business and a balance should be created by perhaps using the formulae for important items only. For other items the risk should be a calculated one. Consideration should be given to the availability of urgent supplies and the effect on completion dates of being without a certain item of stock at a crucial time.

    The number of different items held in stock can be reduced by increased standardisation of parts. Unnecessary variety in the design of products increases the variety of parts to be held in stock.

    Annual Stocktaking. The latest receipts and issues must be recorded on the bin cards before the actual stocktaking takes place. The annual stocktaking often occurs a month before the accounting year-end so as to avoid delay in the preparation of the final accounts. The cost accounts are adjusted to fall in line with the stocktaking results and are used for balance sheet purposes at the end of the financial year.

Perpetual Inventory and Continuous Stocktaking. The features of this system are: balances are recorded on the bin cards after each receipt and issue; a few items of stock are checked each day by cost audit clerks; all items should be checked at least once a year; an element of surprise should be involved and storekeeping staff should not therefore be given notice of which bins are due for checking.

The advantages of this system are as follows:

(a) discrepancies are discovered earlier and can be investigated; annual stocktaking may reveal discrepancies when it is too late;

(b) there is no factory close-down; this is often costly as production is held up. Also weekend overtime in order to carry out the stocktaking is avoided.

(c) the stocks are checked by personnel from the costing department who, because they check a few items each day, become experienced in this activity;

(d) the presence of cost audit clerks in the store acts as a deterrent.

Differences will invariably occur between the balance on the bin card and the physical stock balance. These discrepancies arise because of :

(a) incorrect entries on the bin card from the goods received note, material requisition, material returned note, etc. ;

(b) pilferage, evaporation, breaking of bulk, short issues, excess issues, returning of materials to the wrong bin or placing materials in the wrong bin originally;

(c) the difficulty of precise measurement where materials are issued by weight or in lengths;

(d) errors of procedure, e.g. issuing stock without a material requisition.

Discrepancies should be investigated and the bin card brought into line with the actual quantity of material in stock. Where a difference occurs between the bin card balance and the stores ledger balance,they should both be adjusted to conform to the physical balance. Discrepancies should be credited to the stores ledger account (in the case of a deficiency) and a corresponding debit made in the stock adjustment account. The balance of stock adjustment account is written of to costing profit and loss account at the end of the financial year.

Work in Progress and Finished Goods Stock. Control of these stocks is not within the responsibility of the storekeeper. Work in progress is the responsibility of the production manager, whilst the distribution manager is responsible for the control of finished goods.

Turnover of Stock. This is the rate at which stocks are consumed. It is possible to calculate the number of times stock is turned over during the year by using the formula :

$$\frac{\text{Cost of materials sold}}{\text{Average stock of materials}}$$

Example:

$$\text{Stock at January 1st} \quad = \quad £9,000$$
$$\text{Stock at following Dec 31} = \quad £5,000$$
$$\text{Purchases during the year} \quad = \quad £38,000$$

Calculate the number of times stock has been turned over during the year.

Cost of materials sold = £42,000, i.e. £9,000 plus £38,000 less £5,000

Average stock of materials = £7,000, i.e. $\dfrac{£9,000 + £5,000}{2}$

Therefore, the stock has been turned over six times during the year, i.e. $\dfrac{£42,000}{£\ 7,000}$

It could also be stated that, on average, stock has been held for two months.

The purpose of this calculation is to identify slow-moving, dormant and obsolete stocks. It can be used for a single item of material, groups of materials or for the total stock.

Issue of Materials. In most cases it is wise to issue the oldest stock first to avoid deterioration. In other words, the stock that is received first is issued first. Slow-moving, dormant and obsolete stocks should be reviewed periodically and disposed of where necessary to make storage space available.

Valuation of Stores Issues

After materials have been issued from stores the material requisition is forwarded to the cost department for pricing so that the material issued can be valued and an amount entered in the stores ledger. However, a problem arises in that once materials have been placed in receptacles in the stores department they lose their identity.

If material prices remained static for long periods there would be no difficulty. Unfortunately in times of rapid inflation the price of material can fluctuate wildly. A consignment of goods at one price is succeeded by a consignment at a much higher price. Which price does one use therefore when valuing stores issues? Does one value stock issues at the price of the first or the second consignment, or is some average used?

There are a number of methods used for the pricing of material iss - ues and these are considered in the following paragraphs. As the method of pricing chosen affects production costs and stock valuation it is important to look closely at each method and to understand the advan-tages and disadvantages of each.

First in, First out (F.I.F.O.) In this method the assumption is that the materials are issued in the same order in which they were received into stock. The valuation of the remaining stock is therefore on the basis that the quanities in hand represent the latest purchases.

The student should be careful not to confuse pricing methods with stock issuing procedures, where the oldest stocks are moved first to avoid deterioration. It is possible for stores to be issued on the first in, first out basis and at the same time to price those same issues using the last in, first out basis. The method of pricing does not have to be consistent with the method of issuing the materials.

Last In, First out (L.I.F.O.) In this method it is presumed that the last stocks received are the first to be issued. Consequently the valuation of the remaining stock is determined by using out-of-date prices.

Weighted average price. This is calculated by dividing the present value of material in stock by the quantity in stock. However this method differs from F.I.F.O. and L.I.F.O. in that the issue price is calculated after each receipt of material.

Standard price. A pre-determined price is calculated for each material in stock and this price is used for all issues over a given period, usually a year. The standard price must take into account the expected level of prices during the year due to such factors as inflation and changes in market conditions. It is possible to use this method of pricing material issues even though a full system of Standard Costing is not in operation.

Replacement price. This is the current market price at the date the material is issued from stores.

Example. The following information refers to the receipt and issue of a certain item of material.

| Date | Receipts | | Issues |
	Quantity	Price per unit (£)	Quantity
Sept 1	100	1.00	
Sept 8	100	1.10	
Sept 12			50
Sept 15	160	1.15	
Sept 17			120
Sept 18			150
Sept 22	150	1.20	
Sept 29			20

The entries in the Stores Ledger Account using the different methods of pricing issues are illustrated in the following pages and show the following balances:

Stock Valuation Method	£
First in first out	203.00
Last in first out	196.00
Weighted average price	200.48
Standard price	200.00
Replacement price	168.50

The methods compared

F.I.F.O.

Advantages :
(a) It is a realistic method of pricing as it conforms to the normal method of issuing stock, i.e. the oldest items are usually issued first;
(b) As the quantities in stock represent the latest purchases, stock is valued using the most recent market prices.

Disadvantages :
(a) The comparison of the cost of one job with another is difficult because different price issues are often used. The cost of a job therefore very much depends on when a person goes to the stores for a new issue of material;
(b) The issue price may not reflect current economic values;
(c) Frequent calculations are required and this causes additional clerical work.

L.I.F.O.

Advantages :
(a) The issue price is near to current economic values;
(b) During a period of rising prices, stock balance values are conservative.

Illustration of stores issues using the First in First Out (FIFO) method

Date	Receipts			Issues			Balance		
	Quantity	Price £	Amount £	Quantity	Price £	Amount £	Quantity	Price £	Amount £
Sept 1	100	1.00	100				100	1.00	100
Sept 8	100	1.10	110				200	-	210
Sept12				50	1.00	50	150	-	160
Sept15	160	1.15	184				310	-	344
Sept17				50	1.00	50			
				70	1.10	77			
Sept18				30	1.10	33	190	-	217
				120	1.15	138			
Sept22	150	1.20	180				40	1.15	46
							190	-	226
Sept29				20	1.15	23	170	-	203

Notes: (a) The remaining balance of £203 is represented by :

$$150 \text{ at } £1.20 = £180$$
$$20 \text{ at } £1.15 = £\ 23$$
$$\overline{£203}$$

(b) The individual prices are rarely stated in the balance column. This is because the quantity in stock often comprises material bought at different prices. However, on September 18th the 40 items remaining in stock are part of one consignment only, the material received on September 15th.

Illustration of stores issues using the Last in First Out (LIFO) method

Date	Receipts			Issues			Balance		
	Quantity	Price £	Amount £	Quantity	Price £	Amount £	Quantity	Price £	Amount £
Sept 1	100	1.00	100				100	1.00	100
Sept 8	100	1.10	110				200	-	210
Sept 12				50	1.10	55	150	-	155
Sept 15	160	1.15	184				310	-	339
Sept 17				120	1.15	138	190	-	201
Sept 18				40	1.15	46			
				50	1.10	55			
				60	1.00	60	40	1.00	40
Sept 22	150	1.20	180				190	-	220
Sept 29				20	1.20	24	170	-	196

Note: The balance of £196 is represented by :

130 at £1.20 = £156
40 at £1.00 = £ 40
      £196

Illustration of stores issues using the Weighted Average Price (WAP) method

Date	Receipts			Issues			Balance		
	Quantity	Price £	Amount £	Quantity	Price £	Amount £	Quantity	Price £	Amount £
Sept 1	100	1.001	100				100	1.00	100
Sept 8	100	1.10	110				200	1.05	210
Sept 12				50	1.05	52.50	150	1.05	157.50
Sept 15	160	1.15	184				310	1.1016	314.50
Sept 17				120	1.1016	132.19	190	1.1016	209.31
Sept 18				150	1.1016	165.24	40	1.1016	44.07
Sept 22	150	1.20	180				190	1.1793	224.07
Sept 29				20	1.1793	23.59	170	1.1793	200.48

Note: The average price is calculated after each receipt. This is computed by taking the value of the items in stock and dividing by the quantity in stock.

Illustration of stores issues using the Standard Price method

Date	Receipts			Issues			Balance		
	Quantity	Price £	Amount £	Quantity	Price £	Amount £	Quantity	Price £	Amount £
Sept 1	100	1.00	100				100	1.00	100
Sept 8	100	1.10	110				200	-	210
Sept 12				50	1.10	55	150	-	155
Sept 15	160	1.15	184				310	-	339
Sept 17				120	1.10	132	190	-	207
Sept 18				150	1.10	165	40	-	42
Sept 22	150	1.20	180				190	-	222
Sept 29				20	1.10	22	170	-	200

Note: (a) The information above is based on a standard price of £1.10.
(b) The closing valuation of stock should be £187, i.e. 170 at £1.10. It is necessary therefore to credit the stores ledger account with £13 and debit a materials price variance account with the same amount

Illustration of stores issues using the Replacement Price method

Date	Receipts			Issues			Balance		
	Quantity	Price £	Amount £	Quantity	Price £	Amount £	Quantity	Price £	Amount £
Sept 1	100	1.00	100				100	1.00	100
Sept 8	100	1.10	110				200	-	210
Sept 12				50	1.15	57.50	150	-	152.50
Sept 15	160	1.15	184				310	-	336.50
Sept 17				120	1.20	144	190	-	192.50
Sept 18				150	1.20	180	40	-	12.50
Sept 22	150	1.20	180				190	-	192.50
Sept 29				20	1.20	24	170	-	168.50

Note: (a) It is assumed that the current market prices were:

Sept 12	£1.15	Sept 18	£1.20
Sept 17	£1.20	Sept 29	£1.20

(b) Some advise that the valuation of stock should not be calculated after each issue, but it has been included here to show the shortcomings of this particular method. If one refers to the balance on September 18th, it can be seen that the quantity of 40 is valued at £12.50. This represents a unit price of 31¼ pence, which is quite meaningless. Indeed, it is easy to obtain a negative valuation. For example, if 190 had been issued on September 18th, the balance column would show a quantity of nil and a negative valuation of £35.50.

(c) The closing valuation of stock should be £204, i.e. 170 at £1.20. The adjustment is made in the accounts by a debit entry in the stores ledger account of £35.50 and a corresponding

Disadvantages :
(a) The method is not realistic as it is contrary to normal issue procedures;
(b) Stock can be valued at out-of-date prices;
(c) Comparison of one job with another is difficult;
(d) Frequent calculations cause much clerical work.

WEIGHTED AVERAGE PRICE

Advantages :
(a) It smooths out fluctuations in issue prices;
(b) The comparison of different jobs is easier.

Disadvantages :
(a) Calculations have to be made to approximately four decimal places to achieve a fair degree of accuracy;
(b) The issue price may not reflect current economic values.

STANDARD PRICE

Advantages :
(a) It is easier to operate as there is no variation of the issue price over long periods;
(b) The efficiency of purchasing is checked as actual prices paid are compared with standard prices.

Disadvantages :
(a) The setting of standards takes time;
(b) It is often difficult to forecast price levels over a period of a year, especially in times of inflation when standards have to be reviewed and altered causing an excessive amount of work.

REPLACEMENT PRICE

Advantages :
(a) Issues are at current prices.

Disadvantages :
(a) The issue price is not at cost, so where there is a long interval between each receipt of material, estimates have to be made;
(b) There is often difficulty and much work involved in ascertaining current market prices.

The effect on stock valuation of using the various methods

The student will notice from the above stores ledger accounts that in a period of rising prices the use of F.I.F.O. will give a higher stock valuation than the use of L.I.F.O. and that the weighted average price method gives a valuation in between the two. Of course the reverse is true during a period of falling prices. It has already been pointed out that the stock valuation using the replacement price method is meaningless unless frequent revaluations of stock are undertaken.

The student will appreciate that a higher stock valuation will result in a higher net profit in the profit and loss account.

Effect on costs

During a period of rising prices, the charge to production will be greater using the L.I.F.O. method, as the latest price, and consequently the highest price, is used first. In the above example, the charge to production during the month of September using F.I.F.O. was £371. Using L.I.F.O. the amount was £378. Naturally if prices are falling the charge to production would be greater using the F.I.F.O. method.

Inflated price

It is sometimes suitable to charge materials to production at an inflated price to compensate for evaporation, deterioration and other acceptable losses. This procedure should only be used for those stock items which are subject to such losses and should be used in conjunction with some other method, for example F.I.F.O.

Example: The original cost of 100 lbs of a certain material is 49 pence per lb. There is considered to be a normal wastage of 2 per cent. The formula for calculating the issue price to compensate for the 2 per cent wastage is:-

$$\text{Unit cost x } \frac{100}{\text{Normal usage percentage}}$$

$$= 49 \text{ pence x } \frac{100}{98}$$

$$= 50 \text{ pence per lb.}$$

The student will note that the original cost is £49 (49 pence x 100lbs), and the amount charged out is also £49 (50 pence x 98lbs). A disadvantage of using an inflated price is that the cause of loss may often be hidden.

EXAMINATION PRACTICE

Students are advised to attempt the questions under simulated examination conditions. Then check their answers with the suggested answers at the back of the book.

••

Question 3   Stock control procedures   Answer page 249

••

In a costing system, differences may arise as follows:

(a)   between bin card balances and actual stores in hand;

(b)   between bin card balances and balances on stores
      ledger accounts.

You are required to explain likely causes for these differences and suggest what action should be taken.

(Institute of Accounting Staff)

A boutique stocks leather coats. In a month when there was no opening balance, the records show the following:

Leather Coats

May	1	Purchases	50 coats at £30 per coat.
	6	Sales	40 coats
	8	Purchases	40 coats at £35 per coat
	13	Sales	20 coats
	15	Purchases	70 coats at £42 per coat
	20	Sales	80 coats
	22	Purchases	60 coats at £28 per coat
	27	Sales	70 coats
	29	Purchases	30 coats at £32 per coat

The boutique owner has heard that there are different methods of pricing out stock and has asked you to write up his records for the above items using the following three methods as alternatives: 1) F.I.F.O.; 2) L.I.F.O.; 3) Weighted average.

You are required to show the relevant stock calculations for each method.

(Institute of Accounting Staff)

The stock ledger analysis for a type of material used in a manufacturing process shows:

	Units	Cost per unit £	Issues during month	
Stock at 1/1/78	60	15.00	Jan.78	50 units
Purchases 31/1/78	80	15.50	Feb.78	60 units
Purchases 28/2/78	50	15.75	Mar.78	60 units
Purchases 31/3/78	100	15.50	Apr.78	90 units
Purchases 30/4/78	60	15.25		

You are required i) to show the stores ledger account from 1/1/78 to 30/4/78 using a) the weighted average method;
b) the first in first out method;
ii) to comment on the effect of each method on stock valuation and cost of production.

(Institute of Accounting Staff)

From the information shown below which relates to component ABC, prepare statements using each of the following methods of stock accounting, viz.

i)   weighted average cost
ii)   standard cost
iii) replacement cost

to show the following

a) the amount to be charged to cost of production
b) the value of the closing stock
c) the difference, if any, between purchase cost and the aggregate of (a) and (b), indicating how (c) would be dealt with in the accounts.

	Receipts into Stores	Unit Cost	Issues to production	Market unit price
	units	£	units	£
May 1	100	41		41
10	75	42		42
15			50	43
20			65	44
23	40	45		45
30			50	46

You may assume the company had no opening stock of component ABC and that in the case of method (ii) it is the company's practice to account for component ABC in terms of a standard unit cost of £40

(Association of Certified Accountants)

(a) Shown below are the forecasted consumption figures for FC Limited in respect of material 426. You are required to calculate the estimated average stock level for the year.

Forecast Consumption

Material 426		Re-order Quantity: 8,000 units	
Month	Consumption	Month	Consumption
January	2,000	July	3,000
February	2,000	August	3,000
March	2,800	September	2,200
April	2,800	October	2,200
May	3,000	November	2,000
June	3,000	December	2,000

Delivery period from suppliers : minimum 2 months
maximum 4 months

(b) How would you ensure that the average stock level is
maintained at the level most favourable to FC Limited?

(Institute of Cost & Management Accountants)

Question 8   Valuation of stores issues   Answer page 255

For the six months ended 31st October, an importer and distrib
distributor of one type of washing machine has the following
transactions in his records. There was an opening balance of
100 units which had a value of £3,900.

Bought

Date	Quantity in units	Cost per unit £
May	100	41
June	200	50
August	400	51.875

The price of £51.875 each for the August receipt was £6.125
per unit less than the normal price because of the large quantity
ordered.

Sold

Date	Quantity in units	Cost per unit £
July	250	64
September	350	70
October	100	74

From the information given above and using weighted average,
F.I.F.O. and L.I.F.O. methods for pricing issues, you are required
for each method to:

(a)   show the stores ledger records including the closing
stock balance and stock valuation;

(b)   prepare in columnar format, trading accounts for the
period to show the gross profit using each of the three
methods of pricing issues;

(c)   comment on which method, in the situation depicted, is
regarded as the best measure of profit, and why.

(Institute of Cost & Management Accountants)

3
Labour

Introduction

Wages (or Labour) is the second of the three elements of cost and, like Materials, it is the responsibility of the cost accountant to direct the attention of management to areas where savings can be made.

The importance of labour in cost control can be appreciated if one considers the manner in which costs are influenced by the addition of just one employee. As well as paying the employee's wages, the employer has to contribute to the national insurance scheme and possibly to a superannuation fund and sports and social club. Expenditure is also incurred on holiday and sick pay, and on subsidised mid-day meals. A new employee requires space, furniture, equipment, stationery and sometimes a telephone extension. He is usually slower, produces less and has to be trained and supervised. Advertisements are placed for new personnel, interview expenses have to be met and for some jobs a contribution is made towards the cost of moving house. If the person engaged is not suitable, the whole process of recruitment and training has to be repeated. The effect on costs of failing to select the right person for the right job is therefore considerable.

In view of the many costs associated with recruiting and employing someone, it is important that the number of people employed does not exceed the number actually needed. Those who are essential should only be engaged after they have been through rigorous selection procedures. Much care should be taken to see that employees are placed in a job to which they are best suited. It is therefore appropriate to consider firstly the procedures necessary for the engagement of new personnel.

Appointment of new employees

The task of recruiting new personnel is the responsibility of the Personnel Department. The position of the Personnel Manager is analogous to that of the Buyer. The latter is charged with the responsibility of acquiring suitable materials whereas the former is called upon to acquire suitable labour; and like the buyer, the personnel manager can only act on receipt of a properly authorised requisition.

The process of recruitment is started by a departmental manager in need of labour and the requisition represents a formal request to the personnel manager to fill a particular vacancy. The completed requisi-

-tion will state the job title, the grade (or proposed salary) and a brief description of the job. In addition the experience, qualifications and personal qualities of the person required to execute the work will be specified.

It is usual practice now to create a budget beyond which it is not permitted to recruit. This figure should be stated on the requisition together with the number of employees actually employed at the date of the requisition. The requisition should also indicate the reasons why an employee is being sought; in effect, this is a justification for incurring all the costs associated with the addition of one employee and is often required even if the person covered by the requisition is within the budget entitlement.

The authorisation procedures for labour requisitions are usually more stringent than for purchase requisitions. In many companies all requisitions for labour have to be approved by the managing director. It has been suggested by some that labour cost control begins at the recruitment stage, the inference being that costs are kept under control by selecting suitable applicants. However, it could be argued that labour cost control begins even earlier, at the authorisation stage, the managing director exercising his veto on certain proposed appointments.

It is not wise, however, always to adhere strictly to the budget limits; a more flexible approach to manpower levels is needed and decisions taken in the light of the anticipated work load. If, during the course of the financial year, the demand for a company's product or service has exceeded expectation, it would be folly to turn down work in order to keep within the prescribed budgeted manpower limits. The purpose of creating these levels is to achieve the company's objectives at minimum cost. The manpower levels are not an end in themselves.

In passing, it might be worthwhile stating that there are other factors which influence decisions on the number of employees engaged, for example, the availability of space and the amount of working capital available.

On receipt of a properly authorised requisition, the personnel manager must then seek suitable applicants. This may involve consulting his files to see whether a recent enquiry has been made for the kind of job described in the requisition. Alternatively, he could contact employmen agencies, or place advertisements in newspapers and trade magazines. Suitable applicants are interviewed and a recommendation made to the departmental manager with whom the final decision rests.

A personnel record card is made out for each new employee which contains:

(a)   the employee's name, address, telephone number, date of birth and national insurance number;

(b)   his clock number, department, job title, rate of pay and date of commencement;

(c)   particulars of previous employment, experience and qualifications;

(d)   sufficient space to record details of the employee's history with the firm, e.g. wage increases, appraisals of performance, promotions and transfers to other departments;

(e)   a record of sickness, absenteeism, lateness and holidays;

(f)   a space to record the date of termination and the reason for leaving.

The income tax form, P45, should be handed by the employee to the personnel department. It is then forwarded to the wages department together with the employee's name, clock number, rate of pay, date of commencement, department, hours of employment and details of any deductions from wages authorised by the employee, e.g. trade union contributions, sports and social club subscription, etc.

Recording Attendance Time

The number of hours the employee is present at his place of work must be recorded so that the wages due to him can be calculated. Overtime must be paid for and deductions made for lateness and absenteeism. The recording of the employee's time can be carried out manually by the gatekeeper. Alternatively, the employee can record his own time by signing an attendance book and noting his time of arrival or departure.

However, the most popular method of recording attendance time today involves the use of time-recording clocks, especially where a significant number of workers are employed. Each employee has a clock card (see *Figure 6*) and when it is inserted in the time recorder, the time of arrival or departure is automatically stamped on the card. Thus, the details recorded on the card become the basis for the calculation of the employee's wages.

In addition, two racks are normally installed, one either side of the time-recording clock. The racks house the clock cards, the one nearest the factory gates (the 'out' rack) holding the cards of those workers who are not on the premises, and the one nearest the factory buildings (the 'in' rack) containing the cards of those who are at work.

On arrival the worker takes his card from the 'out' rack and inserts it in the time recorder which automatically prints the day of the week and the time of arrival in the correct position. He then places the card in the 'in' rack. This procedure is often referred to as 'clocking-in'. The employee will then clock out at lunch time and repeat the process for the afternoon session.

It is possible therefore to ascertain whether a worker is present at work or absent simply by examining the in and out racks. Each employee has a clock number and the cards are positioned in the racks in numerical sequence.

A decision has to be made whether to locate the time-recording clock just inside the factory gates or to provide a number of clocks

		In	Out	In	Out	In	Out	Hours worked
Mon.		8.00	12.01	12.59	5.00			8
Tues.		8.12	12.00	1.00	5.01			7¾
Wed.		8.00	12.00	12.58	5.02	5.30	6.45	9¼
Thurs.		7.59	12.01	1.00	5.00	5.30	7.30	10
Fri.		8.00	12.00	1.00	5.01			8
Sat.								
Sun.								

Clock card — Clock No. ___ Name ___ Week ending ___

	Hours	Rate £	Amount £
Basic Time	40	1.60	64.00
Overtime	3	1.60	4.80
Premium time	1	1.60	1.60
Total	44		70.40

Figure 6 - Clock Card. The days and times are stamped by a time-recorder, but the 'Hrs worked' and the bottom section are completed by the wages staff.

and position them in the various departments. To locate the time-recording clock near the factory gates might cause delay if a number of workers arrive at the same time. However, it is necessary to supervise the clocking of time and this can be undertaken more easily at the factory gates where a gatekeeper can ensure that employees stamp only their own cards and not those of other employees.

At the end of each week the clock cards are forwarded to the wages office where the wages staff calculate the hours for each day and complete the bottom section of the card. In the example shown in *Figure 6*, the calculation of gross wages is based on a 40-hour week, a payment of time and a third for overtime and a rate of £1.60 an hour. It will be noted that a quarter of an hour has been deducted for lateness on Tuesday. The premium time represents the extra 'third' which is payable for overtime.

It is important that the premium time is recorded separately as the cost of premium hours is normally, although not always, charged to overhead. This will be discussed more fully later in the chapter.

It is also important that the difference between hours worked and hours paid is fully appreciated. In the example, the hours worked were 43 but payment has been made for 44 hours.

Pieceworkers. Where an employee's pay is based on the quantity produced rather than on the time attended, it is still necessary for him to follow the clocking procedures. There are a number of reasons for this.

(a) It is important to keep an even flow of production and this can only be achieved if pieceworkers are punctual and regular in their attendance.

(b) Overhead is often apportioned on the basis of the number of hours worked and this can only be done if a record is kept of the hours worked by *all* direct employees.

(c) It is advantageous to know the relationship between hours worked and quantity produced as this information will assist in establishing future piecework rates.

Site workers. Where a company employs workers who travel straight from home to a customer's site, it is not possible for them to use the clock card system. Instead they will generally make out hand-written time sheets and forward them to their foreman for signature. By countersigning the time sheets, the foreman is in effect confirming that the hours worked on site are correct. This, of course, may not be so, especially if the foreman is responsible for a number of sites. All he can do in such circumstances is to visit the site periodically and chech whether the employees are arriving and leaving at the correct times.

Advantages of time-recording clocks. If properly supervised, they provide an accurate record of arrival and departure times which is difficult to challenge. The recording of time is carried out quickly and the times stamped on the card form the basis for wage calculations.

Booking Activity Time.

The need to keep a record of attendance times should now be evident. However, every employee enaged on activity of a direct nature, i.e. an employee working directly on a product or saleable service,must allocate his time to jobs, products, or some other cost unit. Where time cannot be allocated directly to a cost unit, it should nevertheless be accounted for in some other way. For instance, a direct worker may be employed for part of the week on work of an indirect nature, such as supervision, cleaning or maintenance. Moreover, there may be occasions when he is unable to proceed with any work at all because he is waiting for materials, or waiting for further instructions, or for some other reason. All indirect work and idle time of direct workers must be recorded and analysed in such a way that management is aware of the nature of the indirect work and the reasons for the idle time. In this way the whole of a direct worker's time can be properly explained. It should be emphasised that the recording of activity time is generally undertaken only by those employees engaged on production. Indirect workers such as cleaners or accounting personnel do not usually acco-unt for their time.

At the end of the week the total of activity time should be reconciled with the total attendance time to ensure that the hours recorded on the clock cards are accounted for. The reconciliation procedure could be carried out by using the following format:

Summary of attendance time.

	Hours
Number of production workers (say 100) at 40 hours per week	4,000
Add overtime hours (excluding premium hours)	200
	4,200

Summary of activity records.

Direct hours (i.e. hours booked to jobs,products,etc)	3,500
Indirect hours (e.g. cleaning machines)	400
Idle time (e.g. due to machine breakdown)	300
	4,200

If the two totals should fail to agree, the difference must be investigated.

The format chosen for the reconciliation procedure will vary from one business to another depending on the various circumstances that exist. If part-time workers are employed, then clearly the total number of employees cannot be multiplied by 40 hours. Also, it should be remembered that new personnel do not always start on a Monday and, likewise, employees who leave do not always do so on a Friday. This would also affect the total attendance time. However, it is hoped that the above format will indicate to the student the lines along which the reconciliation procedure is to be followed.

There are a number of ways in which activity time can be recorded.

Daily Time Sheets. Each employee will submit one time sheet per day which will include the worker's name, his clock number and department, the date, the job number (or cost code number for indirect work and idle time), a brief description of the work undertaken and the hours taken for each job or operation. The time sheet will be submitted daily to the foreman for signature and then forwarded to the cost office.

This is a simple method of recording activity time but it has some disadvantages. The worker normally completes the time sheet himself and will tend to do this at the end of the day. In other words, he is not recording his time at the moment he finishes one job and commences another. So while time sheets can be commended on the grounds of simplicity, they can be faulted because they are not a sufficiently accurate method of recording a worker's daily activity. Also workers are prone to leave out idle time and they may deliberately falsify the time sheet in order to cover up inefficiences. Indeed, they may enter against each activity the number of hours they believe the foreman wants to see.

It is of the utmost importance that the information provided by the costing system is accurate. Management must be able to rely on the information received, but if the above practice is allowed to take place, there is a danger that the reports issued to management will be based on meaningless data.

The vast amount of paper generated by using daily time sheets is a further disadvantage.

Weekly Time Sheets. The procedure is the same as for daily time sheets with the exception that a space is provided on the sheet for each day of the week, each employee submitting one time sheet per week. The disadvantage of daily time sheets becomes more accute with weekly time sheets. They are even more inaccurate and there is a likelihood of completely omitting the time spent on some jobs. If the time sheet is not completed until the end of the week or the beginning of the following week, the time booked may bear little relation to the actual time spent on each job, especially if the worker has been engaged on a number of different jobs.

Weekly time sheets are more appropriate for those organisations where workers are normally engaged on only one or two jobs a week. The volume of paperwork produced is significantly less than with daily time sheets and this has the effect of significantly reducing the pressure of work in the cost office.

Job Tickets (or Job Cards). Each employee uses a separate ticket for each job (see *Figure 7*). These tickets are often used in conjunction with time-recording machines, which are usually smaller than the time-recording clocks used for registering attendance time. The machines are often situated on the desk of the shop clerk who inserts the job ticket into the machine and the machine stamps the starting or finishing times. The direct workers are therefore 'booked on' and 'booked off' the various jobs.

Much greater reliability can be placed on this system and the possibility of error is considerably reduced. There is much less opportunity to manipulate the number of hours recorded against each job.

However, like daily time sheets, this method has the disadvantage of producing an enormous amount of paperwork, especially if the worker is constantly booking on and off jobs.

Job Tickets that circulate with the work. One job ticket is used for each job or operation and each worker records his time on the same

Job Ticket

Operator's name ....   Clock No ....

Department ....   Date ....

Works order No. ....   Job/code No ....

Time allowed ....

Date and time started ....

Date and time finished ....

Operation No.	Description of operation	Quantity	For office use
			Hrs. Rate Cost
			£ £

Operator's signature ....   Foreman's signature ....

Figure 7 - Job Ticket

ticket. The job ticket remains with the work until the job is completed when it is forwarded to the cost office. One ticket, therefore, contains the total number of hours worked on a particular job and, in consequence, the analysis work of the cost office is made easier.

This method, though, has a major disadvantage. Because the job tickets are not forwarded to the cost office until the completion of the job, it is difficult to reconcile the activity time with the attendance time.

Idle time cards. These cards are used in conjunction with job tickets and they are made out when an employee cannot proceed with work of a productive nature. It is important that the reason for the idle time is stated, e.g. machine breakdown, waiting for materials, etc.

A further card can be used to record work that is indirect in nature, for example, maintenance, cleaning and so on, using a separate code number for each indirect activity.

It is essential that idle time and bookings to indirect work are analysed properly, for such an analysis will assist management in its efforts to ensure that labour is being employed effectively.

The hours recorded on the job tickets and idle time cards are used as a basis for charging the wages of each direct worker to cost centres and cost units.

Piecework Tickets. When the amount of wages paid to an employee is dependant on the number of pieces produced, then the details are recorded on piecework tickets. The details will include the employee's name, his clock number and department, the piece part number, a description of the work, the job or operation number, the quantity produced, the number of units passed by the inspection department, the number rejected, the agreed piecework price, and the signatures of the employee, foreman and inspector.

Methods of Remuneration

There are three basic methods of remunerating workers; by time-rates, piece - rates or premium bonus systems.

Time-rates. The amount earned by the employee is based on the number of hours spent at his place of work and not on the quantity of work produced. The gross wage is calculated thus: Hours worked x rate per hour.

However, the above formula is not absolutely accurate all the time; when overtime is worked, the payment to the employee will also include premium hours. Using the information given in figure 6, the computation is: 44 hours x £1.60 per hour = £70.40.

It is not necessary to compute an hourly rate for every situation; payment can be based on the day of the week. Alternatively, an employee could be paid an annual salary. Whichever period of time is chosen, the principle remains the same; the wage or salary is related to the time worked and not the amount produced.

This method of remuneration has certain advantages:

(a) It is simple to operate and easy to understand. The wages department does not get involved in complex calculations and consequently less clerical staff are required to compute employees' earnings. In contrast, where a weekly bonus is paid, the amount of time spent working out the bonus can be quite substantial. Furthermore, disputes and queries often arise and these throw an additional burden on the wages office staff. With time rates, the employee has little difficulty in calculating the gross pay due to him.

(b) The quality of the work produced tends to be higher, for the worker is not always in a rush to complete a job in order to maximise his earnings.

However, there are a number of disadvantages inherent in this method.

(a) There is no financial incentive to produce more than a minimum amount. In fact, there is often an incentive to produce as little as possible so that the worker can increase his wages by completing the job during overtime. This has a significant adverse effect on the volume of output.

(b) To minimise this practice, the employer would be obliged to incur higher costs on supervision.

(c) The method is often unfair in that good workers are penalised. They receive no extra payment for producing more than the slow workers and dissatisfaction is likely to emerge. Hence, there may be difficulty in retaining skilled labour; resignations could occur if effort is not rewarded, and the employer must not forget the high cost of recruiting and training personnel.

A close examination of these advantages and disadvantages will show that the use of time-rates might be preferred in the following circumstances:

(a) where a high degree of skill is essential in the work; in other words, where accuracy is more important than speed, and quality more desirable than quantity, e.g. tool-making;

(b) for indirect workers, such as office staff, as it is difficult to measure accurately the amount of work produced by these workers;

(c) where the amount produced is influenced by the speed of the machine and consequently outside the control of the employee;

(d) for trainees and apprentices;

(e) where the employer is reasonably satisfied with the existing rate of production;

(f) where the cost of introducing an incentive scheme is greater than the additional profit expected from increased output.

As the employee's pay remains constant and is not influenced by the quantity of work produced, the employer is the one who loses when there is a low rate of production. Conversely, the employer will benefit when output is at a maximum.

The student should observe that, although the labour cost per unit of production depends on the efficiency of the labour force, there are other factors at work, for example, the age and condition of the machinery and the effectiveness of the management.

High Wages Plan. This method, which is sometimes referred to as the 'high day rate' system, is a variation on the time-rate method. In fact, the method of calculating the employee's remuneration is the same, the only difference being that the rate of pay would be significantly higher than normal.

The advocates of the high wages plan argue that the best workers are tempted to apply for the jobs where high rates of pay are advertised. Because of the high rates of pay offered, the management would feel able to demand high output levels. Indeed, at the interview the employee would be acquainted with the level of performance required; the best candidate would be selected and, it is argued, would respond by making the desired effort in order to keep his highly paid job.

The advantages of time-rates are not lost by adopting the high wages scheme and some of the disadvantages lose their force. There is an incentive to produce more because the employee is anxious to preserve his occupation. Also, the dissatisfaction experienced by good workers is less likely to arise. High wages will attract those who are confident they can maintain the high standard of performance necessary.

Piece-rates. Under this method the amount earned by the employee is based on the number of units (or pieces) produced. Piece-rates can be examined under three headings, namely, straight piece-rates, differential piece-rates and piece-rates with guaranteed time-rates.

Under straight piece-rates the payment to the employee is computed thus:

Number of units produced x rate per unit

The worker receives a fixed rate for each unit produced which does not depend on the time taken to produce it. Earnings therefore depend on the volume of the worker's output.

Example: Normal rate per hour = £1.60

Standard time allowed = 10 units per hour

(Therefore, time rate per unit = 16 pence)

During an 8-hour day, Beaver completes 90 units and Sloth completes 60 units.

Therefore the earnings for each employee are:

Beaver 90 units x 16 pence   = £14.40

Sloth   60 units x 16 pence   = £ 9.60

The remuneration fluctuates in direct proportion to the units produced by each employee. Beaver produces 50 per cent more than Sloth and accordingly his wages are 50 per cent higher. If time-rates were used, both employees would receive £12.80, i.e. 8 hours x £1.60.

The advantages of adopting this method are:

    (a)   effort is rewarded and, in consequence, the employee is given the incentive to produce more; he has the opportunity to earn a higher than average wage which should lead to a more contented labour force, with the employer able to retain his more efficient workers;

(b) because of the above less supervision is required;

(c) as some overhead costs are relatively unaffected by an increase in the volume of output, e.g. rent and rates, administration salaries, etc., the employer benefits from a reduction in the overhead cost per unit of production.

The prospect of obtaining these benefits might cause the employer to commit himself hastily to the introduction of this method of remuneration. However, there are some drawbacks:

(a) There is a danger that quality will be sacrificed and, in order to avoid such a situation, the employer would spend more on inspection and quality control.

(b) Pieceworkers, after earning a certain amount during a week, might be satisfied and slacken their pace, arrive late or absent themselves. Plant is therefore left idle and capacity is under-utilised.

(c) A considerable degree of work is involved in setting standard times and as these are subject to the agreement of trade union representatives, further time is often spent in detailed and protracted negotiations before piece-rates are established.

(d) If an error is made and piece-rates are set too high, it is difficult subsequently to reduce them. This could prove to be extremely costly.

There are occasions when pieceworkers cannot proceed with work of a productive nature because of, for example, machine breakdown, shortage of material, etc. When such a situation occurs which is beyond the control of employees, time-rates are substituted for piece-rates.

It was seen that under time-rates the employer gained when production was above normal and suffered adversely from a low rate of production. With the piecework system, the employee gains from additional production and the labour cost per unit remains the same. Nevertheless the employer gains indirectly by achieving a reduction in the overhead cost per unit.

Under the differential piece-rate method, two piece-work rates are used. If the worker completes the work in less than the standard time, he receives the higher rate, and conversely if he takes longer than the standard time he receives the lower rate. It is possible to adopt a number of piecework rates on an ascending scale. The purpose is to encourage workers to achieve very high rates of production by stimulating them at that point when they are becoming satisfied with a certain level and start to slow down.

Using the information given in the previous example and introducing a higher rate of 120 per cent and a lower rate of 80 per cent, the earnings for Beaver and Sloth would be:

Beaver 120 per cent of £14.40 = £17.28

Sloth 80 per cent of £ 9.60 = £ 7.68

Although this method has the advantage of providing a worthwhile inducement to achieve a high level of output, it is manifestly unfair to have such a vast difference between the wages of the two employees. Beaver produces 1½ times the units produced by Sloth but receives 2¼ times the payment. Consequently, this methid is not widely used.

A possible solution is to pay Beaver the higher rate for the excess production rather than for all the production, and to withdraw the lower rate. Sloth would therefore receive £9.60 as he did under the straight piecework method but Beaver's wage would be as follows:

80 units x 16 pence = £12.80

120 per cent of

(10 units x 16 pence)

£ 1.92

£14.72

The inducement however has been considerably diluted.

Piece-rates with guaranteed time-rates is a slight variation on the straight piece-rate method, the only difference being that if the worker falls below the amount he would have received for a given week under the time-rate method, then time-rates are substituted. For example, Sloth would receive £12.80. A worker therefore is guaranteed a minimum wage per week. The knowledge that a guaranteed wage is paid benefits those employees who are likely to worry because of the possibility of receiving low wages. Because of this concern, the amount they produce might be even further affected. However, the spur to work harder is significantly reduced.

Premium bonus systems The main feature of premium bonus systems is that, in addition to normal time-rages, the employee is paid a bonus based on the amount of time saved. It is therefore necessary to establish a time allowance for each job and to record the time actually taken to complete it. The difference between the time allowed and the time taken represents the time saved. It must be emphasised that the bonus is in addition to the normal time-rates and if the employee fails to finish a job in the time allowed, he nevertheless receives his normal wage based on time-rates.

There are two main examples of premium bonus schemes.

(a) The Halsey Scheme. In this scheme the employee receives a bonus of 50 per cent of the time saved and this can be expressed as:

$$\tfrac{1}{2}TS \text{ x hourly rate}$$

Using the Beaver illustration once again, the time allowance for the 90 units produced is 9 hours (Note that the standard time is 10 units per hour). Beaver completes the 90 units in 8 hours and thereby saves 1 hour. As he receives half of the time saved, his bonus payment for that particular day is 80 pence, i.e. 0.5 hours x £1.60. In addition, Beaver receives his normal daily rate of £12.80. His total payment for the day is therefore £13.60.

A similar scheme is the Halsey-Weir plan, the only difference being that the proportion of time saved received by the employee is one third instead of a half.

(b)   The Rowan Scheme. Under this method the bonus is calculated thus:

$$\frac{\text{Time taken}}{\text{Time allowed}} \text{ x time saved x hourly rate}$$

Beaver's bonus would therefore be: $\dfrac{8}{9}$ x 1 x £1.60 = £1.42.

The bonus supplements the daily wage making a total of £14.22.

Premium bonus schemes combine the piece-rate and the time-rate methods and the savings made are shared between the employer and the employee. Hence, this method of remuneration produces lower earnings than the piece-rate method.

The student will be able to work out the advantages and disadvant - ages of premium bonus systems by referring back to the sections on time-rates and piece-rates. However, it is worth stressing that the emp- loyer derives a major advantage from the sharing of the time saved. This in turn means that any errors made in the setting of the initial standard are less crucial. A major disadvantage is the complexity of the bonus calculations and the disputes and queries which might follow.

In some organisations the employee's individual hourly rate is not used and in its place a special bonus rate is used for all employees. This does not make matters easier for the wages office.

Group Bonus Schemes. The incentive schemes explained above are relevant to groups of workers as well as to individuals. The output of the entire group is ascertained, the bonus calculated, and then divided between the workers on some agreed basis. The size of the group can vary. In some cases just a few workers could constitute a group, but in other cases a whole factory might be a single group.

Group bonus schemes have the following advantages:

(a)   co-operation between workers is developed as they are striving towards the same end;

(b)   less supervision is necessary as any lazy workers will be encouraged by their colleagues to work harder.

However, the disadvantage of this type of scheme is apparent. The good workers receive the same payment as the slow workers and as the bonus paid is dependant on the performance of the group as a whole, the motive for the good worker to exert himself is weakened.

Nevertheless, group bonus schemes might be suitable in circumstances when it is difficult to measure the amount produced by individual workers, for example, on an assembly line.

Profit Sharing Schemes. These are schemes in which the employee receives a bonus based on the profits of the organisation. This payment is in addition to the employee's normal wages and the factors that determine the amount of each employee's bonus include (a) his normal wage and (b) his length of service. Sometimes the bonus takes the form of shares in the company which are either given to the employees or set aside for them to buy. Alternatively, a loan could be granted to enable employees to purchase the company's shares.

The purpose of profit-sharing schemes is to encourage the worker to perform well, in the knowledge that he will share in the firm's success. However, profit is not solely dependant on the contribution made by the workers. Profits earned by workers can be quickly eroded by poor management.

Bonus Schemes for Indirect Workers. If a direct worker can be stimulated to produce more by the introduction of an incentive scheme, it follows that clerical workers, typists, foremen and other indirect workers would also work harder and more efficiently if they were to be similarly rewarded. However, the difficulty is to find some appropriate method of measuring the amount of work carried out by these workers and consequently most indirect workers are paid on the time-rate basis. In some cases, it is possible to find a suitable method of creating an incentive, for example:

(a)   foremen and supervisors can be paid a bonus that is allied to the amount produced by their subordinates;

(b)   salesmen are paid a commission which is based on the value of the goods they sell;

(c)   heads of department are sometimes paid a bonus which depends on the level of costs in their department compared with budget.

Installation of an Incentive Scheme. A financial incentive scheme is a scheme in which the payment to employees is linked in some way to the results achieved. Accordingly, it is sometimes referred to as Payment by Results. The object of a scheme of this nature is to raise the level of output, and therefore, it is desirable to consider the principles which should be applied to incentive schemes.

(a) A scheme has little chance of success unless the collaboration of the work force is obtained. Many workers may be suspicious of a proposed scheme on the grouds that its introduction will be followed by redundancies. They reason that if each worker increases his output, then fewer workers are required. If management cannot allay these fears, the support of the employees will not be forthcoming. Full discussions must therefore take place between the employer and the employees' representatives prior to the introduction of an incentive scheme.

(b) The details of the scheme should be fully explained to the work force. The scheme therefore should not be too complicated. It .must be capable of being understood, and it must be possible for the employees to check whether the bonus has been calculated correctly.

(c) The amount of the bonus should be sufficient to stimulate the employees to greater effort. The standards set must be realistic and it should be possible for an average employee to attain the required standard.

(d) In order that increased output is not attained at the expense of quality, an adequate programme of inspection must be provided.

(e) Workers should not be penalised if a situation arises which is beyond their control. The scheme should therefore provide for an 'in lieu' bonus to be paid at times when the employer cannot supply sufficient work of a productive nature for the employee to earn his normal bonus.

(f) The payment of the bonus to the employee should be made as soon as possible after the completion of the work. A bonus payable at thirteen week intervals is not recommended, for some employees find it difficult to sustain an effort for such an extended period.

(g) The scheme should provide the employer with a reduction in the cost per unit produced. An increase in the labour cost per unit should be more than compensated for by a reduction in the overhead cost per unit.

Work Study, Job Evaluation and Merit Rating.

The size of an employee's remuneration and consequently the unit cost of labour are influenced by the extent to which the techniques of work study, job evaluation and merit rating are applied. Work study comprises the two techniques of Method Study and Work Management.

Method Study. This technique is concerned with the detailed investigation by work-study engineers of the way in which the production process is carried on. This will include the examination of the various tasks which are undertaken, the methods used, the sequence in which operations are performed, the plant available and the layout of the factory. All the relevant details are recorded and considered in order to determine whether the best use is being made of the resources available. Improvements are introduced which should have the effect of lowering the unit cost of production.

Work Measurement. Once the improved methods have been adopted, the work-study engineers can then turn their attention towards fixing the time it should take to complete a particular task. This involves the use of time-study in which the time-study engineer, often with the aid of a stop-watch, records the time taken by an operator under normal conditions. To this time is added an allowance for rest periods and personal requirements. Time is deducted if the purpose of the work measurement is to establish allowed times which are to be used in conjunction with sn incentive scheme. This deduction converts the normal estimated time into the time it should take under incentive conditions.

It will be observed that some estimating has to be carried out by the time-study engineer before standards are established. It is essential, therefore, in the first place to obtain the agreement of the employees' representatives and possibly a period of negotiation will take place before time allowances are introduced.

Job Evaluation. In this technique the value of each job is considered in order to rank the various jobs in some order of importance. The course of action to follow in order to evaluate each job is:

(a) consider the skill, training, experience and intelligence required to perform a particular job, the physical and mental effort necessary and the degree of responsibility borne by the job-holder;

(b) establish for each characteristic a maximum number of points which reflects its importance relative to the other characteristics; for instance, if responsibility is considered to be twice as important as physical effort, responsibility can be awarded a maximum value of 10 points and the physical effort at its maximum will be worth 5 points;

(c) taking one job at a time, determine the number of points to be given for each characteristic; for example, the job of the cost accountant might be given 7 out of 10 for responsibility and 1 out of 5 for physical effort;

(d) total of points for each job;

(e) fix the salary or wage to be paid according to the total points earned.

Job evaluation has its critics. The valuation of each characteristic and the awarding of points are purely subjective and in practice wage and salary rates are influenced by many other factors, for example, supply and demand, collective bargaining and government pay guidelines.

Merit Rating. This is a technique which is used to appraise the individual himself, whereas the technique of job evaluation was concerned with placing a value on the job regardless of the person who performs it. A points system is also used in merit rating and the procedure is as follows :

(a) determine the desirable qualities to be found in a good employee, e.g. ability, initiative, reliability, punctuality, etc;

(b) weight the various qualities to reflect the importance of each; for example, initiative might be considered by some to be more important than punctuality;

(c) for each employee, decide on the number of points earned for each quality and arrive at a total.

A system of merit rating can be used for the purpose of determining annual salary increases and also as an aid to decisions on promotion. In some organisations a system of yearly or half-yearly appraisals is in operation where an employee discusses his performance with his superior. This would present an opportunity for the departmental head to inform the employee of his merit rating which the employee could perhaps try to improve upon during the subsequent period. If the points scored by a large number of employees are on the low side, this might give an indication that the selection procedures are not adequate.

Like the technique of job evaluation, the merit rating of employees involves managers and personnel officers making subjective judgments on the relative importance of personal qualities and on the points to be awarded to each employee. However, the system might be appropriate for those employees whose pay is not influenced by any other form of incentive.

Payroll Preparation and Payment of Wages.

The payroll (see *Figure 8*) consists of a sheet or number of sheets on which are entered the names of the employees and the various details necessary to compute the net wages payable to each of them. The payroll procedure can be conveniently broken down into a number of separate stages.

Ascertaining the Gross Pay. The reader will have noted the example given in *Figure 6* which included the calculation of overtime. The wages office must ensure that all overtime has been properly authorised. This check must be carried out by using a document known as an overtime permit which must be completed by the employee's supervisor before the overtime is undertaken. A copy of the permit is forwarded to the wages office and matched against the overtime details recorded on the clock card.

Payroll

Department ....

Week ending ....

Week No ....

Sheet No. ....

Clock No	Name	Hours worked	Overtime premium hours	Total paid hours	Basic pay £	Overtime premium £	Bonus £	Sickness and holiday pay £	Gross pay £

Total Gross Pay to date £	Total Free Pay to date £	Total Taxable pay to date £	Tax this week £	Deductions					Net Pay £	Employer's	
				N.I. £	Pension fund £	Other £	Total £			N.I. £	Pension fund £

Figure 8 - Payroll.

If the worker has earned a bonus payment, this will be added to the wages indicated at the bottom of the card.

The gross wages due to pieceworkers are computed from completed piecework tickets, but where the method of remuneration for pieceworkers includes the payment of a guaranteed minimum wage, reference will be made to the clock cards if the piecework earnings are below the basic wage.

In order to enter the employee's rate of pay on the clock card, the wages clerk will consult the employee's wage record card, which also includes such details as the employee's clock number, department, P.A.Y.E. code number and a record of the employee's earnings and deductions during the current tax year. Entries are made on the card when the employee commences work with the company, the information being supplied by the personnel department. The card will be updated at various times during the employee's period of employment, for example, when an increase in pay is awarded or when a change in the P.A.Y.E. code number is notified by the Inland Revenue.

Ascertaining the Net Pay. The main purpose of preparing the pay - roll is to ascertain the net wages payable to each employee. To arrive at the net wages, certain deductions are made from the gross pay, for example:

(a) income tax under the pay-as-you-earn system;

(b) national insurance contributions;

(c) contributions to a superannuation fund designed to provide the employee with a pension on retirement.

(d) trade union contributions;

(e) subscriptions to the sports and social club;

(f) charitable donations.

The employer is legally compelled to make the deductions in (a) and (b) above. With regard to (e) and (f) the deductions are usually only made with the employee's agreement. In the case of (c) and (d) the situation varies; it is a condition of employment in some organisations that the prospective employee agrees to join a trade union and also to contribute to a superannuation scheme.

Cash Analysis. On the assumption that the net wages are to be paid in cash, an analysis of the note and cash requirements is prepared, i.e. the number of £10, £5 and £1 notes, the quantity of 50 pence pieces, etc. The information obtained by the preparation of the cash analysis is telephoned through to the company's bank so that the money can be ready for collection. A cheque is drawn for the cash required and delivered to the bank, usually by a security firm, in exchange for the cash.

Preparation of Wage Packets. This job is usually carried out by two people, one counting the net wage due to each employee and the other checking the cash and inserting it into the employee's wage packet or envelope. A wage slip is also included in the wage packet which gives details of the employee's gross wages, the various deductions from pay and the net wage. The wage slip is often a duplicate copy of the employee's line on the payroll.

Payment of net wages. It is important that each employee is correctly identified before he receives his pay. If an employee is absent and cannot collect his pay, it can be sent to him by registered post or collected by a relative or colleague, or left in the safe until he returns to work. On no account should a wage packet be handed to another person unless the employee has given that person authority to collect the money on his behalf. In addition, a signature should be requested from the person collecting the money.

Internal Check and Payroll Fraud. There is ample scope for perpetrating fraud at some stage during the preparation and payment of wages. For this reason, it is essential that some form of control exists to prevent fraud or to detect it in its infancy. The dangers to be avoided are: the payment of wages to employees who do not exist i.e. 'dummy' workers; and the payment to an employee of an amount which is more than he is entitled to receive.

These risks can be minimised by:

(a) segregating the work so that the payroll procedures are not the responsibility of only one or two persons; for example, the clerks who prepare the wage sheets should not also make up or distribute the wage packets;

(b) adopting adequate authorisation procedures: piecework tickets and job tickets which are the basis of incentive payments should be signed by an inspector and the employee's foreman; only overtime properly authorised should be paid; changes in wage rates and salaries should only be processed if the personnel manager completes and signs the appropriate form;

(c) proper supervision; the distribution of the pay envelopes must be supervised by a senior official and preferably by one who can identify the recipient;

(d) instituting suitable procedures, for instance, a procedure should be laid down for dealing with unclaimed wages;

(e) creating a programme for internal checks. As part of the programme the personnel officer might periodically check the payroll to ensure that payments are not being made to fictitious employees. If the organisation is sufficiently large, the internal audit department will be very much involved in the creating and working of the internal check programme.

Accounting for Wages

The cost to an employer is the gross wages plus the employer's share of the national insurance and pension fund contributions and consequently they are shown as debit entries in the financial accounts. Bank account is credited, as are the accounts of the Inland Revenue and other creditors:

Example: The following totals were extracted from the payroll for a particular week:

	£	£
Gross wages		10,000
Deductions -		
Tax this week	1,350	
National Insurance	450	
Pension Fund	500	
Trade union subscriptions	30	
Total deductions		2,330
Net wages		7,670
Employer's national insurance contributions		600
Employer's pension fund contributions		500

The entries in the financial books are:

	Dr.	Cr.
	£	£
Gross wages (including employer's national insurance and pension fund contributions)	11,100	
Inland Revenue		2,400
Pension Fund		1,000
Trade union		30
Bank		7,670
	11,100	11,100

Notes:

(a) The employees' and employer's national insurance contributions are payable to the Inland Revenue as well as the tax deducted under the P.A.Y.E. system. The amount of £2,400 posted to the credit side of the Inland Revenue account is made up of £1,350 + £450 + £600.

(b) The various personal accounts will be debited and the bank account credited when cheques are drawn for the amounts due, i.e. £2,400, £1,000 and £30.

Cost Accounts. The employment costs, £11,100, are posted to the cost accounts and to do this it is necessary to analyse the costs between direct wages and indirect wages. Direct wages are allocated to jobs (or products or some other cost unit), indirect functions or idle time, the basis for the apportionment being the hours recorded on the job cards or time sheets. The values of the bookings to indirect functions and idle time are transferred from direct wages to overhead. Other items which are included in overhead are:

> Indirect wages and salaries
>
> Employer's national insurance contributions
>
> Employer's pension fund contributions

Overtime Premium. It was stated earlier in the chapter that the cost of premium hours is normally, though not always, charged to overhead. The position is that where the overtime is worked on a regular basis and is not undertaken in order to complete one specific job, the cost of overhead premium is charged to overhead. Where, on the other hand, the overtime is worked in order to meet the specific delivery requirements of one customer, the cost of overtime is directly attributable to that order and overtime premium should be charged to the job.

Labour Turnover

Labour turnover is a term which signifies the extent to which employees leave an organisation. It can be measured by using the following formula:

$$\frac{\text{Number of employees leaving during a period}}{\text{Average number of employees}} \times 100$$

The percentage calculated is referred to as the Labour Turnover Ratio (or Rate).

Example: The details below relate to the month of March.

Total number of employees at the beginning of month - 201

Number of employees who started during the month - 3

Number of employees leaving during the month - 5

Therefore, total number of employees at end of month - 199

The labour turnover rate for March is therefore $\dfrac{5}{\frac{1}{2}(201 + 199)} \times 100 = 2\frac{1}{2}\%$

To obtain the maximum benefit from the calculation, the rate of labour turnover should be compared with the rate for previous periods and, if available, the rate for other businesses in the area and in the industry as a whole.

If the number of leavers is high relative to the total number of employees, a high ratio will emerge. An increase in the number of employees leaving and/or a reduction in the total workforce will cause a increase in the rate compared with previous periods. The effect of a high rate is reflected in loss of output, a lowering of morale and higher costs.

Loss of output occurs because of:

(a) the gap between a person leaving and his replacement starting, which one report put at twelve working days on average;

(b) the length of time taken to train a new employee to the level of efficiency of the previous employee;

(c) the reduced effort given by an employee during the days or weeks immediately prior to the date of departure.

Cost of Labour Turnover. In addition to the increase in the cost per unit which results from reduced production and low morale, the following costs are likely to be higher when the rate of labour turnover is on the increase:

(a) advertising for personnel and interviewing expenses;

(b) the reimbursement of removal and settling-in expenses, for example, solicitors' and house agents' fees, removal of furniture to new house, and subsistence allowance between date of commencement and date of moving;

(c) training, including the new employee's wages during the training period, the wages and salaries of instructors, supervisors and other experienced employees who spend time guiding the new recruit during the early weeks, materials used in the training school and the cost of sending new employees to college or on courses;

(d) scrap and defective work;

(e) machine breakdown;

(f) administration of personnel department, e.g. stationery, additional staff;

(g) pension scheme administration.

It is difficult however to calculate the true cost of labour turnover. One can appreciate that a high rate is costly but it would be more helpful if a value could be given. It is possible to go some of the way by creating cost centres in order to segregate those costs which are affected by the number of employees leaving. Separate cost codes can be issued for items such as advertising for personnel, scrap, and training. However, the cost of advertising for personnel would include advertising for additional staff because of expansion, as well as replacements. It must be left to the cost accountant to analyse the expenditure included in the various cost centres in order to value the extent of labour turnover.

Causes of Labour Turnover. Although labour turnover cannot be eliminated completely, the problem can be tackled by an understanding of the events and circumstances by which it is caused. Why do people leave? The following are some of the reasons given:

(a) dissatisfaction with the job, wages, hours of work or working conditions;

(b) discontent due to the relationship with the employee's supervisor and/or colleagues;

(c) lack of promotion opportunities;

(d) personal matters, e.g. ill health, marriage, pregnancy, moving to a new area.

Of course, employees do not always leave voluntarily. They are sometimes discharged due to redundancy, incompetence, lateness, absenteeism and for disciplinary reasons.

Reduction in the Labour Turnover Rate. It is the responsibility of the personnel manager to find ways in which the rate can be reduced or kept to a minimum. The following should be considered:

(a) regular statistics should be provided analysing labour turnover by cause and indicating whether the cause was avoidable or unavoidable and whether the person left voluntarily or was dismissed; nevertheless, there are dangers inherent in such an analysis because employees who leave do not always give the true reasons for leaving;

(b) seek ways in which the selection of applicants can be improved in order to prevent situations arising where employees are discontented or unsuitable;

(c) ensure that the labour requirements are properly planned in order to avoid redundancies;

(d) consider the introduction of a high wages plan or some other form of incentive;

(e) see that the working environment is congenial;

(f) consider whether the transfer of a dissatisfied employee to another department will remove the cause of the dissatisfaction;

(g) hold annual medical check-ups in order to prevent ill-health at a later date;

(h) consider whether the fringe benefits are competitive, e.g. pension scheme, subsidised meals, sports and social facilities;

(i) develop better human relationships between management and workers.

As it is important for an organisation to keep its skilled and experienced employees, a target labour turnover rate could be set, with the personnel manager being responsible if the rate is higher than target .

EXAMINATION PRACTICE

Students are advised to attempt the questions under simulated examination conditions. Then check their answers with the suggested answers at the back of the book.

Question 9   Labour rate calculations   Answer page 257

A contractor uses a labour group of two skilled and three unskilled workers to do small contract jobs. The contractor wishes to charge out the work done by this group on an hourly basis. The information for the group is as follows:

	One skilled worker	One unskilled worker
Working hours per week	40	40
Normal idle time	10% of working hours	10% of working hours
Holidays per annum	Three weeks on full pay plus bonus of £30 per annum	Three weeks on full pay
Wage rate per hour	£1.20	80p
Food allowance per working week	£6	£4
Lodging allowance per working week	£9	£6
Non-contributory pension fund - employer's payment per annum	£123	-

You are required to calculate a labour hour rate for the group assuming fifty two weeks per year.

(Institute of Accounting Staff)

Question 10   Labour cost calculations   Answer page 257

An item passes through five successive hand operations in sequence as follows:

Operation	Time per article (minutes)	Grade of employee	Wages rate per hour
1	12	A	50p
2	20	B	55p
3	30	C	60p

4	10	D	70p
5	15	E	80p

A 36 hour week is worked and a production target of 720 dozen items has been set.

You are required to calculate:

(a) the total number of workers required;

(b) the weekly cost of each operation;

(c) the total labour cost for a week.

(Institute of Accounting Staf,

Question 11   Principles of labour costing   Answer page 25'

Assume that you are dealing with a manufacturing concern which employs a large labour force in a factory with many departments and different activities.

You are required to discuss the involvement of the cost department in the timekeeping and payroll preparation in such an organisation.

(Institute of Accounting Staf,

Question 12   Employee remuneration calculations   Answer page 2!

(a) Based on the data shown below, you are required to calculate the remuneration of each employee, as determined by each of the following methods:

(i) hourly rate;

(ii) basic piece rate;

(iii) individual bonus scheme, where the employee receives a bonus in proportion of the time saved to the time allowed:

Data

Name of employee	Salmon	Roach	Pike
Units produced	270	200	220
Time allowed in minutes per unit	10	15	12
Time taken in hours	40	38	36
	£	£	£
Rate per hour	1.25	1.05	1.20
Rate per unit	0.20	0.25	0.24

(b) Comment briefly on the effectiveness of method (iii).

(Institute of Cost & Management Accountants)

Question 13   Labour incentive schemes   Answer page 259

(a) Recent regulations affecting pay policies are causing many businesses to re-examine the use of incentive schemes as a method of remunerating employees. Discuss the general principles which should be applied to incentive schemes.

(b) Certain organisations, for example car manufacturers, have abandoned premium bonus schemes and piece work schemes and substituted a 'high day rate' system. List the advantages and disadvantages expected from following such a policy.

(Institute of Cost & Management Accountants)

Question 14   Labour incentive schemes   Answer page 260

Bonus systems are often introduced as part of labour remuneration. These are generally for direct workers and on the individual or group basis.

You are required to state when the individual basis would be preferable and the features and effects of such schemes.

(Institute of Accounting Staff)

Question 15   Principles of labour and stock turnover   Answer page 260

'Labour turnover should be low whereas stores turnover should be high'. Analyse critically this statement, and discuss the problems inherent in calculating turnover rates for labour and stores, and the importance of these in controlling costs.

(Institute of Cost & Management Accountants)

Question 16   Prevention of fraud and labour turnover   Answer page 261

The total cost of production of X Limited has risen considerably in the last year, despite the fact that output has not risen significantly. As cost accountant, assume you have completed an investigation and have established that two of the major factors were: (a) fraud in connection with wages; and (b) labour turnover.

You are required to prepare a report for the directors to explain:
- (a) the steps to be taken to minimise fraud in connection with wages;
- (b) how a high labour turnover affects the cost of production.

(Institute of Cost & Management Accountants)

4
Overheads

Introduction

It has already been stated that Overhead is the total cost of indirect materials, indirect wages and indirect expenses. Each of these elements of indirect cost will now be examined in more detail.

Indirect Materials Cost. This term is defined by the I.C.M.A. Terminology simply as 'materials cost other than direct materials cost'. It is necessary therefore to refer again to the definition of direct materials cost in order to understand what is meant by indirect materials cost. Put simply, direct materials comprise those materials which become part of a particular product or service which a business sells to its customers. All other materials are indirect materials. In other words, indirect materials can be defined as materials which do not become part of a product or saleable service, for example, rags to clean machines, soap for use in the washrooms, floor polish, books for the technical library, stationery, fuel oil and so on.

It must be remembered that there are some materials which, although direct in nature, are treated as indirect for costing purposes. Screws, nuts and washers, for example, represent an insignificant part of the material content of the product as a whole, and the cost and effort involved in trying to determine accurately the quantity that becomes part of the finished product cannot reasonably be justified. The cost of materials of small value therefore is normally charged to production overhead.

Indirect Wages Cost. The definition given by the I.C.M.A. Terminology is 'wages cost other than direct wages cost'. By referring back to the definition of direct wages cost it is possible to give a more detailed definition of indirect wages cost. It can be defined as the remuneration paid to those employees who do not work directly on a product or saleable service, e.g. production foremen and office typists.

However, a note of caution needs to be sounded here. If, for instance, a foreman is responsible for a group of workers who are engaged in the manufacture of a single product, there is no reason why the remuneration paid to him should be treated as indirect wages. His effort and skill are applied to one product and consequently his wages can be charged to the product for which he is responsible.

Again, the work of a typist in a research laboratory may consist entirely of typing reports for a customer who has placed a large research contract with her employer. She is therefore working on one particular contract. There is no element of sharing involved, so her wages can be allocated entirely to the contract that consumes her time.

The definition of indirect wages includes the proportion of the wages paid to direct workers which is attributable to idle time and work of an indirect nature. For example, assume that a direct employee earned £60 for a 40-hour week and his time bookings for the week were as follows:

	Hours
Job No.123	30
Idle time due to machine breakdown	4
Cleaning machines	1
Maintenance	5
	40

An amount of £15, i.e. £60 x 10/40, would be charged to production overhead in respect of indirect wages, and £45 would be treated as direct wages.

Also included in the category of indirect wages are the employer's national insurance and pension fund contributions, for direct as well as indirect employees. The cost of overtime premium is also included, except in those circumstances where overtime is worked in order to satisfy the specific delivery requirements of an individual customer.

Indirect expenses. The I.C.M.A. definition is 'expenses, other than direct expenses'. Costs included in this category include rent and rates, electricity, telephone rental and calls, and repairs to buildings.

Overhead, then, comprises those costs which cannot be easily identified with one particular product or saleable service.

Collection of Overhead

The collection of overhead involves the processing of various documents from which the necessary data can be extracted.

Information relating to indirect materials is found by referring to suppliers' invoices, goods received notes and material requisitions. For example, the details of a consignment of stationery would be recorded on a goods received note.

The wages and salaries paid to employees, such as salesmen and storekeepers who are engaged on work of an indirect nature, can be extracted from the payroll. Details of indirect bookings made by direct workers can be taken from idle time cards, time sheets, or from some other time record. The cost of overtime premium is collected from the appropriate column on the payroll.

The particulars of travelling and entertaining expenses incurred by employees engaged on company business are normally recorded in the petty cash book. The entries in this book must be supported by properly authorised expense claim forms, to which should be attached the relevant documentary evidence, for example hotel and restaurant bills.

The end of the costing period will often precede the receipt of some invoices. In order to include in the cost accounts for the period an appropriate charge for a service received, it is necessary to prepare a journal voucher and to make an estimate of the amount of expenditure which has accrued. This procedure is required in the case of electricity because invoices are generally received at three-monthly intervals. An estimated amount can be arrived at by taking the meter readings at the end of the costing period and multiplying the units consumed by the price per unit, adding a proportion of the standing charge to the result.

Similarly, a journal voucher should be prepared where an invoice has been passed that covers future periods, so that the proportion of the charge that refers to later months is credited in the cost accounts. This is necessary for expenses such as rates and insurance. With regard to telephone costs, both accured charges and prepayments may have to be included on the journal voucher because calls are charged for in arrears whereas rental is charged for in advance.

Classification of Overhead

It was pointed out in chapter one that there are various ways in which the same cost can be classified. A company manufacturing a number of different products would probably classify its costs in a manner that would reveal the cost of producing each product. The company may also wish to know the cost of the various functions of the business; production, marketing, administration, and research and development. Another company may manufacture only one product, but if production takes place in a number of different locations, an analysis of costs by factory might be pertinent. It is the responsibility of the cost accountant to provide managers with information that will enable them to manage effectively. The methods of classification chosen must fulfil this objective and there must be sufficient flexibility to meet changes in requirements.

Cost Code Numbers. The collection and classification of overhead costs are made easier by adopting a system of cost code numbers, sometimes referred to as standing order numbers. A schedule, often called a coding manual, is produced which lists the various headings and items of expenditure under which the costs are to be classified. A cost code number is given to each item and this number must be recorded on all documents used in the costing system, e.g. purchase orders, goods received notes, suppliers' invoices, job tickets and idle time cards.

The number of code numbers used will depend on the extent of the analysis required. If too many numbers are employed, the costing system will be burdened with too much detail and employees will spend much of their time searching through a complex coding manual in the hope of finding a suitable code number. On the other hand, if too few numbers are used, the information provided will be insufficient to assist management to plan and control effectively the operation of the business. The cost accountant must try to strike a suitable balance between these two extremes.

The headings adopted will depend on the nature of the business, the manner in which it is organised and the information requirements of management. Each organisation will have its own particular scheme but it is usual to differentiate between the major functions of the business, i.e. production, marketing, administration, and research and development. In addition, there should be a code number for each item of expenditure; for example, stationery, repairs to plant and machinery, electricity and so on.

It is important that the system of coding facilitates the control of labour costs with regard to bookings to indirect work and idle time. Indirect activities, such as supervision, cleaning and maintenance, should each have a separate code number. Individual code numbers should also be issued to record the various reasons for idle time, e.g. waiting for work, waiting for instructions, waiting for material, machine breakdown, etc. Bookings to idle time and indirect work are often the subject of regular reports to management as an aid to the exercise of proper control over labout costs.

Example. A manufacturing company, with a head office in London, has factories in Southampton, Birmingham and Manchester. It has been agreed that overhead costs are to be classified by type of expense, by function and by factory. The cost accountant has decided to use code numbers with five digits in order to facilitate the classification of costs. The first digit denotes the factory, the second specifies the function and the last three digits indicate the nature of the expense. The following are the code numbers chosen:

Code No.	Location	Code No.	Function
1	Southampton	5	Production
2	Birmingham	6	Marketing
3	Manchester	7	Administration
4	Head Office	8	Research and Development
		9	Services

Code No.	Type of expense (extract)
300	Telephone rental
301	Telephone calls
302	Postage
303	Stationery
304	Consumable materials
305	Travel expenses
306	Entertaining expenses

So, if a salesman based in Birmingham entertained a client to lunch, he would enter code number 2.6.306 on his expense claim form. With the ability of the computer to handle large quantities of information, it is possible to extend the number of ways in which the same costs can be classified.

Distribution of Overhead

After being collected and classified, each item of overhead is distributed to a cost centre. For the moment, the procedure for the distribution of production overhead will be examined; consideration of the overhead incurred by other functions will be deferred until later in the chapter.

The distribution of overhead to cost centres consists of the following cost allotment procedure:

(a) the allocation of overhead to cost centres;
(b) the apportionment of overhead to cost centres;
(c) the allocation and apportionment of the total costs of service cost centres to cost centres using the service provided.

The terms 'allocation' and 'apportionment' have been used deliberately because they are given specific meanings in the I.C.M.A. Terminology and the student should make a point of differentiating between the two.

Cost Allocation. 'The allotment of whole items of cost to cost centres or cost units'.

Cost Apportionment. 'The allotment to two or more cost centres of proportions of common items of cost on the estimated basis of benefit received'.

'Allocation' of overhead takes place, therefore, where the amount to be charged to a particular cost centre can be accurately ascertained. For example, the wages of the canteen manager are wholly attributable to the canteen. If the canteen is treated as a separate cost centre, then the wages of the canteen manager are 'allocated' to that cost centre. The wages of the chef and waiters are treated in similar fashion. The employer's national insurance contributions on behalf of the canteen staff can also be allocated to the canteen.

Also, if a plant register is kept which identifies each item of equipment by plant number and gives information regarding the date of purchase, the cost centre in which the plant is located and the rate of depreciation, it is possible to allocate depreciation charges to individual cost centres.

Overhead is 'apportioned' where an item of expenditure benefits two or more cost centres and the amount chargeable to each cannot be calculated with any degree of accuracy. Of course, only those cost centres which benefit from the cost should be charged. It is therefore necessary to find a basis of apportionment in order to distribute the cost. Different bases will be used to distribute the various items of cost. The amount charged to a cost centre must be fair, so the basis of apportionment chosen should divide the overhead as equitably as possible and be acceptable to the departmental manager receiving the charge.

The manner in which the overhead is apportioned is usually the responsibility of the cost accountant, who will from time to time receive advice from those within the organisation who are in a position to give a technical opinion, for example, on the power used by various machines. Although the cost accountant may use sound judgment in selecting appropriate bases, there will be some instances where, at best, an arbitrary distribution will have to be made. Often the information necessary to apportion the costs fairly is not available and the additional accuracy achieved does not warrant the high cost involved in obtaining the necessary details. For example, in order to apportion the cost of electric lighting, a degree of accuracy can be attained by making estimates of electricity consumption based on the wattage of lamps. Alternatively, it is possible to instal meters at various points within the establishment in order to allocate accurately the cost to cost centres. But is the time and expense of going to such lengths justified? The cost accountant must take a decision on the degree of accuracy necessary bearing in mind the costs involved and the benefits received.

Some of the more common bases used for the apportionment of overheads are given below

Basis of apportionment	Type of expenditure
Number of employees	Supervision, welfare, medical costs, charitable donations, employer's liability insurance.
Floor area occupied	Rent, rates, repairs to buildings, heating, lighting.
Book value	Depreciation and insurance of plant and machinery.
Horse power of machines	Power

In the case of lighting and heating, cubic capacity might be a more suitable basis where the height of the ceiling varies from one floor to another

It will be appreciated that the use of some of the bases of apportionment may not lead to a very precise distribution of overhead. This could apply, for example, to supervision. Some sections of the organisation, because of the nature of the work, require a good deal of supervision, whereas in other departments, employees are able to proceed with their work without supervision. Consequently, cost allocation is to be preferred to cost apportionment, if accurate information is easily available.

Example. A company has three production departments, A, B and C, and a service department, S. The overhead costs incurred during a particular four-week costing period were:

	£	£
Indirect wages and salaries -		
Dept.A	4,000	
Dept.B	3,000	
Dept.C	3,500	
Dept.S	2,500	
		13,000
National insurance		780
Rent and rates		600
Repairs to plant and machinery		600
Depreciation of plant and machinery		450
Heating and lighting		300
Power		560
Insurance		350
Medical costs		20

The following information is also available:

	Dept. A	Dept. B	Dept. C	Dept. S
Area in square feet	10,000	8,000	7,000	5,000
Number of employees	20	12	15	13
Book value of plant and machinery	£10,000	£12,000	£6,000	£2,000
Average stock	£2,000	£1,500	£1,500	--
Horse power of machines	120	95	55	10

Carry out the allocation and apportionment of overhead to the four departments.

In order to illustrate the calculations that follow, rent and rates has been chosen as an example.

$$\text{Dept. A} = £600 \times \frac{10,000}{30,000} = \overset{£}{200}$$

$$\text{Dept. B} = £600 \times \frac{8,000}{30,000} = 160$$

$$\text{Dept. C} = £600 \times \frac{7,000}{30,000} = 140$$

$$\text{Dept. S} = £600 \times \frac{5,000}{30,000} = 100$$

$$600$$

Overhead Distribution Sheet

Cost	Amount £	Basis of apportion. ment	Production depts. A £	B £	C £	Service dept. S £
Indirect wages and salaries.	13,000	Allocation	4,000	3,000	3,500	2,500
National insurance	780	Indirect wages and salaries	240	180	210	150
Rent and rates	600	Area (sq.ft.)	200	160	140	100
Repairs to plant and machinery	600	Book value	200	240	120	40
Depreciation of plant & machinery	450	Book value	150	180	90	30
Heating & lighting	300	Area (sq.ft.)	100	80	70	50
Power	560	HP of machines	240	190	110	20
Insurance	350	Book value of plant and machinery plus average stock	120	135	75	20
Medical costs	20	No of employees	7	4	5	4
	16,660		5,257	4,169	4,320	2,914

Service Department Costs. The next step is to allot the total cost of each service department to those departments using the service. The same procedure is adopted; the costs are allocated where possible, otherwise they are apportioned using some suitable basis of apportionment. The objective is to charge all costs to cost units, i.e. products, jobs, etc.

It is possible, for example, to allocate the costs of a maintenance department if employees engaged on maintenance work keep a record of the time spent in each department. The costs of other service departments, the canteen for instance, will have to be apportioned. Examples of bases used for service departments are:

Basis of apportionment	Service department
Number of employees	Canteen, personnel, security, wages
Floor area	Cleaning
Number of material requisitions	Stores
Number of purchase requisitions	Purchasing

Example: Using the information given in the above example and assuming that service department S is a canteen, apportion the total cost of the service department to the production departments, using a suitable basis of apportionment.

Overhead Distribution Sheet (continued)

Cost	Amount £	Basis of apportionment	Production depts. A £	B £	C £	Service dept.S canteen £
Brought forward	16,660		5,257	4,169	4,320	2,914
Canteen	--	Number of employees	1,240	744	930	-2,914
Total	16,660		6,497	4,913	5,250	--

Reciprocal Service Costs. It is a fairly simple exercise to allot the cost of one service department to a number of production departments. However, in practice, it is more likely that a number of service departments will exist, and in addition to providing a service to production departments, they will be performing services for each other. The transfer of overhead between service departments can cause quite a problem. The costs of a service department will be distributed at the end of a costing period but, concurrently, the same service department will receive charges from other service departments. For example, the distribution of canteen costs would presumably include an amount to be charged to the maintenance department but, equally, an allocation may have to be made by the maintenance department to the canteen for, say, repairs to tables and chairs. The total cost of the canteen cannot be ascertained until the costs of maintenance have been received and, similarly, the maintenance department's total cost will not be known until it receives a share of the canteen costs. The problem can be dealt with in one of three ways, by using:

(a) simultaneous equations;
(b) continuous allotment;
(c) a specified order of closing.

Example. A company has three production departments and two service departments. The overhead distribution sheet showed the following totals:

	£
Production departments -	
A	2,500
B	3,100
C	2,800
Service departments -	
S	800
T	1,390

The costs of the service departments are to be distributed using the following bases of apportionment:

	Dept.S %	Dept.T %
A	30	40
B	20	15
C	40	25
S	--	20
T	10	--
	100	100

The service department costs can be apportioned using each of the three methods, thus:

(a) Simultaneous equations (or the Algebraic method). Assume that equals the total cost of department S after receiving 20 per cent of T's costs. Assume also that b equals the total cost of department T after receiving 10 per cent of the costs of department S. Therefore:

$$a = £800 + 0.2b \quad \text{Equation 1}$$
$$b = £1,390 + 0.1a \quad \text{Equation 2}$$

Also:
$$a - 0.2b = £800 \quad \text{Equation 3}$$
$$b - 0.1a = £1,390 \quad \text{Equation 4}$$

Multiply equation 3 by 5, thus;
$$5a - b = £4,000 \quad \text{Equation 5}$$

Add equations 4 and 5
$$4.9a = £5,390$$

Therefore $a = £1,100$

Substitute £1,100 for a in equation 1

Therefore
$$0.2b = £300$$
$$b = £1,500$$

The costs of the service departments can now be distributed to the production departments using the bases of apportionment given:

	Total £	A £	B £	C £
Per overhead distribution sheet	8,400	2,500	3,100	2,8C
Department S	990	330	220	44
Department T	1,200	600	225	37
	10,590	3,430	3,545	3,61

(b) Continuous Allotment (or Repeated Distribution). In this methc the costs of one of the service departments are allotted to the other departments. The costs of the next service department are then allotte to the other departments, including the first service department. The first service department then allots the amount received from the secor service department. This process of distribution is repeated until the amount left is too small to warrant accurate distribution.

	A £	B £	C £	S £	T £
Per overhead distribu- tion sheet	2,500	3,100	2,800	800	1,390
Department S	240	160	320	−800	80
Department T	588	221	367	294	−1,470
Department S	88	59	118	−294	29
Department T	12	4	7	6	−29
Department S	2	1	3	−6	−
	3,430	3,545	3,615	−	−

It will be noticed that this method gives the same result as the previous method.

(c) Specified order of closing. A decision is made concerning the order in which service departments are closed and, once closed, they cannot be re-opened to receive charges from other service departments.

If S were closed first, the distribution would be as follows:

	A £	B £	C £	S £	T £
Per overhead distribution sheet	2,500	3,100	2,800	800	1,390
Department S	240	160	320	−800	80
Department T	735	276	459	-	1,470
	3,475	3,536	3,579	-	-

If T were closed first, the result would be:

	A £	B £	C £	S £	T £
Per overhead distribution sheet	2,500	3,100	2,800	800	1,390
Department T	556	208	348	278	−1,390
Department S	359	240	479	−1,078	-
	3,415	3,548	3,627	-	-

This method is less accurate than the other two, but there is little merit in being too accurate. It is frequently difficult to find bases of apportionment that distribute the overhead accurately and in this example it is apparent that the percentages have been rounded to the nearest five per cent.

Overhead Absorption.

It might be appropriate at this point to recapitulate on the procedure so far with regard to the allotment of production costs to cost units and cost centres. Costs which are easily identifiable with a particular product or saleable service, i.e. direct costs, can be allocated directly to cost units The cost unit could be a product, a job, a contract or a service. All other costs are allocated or apportioned to cost centres. Remember that the term 'allocated' is used when whole items of cost can be charged to a cost centre, and the term 'apportioned' is used where costs need to be shared between two or more cost centres.

It is then necessary to allocate and apportion the costs of service cost centres to cost centres using the service. This is the stage that has now been reached; direct costs have been allocated to cost units, and overhead has been alloted, i.e. allocated and apportioned, to production cost centres.

It is now necessary to allocate the costs of each production cost centre to the cost units passing through the cost centre. In this way cost units will not only receive the direct costs associated with them, but also a share of production overhead. The charging of production overhead to cost units is carried out by the process of Overhead Absorption, which is defined by the I.C.M.A. Terminology as :

'The allotment of overhead to cost units by means of rates separately calculated for each cost centre'.

It is necessary therefore to calculate overhead absorption rates for each cost centre in order to charge the products, jobs and contracts which benefit from the facilities of the cost centre.

But the question arises, how is the rate to be calculated? One of the figures in the calculation must be the total overhead of the cost centre, for it is this total that has to be shared among the cost units. With regard to the other figure, it is necessary to find a suitable basis of apportionment. Once a suitable basis has been selected, an overhead absorption rate for the cost centre can be calculated and then applied to the cost units passing through the cost centre.

Methods of Overhead Absorption. There are a number of methods for calculating absorption rates, each one involving the use of a different base. Those most commonly used are listed below together with the relevant formulae:

Direct labour hour rate $= \dfrac{\text{Total overhead of cost centre}}{\text{Direct labour hours}}$

Machine hour rate $= \dfrac{\text{Total overhead of cost centre}}{\text{Machine hours}}$

Direct materials percentage rate $= \dfrac{\text{Total overhead of cost centre} \times 100}{\text{Direct materials cost}}$

Direct wages percentage rate $= \dfrac{\text{Total overhead of cost centre} \times 100}{\text{Direct wages cost}}$

Prime cost percentage rate $= \dfrac{\text{Total overhead of cost centre} \times 100}{\text{Prime cost}}$

Cost unit rate $= \dfrac{\text{Total overhead of cost centre}}{\text{Cost units produced}}$

The direct labour hours used to compute the direct labour hour rate exclude idle time and any work of an indirect nature, such as maintenance or cleaning. Likewise, the machine hours used to calculate the machine hour rate consist only of operating hours. Time spent on cleaning and resetting is excluded.

The student should note that whichever method is used, the numerator is the same; it is only the denominator (or base) that changes.

The first two rates are based on hours (or time), and are expressed as 'so much per hour'. The next three are shown as percentages and the cost unit rate is expressed as 'so much per unit'.

Example. The following cost statement has been produced for department A, a production cost centre, for the month of March:

	£
Direct materials cost	10,000
Direct wages cost	4,000
Direct expenses	1,000
Prime cost	15,000
Production overhead	3,000
Cost of production	18,000
Number of articles produced	1,500
Direct labour hours employed	2,500
Machine hours	2,000

Calculate an overhead absorption rate for production overhead using the various methods.

Direct labour hour rate $\dfrac{£3000}{2500}$ = £1.20 per direct labour hour

Machine hour rate $\dfrac{£3000}{2000}$ = £1.50 per machine hour

Direct materials percentage rate $\dfrac{£3000 \times 100}{£10000}$ = 30 per cent of direct materials cost

Direct wages percentage rate $\dfrac{£3000 \times 100}{4000}$ = 75 per cent of direct wages

Prime cost percentage rate $\dfrac{£3000 \times 100}{£15000}$ = 20 per cent of prime cost

Cost unit rate $\dfrac{£3000}{1500}$ = £2 per unit

Application of overhead absorption rate. The overhead absorption rate for a cost centre is then applied to the cost units passing through that cost centre.

Example. During the month of March, work was carried out on job No. 123 which involved the manufacture of 3 articles. The following costs and times were recorded:

	£
Direct materials cost	21
Direct wages cost	15
Direct expenses	2
Prime cost	38
Direct labour hours	5
Machine hours	4½

Using the overhead rates computed in the previous example, show the production overhead that would apply to job No. 123 for each method adopted.

Method	Calculation	Overhead absorbed
Direct labour hour rate	5 hours x £1.20	£6.00
Machine hour rate	4½ hours x £1.50	£6.75
Direct materials percentage rate	30 per cent of £21	£6.30
Direct wages percentage rate	75 per cent of £15	£11.25
Prime cost percentage rate	20 per cent of £38	£7.60
Cost unit rate	3 units x £2	£6.00

It will be observed that the amount absorbed by a cost unit very much depends on the method of absorption chosen. Assume that the manufacturer in the above example bases his selling prices on production cost. By taking just two of the methods, it is possible to see the effect that different methods of absorption will have on his selling prices. It is assumed also that 30 per cent is added to the cost of production to cover administration and marketing costs and net profit.

	Direct wages percentage rate	Direct labour hour rate
	£	£
Prime cost	38,00	38.00
Production overhead	11.25	6.00
Cost of production	49.25	44.00
Add 30 per cent to cover other costs and net profit	14.77	13.20
Selling price	64.02	57.20

How has this difference come about? How is it that when using the direct wages percentage method, an amount of £11.25 is charged to job No. 123 for production overhead, whereas with the direct labour hour method the amount is £6.00? By referring back to the cost statement for department A, it will be observed that the average hourly wage rate is

£1.60, i.e. $\dfrac{£4,000}{2,500}$. For job number 123 the rate is £3 per hour, i.e.

$\dfrac{£15}{5}$. Consequently, employees who are more highly paid than average

have been used on this job. This has the effect of increasing the amount of direct wages charged to the job, and it is to this higher figure that the direct wage percentage rate has been applied. Of course, situations will arise where the reverse occurs. There will be those jobs that use employees whose rates of pay are lower than average. In those situations, the amount of production overhead absorbed will be greater using the direct labour hour rate.

But which rate is most suitable? In what circumstances should one rate be adopted in preference to another? When would it be appropriate to use a machine hour rate?

Choice of overhead absorption rate. It is only necessary to compute one rate for each cost centre but the most suitable rate must be chosen. With this in mind, the various methods are examined below in order to discover the circumstances in which each can be used. It is, of course, possible to choose one method for one cost centre and a different method for another cost centre.

Cost unit rate. Where units passing through a cost centre are the same, the best method is to calculate a unit rate so that each cost unit receives an equal share of the overhead. However, this method is clearly unsuitable if cost units are dissimilar. In an organisation that undertakes jobbing work, one job may cost £100, whereas another might cost £5. Clearly, it would be unfair to charge each job with the same amount of production overhead.

Direct labour hour rate. Most production overhead costs fluctuate with the amount of time spent producing the cost units. For example, if the number of direct hours were to increase by, say, fifty per cent, additional indirect staff, such as storekeepers and canteen assistants, would need to be recruited to support the increase in the direct labour force. Equally, the size of other costs, such as lighting and heating, depends to some extent on the number of direct labour hours worked. It seems relevant, therefore, to apportion production overhead on the basis of the length of time taken to produce a cost unit, so that cost units which make the most use of production facilities are charged with a higher share of the overhead.

This method is particularly suitable where the majority of production operations are carried out manually, but it is necessary to ensure that there is a system of booking activity time in order to obtain the number of hours worked on each cost unit.

Machine hour rate. Where production is largely mechanised, many of the overhead costs of a cost centre are caused because of the widespread use of plant and machinery, for example, power, depreciation, maintenance, insurance and so on. In such circumstances, a machine hour rate can be used to absorb the overhead. However, there are two disadvantages; it is necessary to record the number of machine hours worked; and where some jobs are completed without the use of any machinery, they receive no charge whatsoever for overhead.

Direct materials percentage rate. This methos id not usually suitable for the absorption of productior overhead as the overhead is rarely related to the cost of direct material used. However, where the cost of direct materials represents a substantial proportion of prime cost, it may be the only convenient way to absorb the overhead. It could also be employed where the overhead contains a large proportion of costs related to materials, for example, purchasing, receiving, storage and handling. Nevertheless, it will be appreciated that, although the overhead may to some extent be related to material, the amount of overhead is not necessarily influenced by the cost of the material. For instance, the overhead cost incurred to purchase, receive, store and handle an inexpensive piece of material may be greater in some cases than the overhead cost incurred on more expensive material.

Direct wages percentage rate. Where there is only a slight variation in the rates of pay for different grades of workers, this method will produce similar results to the direct labour hour rate. However, where the differentials are wide, then the combination of workers employed on a particular cost unit will affect the amount of overhead absorbed. If the hours worked on two cost units were identical, the one which required employees who receive higher rates of pay would receive a larger share of the production overhead. This method is not particularly suitable therefore where there exists substantial differences in rates of pay.

Prime cost percentage rate. Like the materials percentage rate, over head is rarely related to prime cost. This method is not usually recommended.

Predetermined Overhead Absorption Rates.

It has been seen that, at the end of the costing period, the overhead of each production department is totalled and charged to cost units by means of an overhead absorption rate. Costs are therefore not ascertained until some time after work has been completed. In most cases, this delay is unsatisfactory.

Suppose that the selling price of a particular job is to be arrived at after the costs have been calculated. A garage, for example, will undertake repairs to a motor car and the price to the customer will be based on the cost incurred by the garage. The cost of direct materials is known; the number of hours and the rates of pay are also known. But the proprietor has to include in the total cost an amount for production overhead. He cannot ask the customer to return in, say, four weeks time when the overhead for the month has been collected, classified and alloted to the various jobs passing through the garage. Also, the proprietor would not be prepared to send the customer an invoice when the cost details have been compiled. The invoice has to be prepared the same day, so that the customer can collect the vehicle and settle his account immediately. There is, therefore, a need to calculate an overhead rate in advance, based on estimates, and to apply this predetermined rate to cost units passing through a particular cost centre.

There is a further reason why the use of a predetermined rate is necessary. It has been seen that the overhead rate is influenced by two factors. For example, the direct labour hour rate is affected by the amount of overhead expenditure incurred and the number of direct hours worked. Both these factors will, throughout the year, affect the size of the rate. During the winter, because of increased heating costs, overhead expenditure might be higher than in the summer months. Also, where the trade is seasonal, the number of hours worked would vary from one month to the next. If overhead were absorbed at the end of each month, the overhead rate would fluctuate, possibly wildly. And if selling prices were to be based on a fluctuating monthly overhead rate, the selling price of identical goods and services would vary from month to month.

To overcome this problem, a predetermined rate is usually calculated at the commencement of each accounting year, based on annual budgets, and applied to all cost units throughout the year. This successfully takes away the adverse effects of fluctuating overhead costs and seasonal working.

The procedure for calculating the predetermined rate is similar to that stated above, the only difference being that the figures are based on some prediction, e.g. a budget, a forecast or an estimate, and the period to be covered is usually a year. For example, the formula for calculating a predetermined overhead absorption rate using the direct labour hour method is:

$$\frac{\text{Budgeted overhead of cost centre}}{\text{Budgeted direct labour hours}}$$

The other methods are calculated in the same way as previously mentioned with the exception that the words 'budgeted' or 'estimated' are included in the formula.

Under/over absorption of overhead. Use of predetermined overhead rates based as they are on predictions of future events will result in an under-absorption or an over-absorption of overhead. Events never turn out exactly as forecast and it is therefore necessary to compare the actual overhead incurred with the overhead absorbed to find out the extent of under/over absorption.

Example. The following information was extracted from the budget for a particular year:

Budgeted overhead   £100,000
Budgeted direct labour hours   50,000

At the end of the accounting year in question, it was revealed that overhead expenditure had amounted to £105,000 and that 48,000 hours had been worked.

Calculate the under/over absorption of overhead for the year.

Note firstly that the predetermined overhead absorption rate is £2 per direct labour hour, i.e. $\frac{£100,000}{50,000}$. The overhead absorbed during the year is therefore:

$$48,000 \text{ hours} \times £2 = £96,000$$

Consequently, the under-absorption of overhead amounts to £9,000, i.e. £105,000 − £96,000.

The student should note particularly (a) the formula for calculating the overhead absorbed by cost units and (b) the method for calculating the under/over absorption of overhead:

    (a)   overhead absorbed = Actual direct labour hours x budgeted overhead rate;

    (b)   overhead under-absorbed = Actual overhead incurred − overhead absorbed;

           overhead over-absorbed = Overhead absorbed − actual overhead incurred.

It is possible to analyse the loss of £9,000 by cause. The overhead incurred exceeded expectations by £5,000, i.e. £105,000 − £100,000, and the direct labour hours worked were 2,000 less than budget, causing a further loss of £4,000, i.e. 2000 x £2 per hour. This analysis by cause can be summarised as follows:

	£
Over-expenditure	5,000
Loss of direct labour hours	4,000
Under-absorbed overhead	9,000

In the cost accounts, overhead expenditure incurred is entered on the debit side of production overhead account, and overhead absorbed is entered on the credit side. The difference between the two sides represents the under/over absorption of overhead and is transferred to overhead adjustment account. The information above would be shown in the production overhead account as follows :

Production Overhead Account

	£		£
Overhead incurred	105,000	Overhead absorbed	96.000
	-	Under-absorbed	9,000
	105,000		105,000

A more detailed explanation will be provided in the chapter on Cost Accounts.

Blanket Rates. As indicated above, overhead absorption rates are calculated for each cost centre and applied to cost units passing through the cost centre. A blanket rate is a single rate that is computed from information relating to two or more cost centres, or a rate embracing all the activities in the entire factory. This practice is not recommended as the amount of overhead incurred will vary from one cost centre to another. For example, the overhead of a cost centre where the manufacturing operations are carried out with the assistance of expensive machinery would be significantly higher than the overhead of a cost centre where the work is processed entirely by hand. Also, the use made of cost centres sometimes varies. The manufacture of one cost unit might be entirely executed in department A, whereas another cost unit could be produced by departments B and C.

It should be the objective when determining overhead rates to ensure an equitable distribution between cost units. It is unlikely that this will be achieved if blanket rates are used.

Increases/decreases in Predetermined Overhead Rates. It is possible for overhead absorption rates to vary considerably from one year to the next It was stated earlier in the chapter that the rate is influenced by two factors: the production overhead costs and the base used to determine the rate. A movement in either of these factors will affect the rate, unless of course they both change in the same proportion.

Before a budget is approved, the reasons which have caused a change in the rate should be examined. The reason could be higher projected overhead costs. Alternatively, a reduction in production activity could be forecast. Budget plans may have to be amended in order to bring about a reduction in the proposed rate.

However, in some circumstances an increase in the rate may be acceptable. For example, production overhead may be higher compared with the previous year due to a deliberate policy of increased mechanisation. This in turn would reduce the number of direct labour hours required to perform the production operations. If the direct labour hour rate was used to absorb overhead, this increase in the numerator and decrease in the denominator would cause a significant increase in the rate. Such a rise might suggest higher costs in the forthcoming year. But is this correct? Take the following illustration :

A company budgets to produce 10,000 units during a year and the expectation is that it takes 2 man-hours to produce each unit. The production overhead costs are forecast at £40,000. The overhead absorption rate is therefore £2 per direct labour hour. The following year, because of depreciation costs associated with additional plant, the overhead is expected to be £48,000, an increase of 20 per cent. It is again expected that 10,000 units will be produced but because of increased mechanisa tion, only 1½ hours will be needed to produce each unit. The overhead rate will, therefore, be £3.20 per direct labour hour, i.e. $\dfrac{£48,000}{15,000}$. The overhead absorption rate has therefore increased from £2.00 to £3.20, an increase of 60 per cent. On the face of it, this looks inefficient, but although the overhead rate has increased by 60 per cent, costs have in fact come down. Assume that the direct workers are paid £2 per hour

Cost of 1 unit:

	Year 1 £	Year 2 £
Labour cost -		
2 hours at £2 per hour	4	
1½ hours at £2 per hour		3
Production overhead -		
2 hours at £2 per hour	4	
1½ hours at £3.20 per hour		4.80
	8	7.80

Similarly, a reduction in the overhead rate does not necessarily imply increased efficiency. It could be that additional activity has increased at a greater rate than overhead expenditure. This will be discussed more fully in chapter 7 when fixed and variable costs are examined.

Individual machine-hour Rates. If the costs of individual machines vary to any great extent, it is not advisable to compute one overall machine hour rate. For example, the depreciation charge can vary considerably between machines. Also, one machine may require an operator's full-time attention whereas elsewhere in the machine shop one operator may be able to supervise two or more machines. Again, if some cost units only pass through machines which incur high costs whilst other units are processed by using low-cost machinery, it would be inequitable to apply a single machine hour rate. In these circumstances it is necessary to compute rates for individual machines (or groups of similar machines), each machine (or group) being a separate cost centre. The method for calculating overhead absorption rates for individual machines is similiar to the method used for calculating one rate for all plant and machinery in a department.

$$\frac{\text{Overhead cost attributable to a machine}}{\text{Number of machine hours}}$$

The overhead cost comprises expenditure which can be directly allocated to the machine, for example depreciation and maintenance, and a share of other overhead costs such as rent and rates, heating and lighting Also included is the cost of any reserve or stand-by equipment necessary in the event of the machine breaking down. The cost of cleaning and resetting the machine are also taken into account. The number of machine hours will only consist of those which are spent on actual production.

Example. A predetermined absorption rate is to be established for a particular machine for the year ending 31st December 19......

(a) The machine was bought two years ago for £12,000 and cost £200 to install; it has an estimated life of 8 years and an estimated residual value of £400.
Depreciation is calculated using the straight-line method.

(b) The maintenance costs during the year are expected to be £536 and it is thought wise to budget an amount of £150 for the possible use of reserve equipment.
Insurance premiums will amount to £60.

(c) Costs extracted from the machine shop budget are:

	£
Rent and rates	2,400
Heating and lighting	900
Supervision	3,000
Consumable materials	600

(d) There are 240 working days during the year and the machine operators work 8 hours each day. Each machine requires the attention of a full-time operator who spends approximately 10 per cent of his time cleaning and resetting the machine. The rest of the time is spent on production.

(e) The labour rate will be £1.50 per hour and power costs are likely to be 8 pence per hour.

(f) The area in square feet is: department 3,000
                                    machine   250

(g) Supervision and consumable materials are to be apportioned on the basis of the number of hours the machine is engaged in production, the budget for the whole of the machine shop being 25,920 hours.

You are required to calculate an overhead absorption rate for the machine for the year ending 31st December 19......

Workings:

Depreciation $= \dfrac{£12,200 - £400}{8} = £1,475$

Rent and rates $= \dfrac{£2,400 \times 250}{3000} = £200$

Heating and lighting $= \dfrac{£900 \times 250}{3000} = £\ 75$

Number of hours the machine is to be used on production $= 90\%$ of $(240 \times 8) = 1728$ hours

Supervision $= \dfrac{£3,000 \times 1,728}{29,920} = £200$

Consumable materials $= \dfrac{£600 \times 1,728}{25,920} = £\ 40$

Calculation of machine hour rate

	£
Depreciation	1,475
Maintenance	536
Reserve equipment	150
Insurance	60
Rent and rates	200
Heating and lighting	75
Supervision	200
Consumable materials	40
Cleaning and resetting, 192 hours x	
£1.50 per hour	288
	3,024

Divide £3,024 by 1,728 production hours	1.75
Add power	0.08
Overhead rate per machine hour	1.83

Marketing Overhead

Earlier in the chapter it was stated that overhead is generally classified by function. Once this has taken place, marketing overhead, which comprises the cost of selling, publicity and distribution, can be alloted to marketing cost centres. For example, the cost centre may consist of various locations in which the marketing function is organised. The process of allotment will include the apportionment of expenditure such as rent, rates, lighting and heating. In addition, there must be added a proportion of service department costs. The service provided by the maintenance department, canteen and other service cost centres benefit, not only the production departments, but the marketing function also. This procedure of allocation and apportionment of overhead is followed for a all the major functions.

However, in the case of absorption a problem arises because there is no satisfactory basis for the absorption of marketing overhead by cost units. It cannot be amalgamated with the production overhead and included in an overall absorption rate because the sale and distribution of products and services takes place at a different time from the production activity. It would not be correct to charge cost units with a share of marketing overhead until they have been sold and distributed to customers.

The following solutions can be adopted:

(a) include marketing overhead in the cost accounts but make no attempt to charge it to cost units; instead, transfer the amount to costing profit and loss account at the end of each month.

(b) absorb marketing overhead by calculating and applying an arbitary rate of absorption, for example -

(i) $\dfrac{\text{Marketing overhead}}{\text{Cost of production}}$ x 100

(ii) $\dfrac{\text{Marketing overhead}}{\text{Sales}}$ x 100

The percentage calculated is then applied to each cost unit when it is sold.

As with production overhead, absorption can take place at the end of a costing period or by using a predetermined rate.

It is important to realise the arbitary nature of the above methods of absorption related to value, for the amount of marketing overhead incurred does not depend on the value of the items being sold. One expensive, established product may require no advertising expenditure, may consume only a small proportion of a salesman's time and involve neglible transport costs. On the other hand, a new, inexpensive product may require much effort and expenditure to sell, publicise and distribute.

Administration Overhead.

Administration overhead costs are costs of general management, accounting and administrative services, which cannot be directly related to the other major functions of the business, i.e. production, marketing, or research and development.

This category does not include the cost of all administrative activities, for some jobs which are administrative in nature are directly related to one of the other main functions. For example, an area sales manager would be concerned with administration, but he is providing a service which benefits the marketing function. Administration is regarded as a separate activity which assists the business as a whole. It cannot usually be associated with any product or saleable service and consequently in most businesses all the general administration costs are treated as overhead.

Because overhead is usually classified by function, administration overhead is separately assembled and the total includes a proportion of the costs of service departments, e.g. maintenance, canteen, cleaning, etc. However, separate cost centres are set up within the administration function and the relevant cost must be alloted to individual cost centres. These cost centres usually include the following:

(a) general management, including the managing director, his staff and other directors;
(b) accounting;
(c) legal and secretarial;
(d) personnel;
(e) data processing;
(f) corporate planning;
(g) internal audit.

Items of expenditure are coded so that costs can also be classified by nature of expense. Examples of administration overhead are :

(a)   wages and salaries of administration personnel;
(b)   rent, rates, insurance, lighting and heating;
(c)   depreciation and maintenance of buildings, furniture and equipment;
(d)   audit fees, bank charges and legal costs;
(e)   telephone costs, stationery, postage.

In some cases costs can be directly allocated to individual cost centres, salaries for instance, whereas in other cases allotment can only take place by apportionment, e.g. rent, rates, etc.

The procedure so far is reasonably straightforward but, like marketing overhead, a problem arises when absorption is considered, for a suitable basis for the absorption of administration overhead by cost units is difficult to find. Indeed, some cost accountants would suggest there exists no case for the absorption of administration overhead by cost units. The arguments will be stated later but for the moment consideration will be given to ways in which the overhead can be absorbed.

(a)   Allot administration overhead between production and marketing. This can either be done scientifically, or on some arbitary basis. If a scientific approach is to be adopted, it is necessary to break down the activities in the cost centres and decide the benefit received by the production and marketing functions. For instance, if one takes the accounting department, it is possible to allocate the cost of the sales ledger section to marketing. Also, most of the costs incurred by the cost office can be identified with the production function, e.g. making entries in the stores and work in progress ledgers, analysing job card bookings, etc. This analysis is carried out for all activities in the administration cost centres until all the costs have been transferred.

To go to such lengths would mean establishing a number of additional cost centres. The accounting function, for example, would have to be divided into sales ledger, bought ledger, costing, wages and so on, in order to accumulate the cost of each activity separately. Even if further cost centres were not set up, a great deal of analysis work would be necessary. Also, there may be a number of production cost centres each with their own overhead absorption rate, each of which would receive a share of the administration overhead.

If administration overhead is to be shared between the production and marketing departments, it is probably better to use some arbitary method of apportionment. After the apportionment, the transferred costs are then included in the production and marketing overhead absorption rates.

(b)   Another method of absorbing administration overhead is to calculate a predetermined administration overhead rate by dividing the total estimated administration cost by the expected cost of production and expressing the result as a percentage. The percentage would then be applied to the production cost of each cost unit. Alternatively, estimated sales could be used as a base and the absorption rate applied to the sales value of each unit.

However, many cost accountants argue that administration costs should not be absorbed, especially in the manner outlined in (a) above. They argue that the majority of administration costs are fixed; they would still be incurred even if there was no production during a costing period. Also, it is further put forward that to transfer administration overhead to production would mean that the valuation of work in progress and finished goods stock would include a share of administration overhead. It is the view of a great many cost accountants that only production overhead should be included in the valuation of finished goods and work in progress. Accordingly, they reason that the total administration costs should be transferred to costing profit and loss account and charged against the sales of the period in which they are incurred. Of course, transferring total administration costs in this way does not obviate the need for cost centres. These are still required for control purposes so that the cost of the various activities can still be related to individuals responsible for the control of those activities.

However, even if absorption is not adopted, there may still be a need to compute an administration overhead recovery rate so that the cost of administration is not forgotten when fixing selling prices.

Research and Development Overhead.

Like marketing costs, research and development expenditure can also be treated as direct. A customer sometimes provides finance so that research can be undertaken on a specific project. However, this section is concerned with expenditure which cannot be recovered against a specific contract, but must be recovered generally from current production.

The following definitions are given by the I.C.M.A. Terminology :

Research cost - 'The cost of seeking new or improved products, applications of materials or methods'.

Development cost - ' The cost of the process which begins with the implementation of the decision to produce a new or improved product or to employ a new or improved method, and ends with the commencement of formal production of that product or by that method.'

The collection, classification and distribution of research and development overhead follows the same pattern as the other overhead functions. The salaries of engineers and scientists and the depreciation of test gear are two costs which can be directly allocated to cost centres. The cost centre could be a research establishment or one particular research project.

Finding a suitable method of absorption is again a problem, even more so, as formal production may not commence for many years. As absorption must take place on the current year's production, the only alternatives are :

(a) transfer research and development overhead to costing profit and loss.

(b) use of an arbitary method of absorption -

(i) $\dfrac{\text{Research and development overhead} \times 100}{\text{Cost of production}}$ or

(ii) $\dfrac{\text{Research and development overhead} \times 100}{\text{Sales}}$

EXAMINATION PRACTICE

Students are advised to attempt the questions under simulated examination conditions. Then check their answers with the suggested answers at the back of the book.

Question 17   Overhead absorption   **Answer page 262**

A company makes two products - Gamma and Delta. The total budget for overheads in the next year is £30,000. Other budget costs and details are:

	Gamma		Delta
Units of production	10,000		5,000
Prime Cost per unit			
Material			
¾lb of X at £1 per lb	£0.75	½lb of Y at £1.80 per lb	£0.90
Labour			
24minutes at 75p per hr	0.30	24minutes at£2.50per hr	1.00
Total Prime Cost	£1.05		£1.90

You are required to:
(a) calculate four different overhead recovery rates;
(b) for one unit of Gamma and one unit of Delta, show the overhead and total cost by each of the four methods.

(Institute of Accounting Staff)

Question 18   Overhead apportionment   **Answer page 263**

A company with three production departments and two service depart. ments has the following balances on a departmental distribution summary of expenses:

Production Departments		Service Departments	
Manufacturing	£24,000	Power	£3,000
Assembly	£21,000	Administr-	
Finishing	£18,000	tion	£5,000

The expenses of the Service Departments are charged out on the follow-ing basis :

Service Department	Production Department Manufac-turing	Assembly	Finishing	Service Department Power	Administration
Power	40%	25%	15%	-	20%
Administr-tion.	35%	30%	20%	15%	-

You are required to show the apportionment of expenses from the service departments to the production departments by an appropriate method.

(Institute of Accounting Staff)

Question 19   Overhead absorption   Answer page 264

You are given the following information relating to Job 99 which is to be processed in a machine shop :

	Previous period	Job 99
Value of materials consumed	£6,600	£14.50
Direct labour cost	£9,900	£22.00
Direct labour hours	8,250	14
Machine hours	11,000	15
Units produced	495	1
Overheads	£3,960	to be added

You are required

a) to calculate four possible prices to be quoted for Job 99, assuming a profit margin of $33\frac{1}{3}\%$ on sale price, and using different methods of overhead recovery.
b) to comment briefly on the merits of each method you have used.

(Institute of Accounting Staff)

Question 20   Overhead absorption   Answer page 265

Your company is contemplating buying a heavy duty site-levelling machine which will be hired out at an hourly rate. Two similar machines, with different cost patterns are being considered. You are given the following data :

Machine	X	Y
Capital cost	£22,000	£18,300
Value estimated after one year	£ 4,000	£ 3,000

Estimated operating time next year	900 hrs	900 hrs
Costs expected to vary with operating time:		
Fuel cost per hour	£3	£3.50
Servicing cost per quarter	£540	£810
Tyres per month	£270	£315
Driver's remuneration per ann.	£7,200	£7,200
Fixed costs for next year including Central Admin. Expenses	£1,530	£1,530

You are required to calculate an hourly rate for each machine and to recommend which should be bought, allowing for a profit margin of 20% of the total cost in each case, and bearing in mind it is a very competitive market.

(Institute of Accounting Staff)

Question 21   Under/over absorption of overhead   Answer page 265

The ABC Company has two production departments, viz. Machining and Finishing, and two service departments, viz. Maintenance and Materials Handling.

The overhead budgets per four week period are £9,000 for the Machining Department, and £7,500 for the Finishing Department. The Machining Department overhead is absorbed on a machine hour basis (300 per period) and Finishing Department overhead is absorbed on the basis of direct labour hours (3,000 per period)

In establishing the overhead budgets of the production departments, service department costs have been dealt with as follows :

Maintenance Dept.	60% to Machining Dept.,
	30% to Finishing Dept., and
	10% to Materials Handling.
Materials Handling:	30% to Machining Dept.,
	50% to Finishing Dept., and
	20% to Maintenance Dept.

During Period VI, the Machining Dept. was in operation for 292 hours and the number of direct hours worked by Finishing Dept. personnel was 3,100. Overhead incurred during Period VI was as follows :

	Machining	Finishing	Maintenance	Materials Handling
Materials	£2,000	£3,000	£1,000	£200
Labour	3,000	900	2,000	3,000
Other allocated costs	600	400	800	300

You are required to

a) write up the overhead accounts for each of the production departments for Period VI showing the disposition of any under/over absorption,

b) state the factors which gave rise to the under/over absorption, and

c) analyse the under/over absorption under the headings you have stated in your answer to (b).

(Association of Certified Accountants)

Question 22   Under/over absorption of overhead   Answer page 266

A manufacturing company has two production departments, viz. Machining and Assembly, and two service departments viz. Tooling and Maintenance

The budgeted monthly activity level of the Machining Department is 400 machine hours and the budgeted overhead cost £16,000. The Assembly Department's overhead budget is £9,600 per month during which 2,400 direct labour hours are expected to be worked.

In determining the overhead budgets of the production departments, the expenses of the service departments were dealt with as follows:

Tooling	70% to Machining
	20% to Assembly
	10% to Maintenance
Maintenance	50% to Machining
	30% to Assembly
	20% to Tooling

During May 1978, the Machining Department booked 415 hours of machine time to production, and the Assembly Department booked 2,350 direct labour hours. Overhead incurred during the month was as follows :

	Machining £	Assembly £	Tooling £	Maintenance £
Material	4,600	5,200	1,800	600
Labour	6,100	1,200	2,700	1,600
Miscellaneous	700	900	500	300

You are required to:

a) prepare the overhead account for each production department showing the amount of any over/under absorption and its disposition;

b) identify the causes which give rise to the over/under absorption in each department, and state the amount attributable to each cause.

(Association of Certified Accountants)

'Generally speaking, there are no difficulties in determining the amount to be charged to a particular job for direct material and direct labour, but the amount of production overhead to be charged gives rise to problems.

Explain this quotation demonstrating in your answer your understanding of:

a) the distinguishing features of direct costs and overhead;

b) the accounting techniques which justify the claim that there are no difficulties in determining the charges to the job for direct material and direct labour;

c) the principle(s) which should determine the amount of production overhead to be included in the cost of the job.

N.B. For the purpose of this question you may assume that the company does not use a marginal costing system.

(Association of Certified Accountants)

Write a short essay on the subject 'Overhead Absorption' paying particular attention to :

a) the meaning of the expression,

b) the basic information required,

c) the methods commonly used, and

d) the problems which arise in practice.

(Association of Certified Accountants)

AC Engineering Company Limited manufactures a wide variety of products. You have recently been appointed management accountant of the company and are concerned with the current method of absorbing production overhead.

You are required to prepare for the next board meeting of the company a report in which you should discuss briefly five methods of overhead absorption, and in respect of each, you should suggest, with reasons, why you would or would not advocate its possible adoption by the company.

(Institute of Cost & Management Accountants)

The chairman of your company has been studying the budgets for the next accounting period and has shown particular interest in the production cost budget. In this the production overhead will increase from the current absorption rate of 200% of direct wages cost to 300%. The production manager protests that this increase is unacceptable.

As company cost accountant prepare a brief report for the chairman, explaining:

a) how the overhead absorption rate is calculated and used;
b) which factors may have contributed to the increase in the rate;
c) the circumstances in which such an increase can be acceptable.

(Institute of Cost & Management Accountants)

Meklect Limited produce two types of lawnmower, a mechanical model, and an electric model. The company's trading summary for the year recently ended is as follows :

	£	£
Sales		550,000
Direct material and labour	389,000	
Factory overhead	40,000	
Administration overhead	30,000	
Marketing overhead	16,500	
		475,500
Profit		74,500

The directors consider the profit/sales ratio (13.54%) to be inadequate and have asked you to analyse the trading summary in order to determine the profitability of each of the two models.
Your investigation reveals :

	£
1. Sales for the year were	
5,000 mechanical models	325,000
3,000 electric models	225,000

2. Opening stocks of raw material were £45,000 and closing stocks 54,000. Purchases during the year were £324,000.

3. £150,000 of material was used in the production of mechanical models and the remainder on the electric models.

4. The piecework labour rate is £10 for a mechanical model and £8 for an electric model.

5. Included in Factory Overhead are the following costs with indications of the directors' views of their apportionment:

	£	Mechanical	Electrical
Indirect labour	15,000	one-third	two-thirds
Power	6,500	three-fifths	two-fifths
Depreciation	12,000	three-sevenths	four-sevenths

The remaining Factory Overhead is to be apportioned equally.

6. Administration Overhead includes a computer bureau's charge of £11,000 for producing sales invoices; this charge is to be apportioned according to invoiced sales value; the remaining Administration Overhea is to be apportioned equally to the two models.

7. Marketing Overhead is to be borne by the two models in proportion t invoiced sales values.

8. Finished Stocks and Work in Progress were the same at the end of the year as they were at the beginning.

You are required to produce statements to show:
a) the trading results for each model
b) the unit cost and profit of each model, analysing cost as follows:
    Direct Material
    Direct Labour
    Factory Overhead
    Administration Overhead
    Marketing Overhead
and to add brief comments which you think may be helpful to the directors.

(Institute of Certified Accountant.

Question 28   Direct and indirect costs   Answer page 27

---

a)   TJ Limited is a manufacturer of hand painted Toby jugs, and is keen to establish a flourishing overseas market. At a recent exhibition of china and pottery, the company's representative was approached by the buyer of a large American departmental store, who offered to place a bulk order with TJ Limited. As cost accountant of the company you are required to evaluate the results of an initial order for 1,000 jugs.

The basic jugs are bought in at £3 each. Raw materials added amount to £0.50 per jug. Direct wages of the employees are £1.50 per hour, but a bonus is also payable of $33\frac{1}{3}\%$ of the hourly rate for each hour saved in painting. A 40 hour week is in operation, and the standard performance expected from each employee is 60 jugs per week.

The initial order is for 1,000 Toby jugs to be painted in the likeness of the American President, and they are to be charged at £10 each, less a bulk discount of 15%. This order was completed in 3 weeks and the output for each employee engaged in painting the jugs was as follows :

Employee	Output (units)
B. Ash	180
T. Yew	240
R. Oak	145
N. Elm	210
S. Fir	225

The buyer arranged for the collection of the order from the company, so no selling and distribution overhead was incurred. However, a special pack was required at a cost of £0.25 for each jug. Processing costs incurred in producing the jugs amount to £85 per 100. Budgeted production overhead for the year amounts to £19,200 and is absorbed by means of a direct labour hour rate. The company operates 48 weeks a year.

(b) Comment briefly on the problems which the company may experience if, on completion of the initial order, it receives a bulk order from the American department store.

(Institute of Cost & Management Accountants)

Question 29 Overhead absorption Answer page 272

A factory with three departments uses a single production overhead absorption rate expressed as a percentage of direct wages cost. It has been suggested that departmental overhead absorption rates would result in more accurate job costs. Set out below are the budgeted and actual data for the previous period, together with information relating to Job No.657

	Direct wages £000s	Direct labour	Machine	Production overhead £000s
Budget:				
Department A	25	10	40	120
B	100	50	10	30
C	25	25	-	75
Total	150	85	50	225
Actual:				
Department A	30	12	45	130
B	80	45	14	28
C	30	30	-	80
Total	140	87	59	238

Hours in thousands (Direct labour / Machine columns)

During this period job No. 657 incurred the actual costs and actual times in the department as shown below :

	Direct material £	Direct wages £	Direct labour hours	Machine hours
Department A	120	100	20	40
B	60	60	40	10
C	10	10	10	-

After adding production overhead to prime cost, one third is added to production cost for gross profit. This assumes that a reasonable profit is earned after deducting administration, selling and distribution costs.

You are required to:

(a)   calculate the current overhead absorption rate;

(b)   using the rate obtained in (a) above, calculate the production overhead charged to job No. 657 and state the production cost and expected gross profit on this job;

(c)   (i)   comment on the suggestion that departmental overhead absorption rates would result in more accurate job costs; and

(ii)   compute such rates, briefly explaining your reason for each rate;

(d)   using the rates calculated in (c) (ii) above, show the overhead, by department and in total, that would apply to job No. 657;

(e)   show the over/under absorption, by department and in total, for the period using:

(i)   the current rate in your answer to (a) above, and

(ii)   your suggested rates in your answer to (c) (ii) above.

(Institute of Cost & Management Accountants)

5
Costing methods

Introduction

The basic methods by which costs are ascertained can be divided into two main categories, namely, Specific Order Costing and Operation Costing. These terms are defined by the I.C.M.A. Terminology as follows:

Specific order costing - 'The category of basic costing methods applicable where the work consists of separate contracts, jobs or batches, each of which is authorised by a special order or contract.'

Operation costing - 'The category of basic costing methods applicable where standardised goods or services result from a sequence of repetitive and more or less continuous operations or processes to which costs are charged before being averaged over the units produced during the period.'

Specific order costing, then, is appropriate for the costing of non-standardised products and services. Each order can be identified and the costing system is designed to find the cost of each order. Operation costing, on the other hand, is a method that is suitable for the costing of standardised goods or services. Individual orders cannot be related to the goods or services being produced and the cost of each unit is ascertained by averaging the total costs over the number of units produced.

The two basic categories can be sub-divided as the following diagram shows:

Basic costing methods

Specific order costing			Operation costing	
Job costing	Contract costing	Batch costing	Process costing	Service costing

Job Costing.

In the I.C.M.A. Terminology, Job Costing is defined as 'that form of specific order costing which applies where work is undertaken to customers' special requirements. As distinct from contract costing, each job is of comparatively short duration. The work is usually carried out within a factory or workshop where each job moves through the processes or operations as a continuously identifiable unit, although the term may also be applied to such work as property repairs carried out on the customer's premises.'

Job costing, therefore, is usually adopted by businesses which receive orders, not for a standardised product or service, but for work peculiar to the needs of individual customers. The job could involve the manufacture of a special item of equipment made to the customer's specification. Alternatively, the task may be to carry out repairs to the customer's own equipment, either in the workshop, as in the case of repairs to a motor car, or on the customer's premises, for example the repair of a washing machine. Whatever the nature of the work performed, where one job differs from the next, job costing is normally employed.

Because each job is different, it can be easily identified as it progresses through the factory. Each job is therefore a distinct and separately identifiable cost unit.

It is possible to combine job costing with some other method of costing. For example, a business may undertake work which is specific to customers' requirements, each completed job consisting of one or two sub-assemblies which are common to all jobs. In such a case, job costing would only commence at that point when the standard sub-assemblies are adapted to the requirements of individual customers.

Job costing procedures. On receipt of a customer's order, the sales department notifies the production control department which raises a production (or works) order. Each job is given a separate works order number. Sometimes a customer's order can be sub-divided into a number of different operations. The cost of each operation can be ascertained by allocating sub-order numbers, one for each operation. The total cost of the various sub-orders would agree with the cost of the main order.

Production orders are also raised when items are to be manufactured for stock, in anticipation of future customer requirements.

A copy of the production order is forwarded to the cost office where a job cost sheet (or account) is created. One account will be made out for each order so that the costs appropriate to each individual job can be separately accumulated. The details recorded will comprise direct materials, direct wages and direct expenses, the term direct in this context being applied to costs which can be easily identified with a particular job. The information is extracted from goods received notes, suppliers' invoices, material requisitions, job tickets and so on; these documents must contain the relevant job numbers to ensure that the costs are posted to the appropriate job cost account. Production overhead is included by the application of overhead absorption rates.

On completion of the job, the production control department will notify the cost office, but the job cost account cannot be closed until all outstanding charges have been received and entered. When the customer has been invoiced, the selling and distribution overhead absorbed by the job is entered on the job cost account and the profit or loss calculated by comparing the total cost with the sales value.

The job cost accounts are included in the work in progress ledger and it is necessary at the end of every costing period to ensure that the total of the balances on the various job cost accounts agrees with the work in progress ledger control account. The agreed balance can then be incorporated in the balance sheet.

Cost Accounting Entries. The postings to the job cost accounts are as follows :

Debit	Credit
Purchases	Materials returned to stores
Materials issued from stores	Materials transferred to other jobs
Direct wages	Cost of completed jobs transferred
Overhead absorbed	to finished goods account
Materials transferred from other jobs	

Note: Each of the entries in the job cost account will have a corresponding entry in another account. Double entry principles as applied to cost accounting will be discussed more fully in chapter six; for the moment that part of the double entry which affects the job cost account has been shown.

The above costs, with the exception of materials transferred between jobs, are also included in the work in progress control account

Example. In March, a manufacturer was engaged on three jobs, all of which were started during the month. The following details relating to March are available :

	Job No.123 £	Job No.124 £	Job No.125 £
Purchases	1,000	1,050	700
Stores issues	120	-	350
Direct wages	450	350	300
Direct expenses	-	50	-
Materials returned to stores	-	-	20

Also, materials valued at £40 were transferred from job No.123 to job No. 125. Overhead expenditure for the month amounted to £1,400 and overhead is absorbed by applying a rate of 120 per cent to direct wages. Job No. 124 was completed during the month and invoiced to the customer at £12,100. Work on the other two jobs will continue during April.

You are required to prepare:
(a) job cost accounts for each job;
(b) a work in progress control account;
(c) an overhead control account;
(d) the costing profit and loss account for March

Job Cost Accounts
Job No. 123

Month	Direct materials £	Direct wages £	Direct expenses £	Overhead £	Total £	Profit £	Sales £
March	1,000 120 − 40	450		540			
	1,080	450	—	540	2,070	—	—

Job No. 124

Month	Direct materials £	Direct wages £	Direct expenses £	Overhead £	Total £	Profit £	Sales £
March	1,050	350	50	420	1,870	230	2,100

Job No. 125

Month	Direct materials £	Direct wages £	Direct expenses £	Overhead £	Total £	Profit £	Sales £
March	700 350 − 20 40	300		360			
	1,070	300	—	360	1,730	—	—

Work in Progress Control Account

	£		£
Purchases	2,750	Returns to stores	20
Stores issues	470	Costing profit and loss	1,870
Direct wages	1,100	Balance c.d	3,800
Direct expenses	50		
Overhead (120% of direct wages)	1,320		
	5,690		5.690
Balance b.d.	3,800		

Reconciliation of job account balances:

Job No. 123	£2,070
Job No. 125	£1,730
	£3,800

Overhead Control Account

	£		£
Overhead incurred	1,400	Overhead absorbed	1,320
		Under absorbed	80
	1,400		1,400

Costing Profit and Loss Account

	£		£
Overhead under-estimated	80	Profit on job No.124:	
Net profit	150	Sales £2,100	
		Cost £1,870	
			230
	230		230

Advantages of Job Costing. It is possible to ascertain the profit or loss earned by each job. Also the details of the costs incurred are recorded; a comparison with the original estimate might disclose where inefficiencies occured. Information revealed in this way would provide a basis for future estimating.

In some cases, however, the profit is not the final figure to be obtained Instead of quoting a price before commencing a job, a firm may fix the selling price after the work has been completed. In other words, once the final cost is known, profit will be added and the selling price ascertained. Job costing in such circumstances provides a basis for fixing selling prices.

Contract Costing.

The I.C.M.A. Terminology defines Contract Costing as 'that form of specific order costing which applies where work is undertaken to customers' special requirements and each order is of long duration (compared with those to which job costing applies). The work is usually of a constructional nature. In general the method is similar to job costing, although it has certain distinctive features.'

It will be noticed that a similarity exists between job costing and contract costing. Both methods are concerned with the costing of specific orders, but the term contract costing is used where the work to be carried out is likely to take a long time to complete. Also, as contract work is usually of a constructional nature, the major part of the activity is carried out away from the contractor's premises. Contract costing, therefore, is applicable to builders, civil engineering firms and companies concerned with road construction and the work may, in some cases, take a number of years to complete.

Each contract is given a separate number and as the cost units, i.e. the individual contracts, are likely to be large, in order to maintain adequate control there is a need to break down the work and allocate a series of sub-orders to each contract. Costs are recorded against each sub-order and the postings to the various sub-orders will be summarised on the main order, the total representing the cost of the contract to date.

Another distinguishing feature of contract costing is that a greater proportion of costs can be directly allocated to the cost units and, accordingly, the overhead to be absorbed is relatively small. Furthermore, many costs which have previously been considered as indirect are treated as direct in the context of contract costing. This aspect will be considered below under the headings of direct wages, direct expenses and plant.

Direct materials. In contract work, materials are normally ordered for specific contracts and delivered to the site where the work is being undertaken. Consequently, the cost of materials is charged directly to the individual contract. Smaller items of material are usually obtained from a central store and these will be requisitioned in the manner already outlined in chapter 2.

Direct wages. The wages of those workers whose efforts and skills are applied directly to contracts are treated as direct and are allocated to the contracts. Where work on site is to continue for a lengthy period, consideration might be given to the possibility of installing time-recording clocks for the purpose of recording attendance times. Alternatively, time sheets can be used for the dual purpose of recording attendance time and booking activity time. Where employees are working on one site for many months, there will still be a need to use the time sheet in order to analyse activity time; if the contract is broken down into a number of distinct stages, each stage will have a separate sub-order number.

In contract costing, the remuneration paid to foremen, site clerks, timekeepers, security staff and nightwatchmen can be treated as direct wages if their work is appropriate to one contract.

Direct expenses. It is often necessary in contract work to sub-contract a proportion of the work to specialists, for example, the installation of central heating. The invoiced amounts can be treated as direct expenses and charged to the contract. Site costs such as electricity and telephone charges can also be posted directly to contract accounts. Seeing that the invoiced amounts are appropriate to one site, no apportionment is required. Other items of direct expenses include architects' fees, postage, insurance and the hire of plant and equipment from other businesses.

Plant and machinery. Items which would normally be treated as capital expenditure can also be charged to the contract accounts. One of two methods can be adopted in order to charge contracts for the use of plant and machinery such as bulldozers, cement mixers and cranes.

(a) When an item of a capital nature is bought specifically for one individual contract, the cost can be treated as direct and allocated to the contract. If the equipment has been used previously on other work, then the written down value can be debited instead. At the end of the contract or at a time when the plant is no longer required, the plant can be revalued and the contract credited accordingly. Alternatively, if the plant is sold, the sale proceeds are credited to the contract. Some organisations keep a stock of plant in a central pool and transfer the plant to sites when it is needed. The entries in the cost accounts to record this transfer are, debit contract account, credit plant account, the amount being the valuation of the plant at the time of the transfer. The entries are reversed when the plant is returned to the central pool but only after a further revaluation has taken place. The contract has been charged therefore, with the monetary loss due to the wear and tear that has taken place during the plant's use on a particular site. The cost of maintenance carried out on the site will also be charged to the contract.

This method is particularly suitable where plant is used on individual contracts for long periods and a considerable loss in value has occured in the time it has been used.

In addition to the revaluation mentioned already, the plant must also be revalued at the end of each accounting year or alternatively some provision made for depreciation so that the year's charge reflects only the loss in value of the plant and not the full value.

Example. Work commenced on a particular contract on April 1st and during the succeeding nine months the following costs were incurred:

	£
Direct materials	60,000
Direct wages	15,000
Direct expenses	5,000

Also on April 1st, plant and machinery costing £10,000 was bought to be used entirely on the contract. The accounting year ends on December 31st and depreciation is to be provided at the rate of 20 per cent per anum. Write up the contract account in the cost ledger for the nine months.

Contract Account	£		£
Plant and machinery	10,000	Plant and machinery c.d.	8,500
Direct materials	60,000	Work in progress c.d.	81,500
Direct wages	15,000		
Direct expenses	5,000		
	90,000		90,000
Plant and machinery b.d.	8,500		
Work in progress b.d.	81,500		

Note: The depreciation amounts to £2,000 per annum and the charge for nine months is therefore £1,500. This £1,500 is included in the work in progress figure of £81,500. The written down value in brought down to the beginning of the following year.

(b) The other method for dealing with plant and machinery in the contract accounts is more suitable when plant is required for short periods and is transferred from one contract to another at frequent intervals. The plant is in effect hired from a central pool and the contract is charged an hourly rate for its use. The hourly rate is calculated in the same way as individual machine hour rates in chapter 4. A cost centre is set up for each type of machine to be hired. An estimate is made of the costs expected to be incurred by a cost centre for the coming year, e.g. depreciation, maintenance, fuel, driver's wages, etc. and the total of thes costs is divided by the number of hours that the plant is expected to be used. An hourly rate is established for each type of machine and this is applied to contracts, which are charged on the basis of hours used. The plant account will then be debited throughout the year as costs occur an will be credited with the charges made to contracts for hire. This methoc gives a site foreman an incentive to transfer the plant back to the central pool as soon as its use is no longer required, for the plant lying idle on site would mean that the contract for which he is responsible would be charged for hours when the plant is idle. By returning the plant, the fore man will be keeping the costs on his contract as low as possible and at th same time releasing the plant for use elsewhere. This should lead to the effective use of available plant.

Services. Plant hire and stores are not the only services provided centrall In some businesses, window frames and doors are made at a central work shop and the manufactured items despatched to site. A cost centre will be established to collect the cost of materials, wages and expenses incurred for subsequent distribution to contracts.

Overhead. As so many of the costs can be charged directly to contracts, the overhead will be relatively small and will be confined to the cost of running the stores, head office administration expenses, costs incurred i negotiating future contracts, etc. These can be charged to contracts usin an overhead absorption rate or, alternatively, written off to costing prof and loss account.

Progress Payments. Where a contract is of long duration, it is usual to include a clause that makes provision for payments to be made by the customer as the work proceeds. If payment was not received until the e of the contract, the contractor would be unable to finance the work. Sc at regular intervals or as the work reaches particular stages, the contract issues an invoice based on the value of work completed to date. The cus omer will require the valuation to be supported by an architect's certif-icate. However, although the invoice is based on the architect's valuatio a percentage is usually deducted and will not be payable for a specified period, say six months, after the completion of the contract. This perce age, e.g. 10 per cent, is known as retention money and it protects the customer from faulty work that might not be evident at the time. The contract will specify that the contractor must put right any defects that are revealed between completion and the end of the specified period before the retention money is paid.

Profit on uncompleted contracts. In job costing, because the work is of comparatively short duration, the profit on each job is not calculated until the work has been completed and the final costs are ascertained. To follow the same procedure in contract costing would mean that where companies only undertook large contracts, no profit would be recorded at all if no contracts were completed during an accounting year. This is tantamount to stating that the work is unprofitable. However, it is normally imprudent to anticipate profits and this concept also applies in contract costing, for the possibility of problems arising in the future must always be kept in mind. In order to make some compromise, it is recommended that a conservative estimate is made at the end of the accounting year of the profit that has been earned on long term contracts. The amount estimated will depend on circumstances, for example, how near the contract is to completion and the likelihood of major defects occurring. The following formula can provide a basis for making an estimate.

$$\text{Estimated profit} = \frac{2}{3} \times \text{Notional profit} \times \frac{\text{Cash received}}{\text{Value of work certified}}$$

'Notional profit' is calculated by subtracting the costs to date from the value of work certified. The 'cash received' will be the amount invoiced after a percentage for retention has been deducted.

Cost accounting entries. The contract account is made out in similar fashion to a job cost account but with certain additions, thus :

Debit	Credit
Purchases	Materials returned to stores
Materials issued from stores	Materials transferred to other contracts
Direct wages	Valuation of work certified
Direct expenses	
Overhead absorbed	
Materials transferred from other contracts	
Plant and machinery at valuation	

If the contract is uncompleted at the end of the accounting period, the credit side will also include the following valuations:

Materials in stock
Work in progress
Plant and machinery

All these items will be brought down to the debit side of the new period.

An estimate of profit earned will be made, using the formula mentioned above and this will be entered on the debit side of the contract account, the corresponding credit entry being posted to costing profit and loss account. The difference between the notional profit and the profit earned is known as profit in suspense and will be entered on the debit side of the contract account, but it will also be carried down to the credit side of the new period.

Example. Prepare a contract cost account from the following data :

	£
Materials purchased specifically for the contract	60,500
Stores issues	4,750
Materials returned to stores	220
Materials transferred to other contracts	180
Written down value on plant sent to site	12,000
Sub-contract work	4,000
Direct wages	18,500
Direct expenses	2,300
Architect's fees	1,250
Overhead absorbed	3,100
Valuation of work certified by architect	100,000

At the end of the accounting year the following valuations were made:

	£
Materials on site	4,850
Cost of work done not yet certified	3,500
Plant on site	9,000
Accrued charges	320
Prepayments	100

The amount invoiced to the customer is based on the valuation of the work certified by the architect less a retention of 10 per cent.

Contract Cost Account

	£		£
Purchases (a)	60,500	Materials returned to stores(a)	220
Stores issues (a)	4,750	Materials transferred (a)	180
Plant (a)	12,000	Value of work certified	100,000
Sub-contract work (a)	4,000	Stock c.d. (a)	4,850
Direct wages (a)	18,500	Work in progress c.d. (a)	3,500
Direct expenses (a)	2,300	Plant c.d. (a)	9,000
Architect's fees (a)	1,250	Prepayments c.d. (a)	100
Overhead absorbed (a)	3,100		
Accrued charges c.d. (a)	320		
Costing profit and loss	6,678		
Profit is suspense c.d.	4,452		

	117,850		117,850
Stock b.d.	4,850	Accrued charges b.d.	320
Work in progress b.d.	3,500	Profit in suspense b.d.	4,452
Plant b.d.	9,000		
Prepayments b.d.	100		

Note:

	£
Value of work certified	100,000
less cost of work - items marked (a)	88,870
Therefore, notional profit	11,130

$$\text{Profit earned} = \frac{2}{3} \times £11,130 \times \frac{£90,000}{£100,000} = £6,678$$

$$\text{Profit in suspense} = £11,130 - £6,678 = £4,452$$

Batch Costing.

This is defined by the I.C.M.A. Terminology as 'that form of specific order costing which applies where similar articles are manufactured in batches either for sale or for use within the undertaking. In most cases the costing is similiar to job costing.'

Instead of manufacturing an article to a customer's specification, some organisations produce a batch of standardised articles, say 1,000 at a time The advantage to the manufacturer and the customer is that the unit cost is likely to be less than under jobbing production. Machines are reset less frequently and consequently they are employed for longer periods in production. However, there is a risk of obsolescence. Consider the clothing industry, for example. If a manufacturer, in order to have the advantage of longer production runs, decided to make his batch size as large as possible, there is a likelihood that, due to a sudden change in fashion, he will have in stock finished articles which are obsolete.

A production order is raised for each batch and a cost account is opened, not for each article as in job costing, but for the batch as a whole. The unit cost can be calculated by dividing the total cost of the batch by the number of good units produced.

Process Costing.

Process costing is defined as, 'that form of operation costing which applies where standardised goods are produced.' (I.C.M.A. Terminology).

This method of costing is used, for example, in industries which are engaged in the manufacture of chemicals, paper, food and paint. It is also employed by companies in oil refining. These industries do not manufact ure individual items to the specific requirements of customers, but instead create uniform products. A consumer can take a tin of paint or soup in the form in which it is sold, or leave it. The range of products manufactured is usually limited, the industries being chiefly concerned with large quantities for the mass market.

Production in these industries consists of a succession of continuous operations or processes and it is this continuous flow of production which distinguishes it from batch production.

Batch production is a kind of half-way house between jobbing work and mass production. Instead of manufacturing a single item to a customer's specification, a batch of articles is made. But after the completion of the batch, machines have to be altered in order to produce a different article. Production is intermittent; there is no continuous flow. However, in the industries where process costing is employed, production continues almost uninterrupted.

Each process represents a distinct stage of manufacture and the output of one process becomes the input of the following process and so on until the articles are complete. A process is generally the responsibility of one person, and a cost centre is set up for each process so that costs can be collected and related to individual responsibility. The I.C.M.A. Terminology defines a process cost centre as 'a cost centre in which a specific process or a continuous sequence of operations is carried out.'

Direct and indirect costs are debited to the process cost centre (or process account), and as it is impossible to identify the individual units of output, the unit cost is calculated by averaging the costs over the units produced, a cost per unit being ascertained for each process.

Example. In the course of manufacture, a product passes through three distinct processes, A, B and C. During a four week period, 1,000 units are produced and the following information is available :

	Process A £	Process B £	Process C £
Direct materials	2,000	1,000	-
Direct wages	1,500	700	800
Direct expenses	300	100	-

Indirect production costs were £4,500 and these are to be apportioned to the processes on the basis of direct wages cost. Prepare the process accounts, ignoring the possibility of work in progress.

Process A Account

	Cost per unit £	Amount £		Cost per unit £	Amount £
Direct materials	2.00	2,000	Output transferred to Process B	6.05	6,050

Direct wages	1.50	1,500				
Direct expenses	0.30	300				
Production overhead	2.25	2,250				
	6.05	6,050		6.05	6,050	

Process B Account

	Cost per unit £	Amount £		Cost per unit £	Amount £
Output transferred from Process A	6.05	6,050	Output transferred to Process C	8.90	8,900
Direct materials	1.00	1,000			
Direct wages	0.70	700			
Direct expenses	0.10	100			
Production overhead	1.05	1,050			
	8.90	8,900		8.90	8,900

Process C Account

	Cost per unit £	Amount £		Cost per unit £	Amount £
Output transferred from Process B	8.90	8,900	Output transferred to Finished Stock	10.90	10,900
Direct wages	0.80	800			
Production overhead	1.20	1,200			
	10.90	10,900		10.90	10,900

Notes:

(a) The cost per unit is ascertained by using the formula

$$\frac{\text{Costs incurred during the period}}{\text{Number of units produced during the period}}$$

(b) The output of one process becomes the raw material of the following process and further direct materials can be added at each stage of production

(c)   A cost per unit is calculated for each process, but it is a cumulative cost per unit. For example, the cost per unit of £8.90 for the output transferred from process B is the cost of manufacture for processes A and B, not for B alone.

(d)   In the above example, the cost is expressed as 'so much per single item' However, in some cases, output can be measured, not by counting the quantity produced, but by weight, value or length. The 'cost per unit' colum therefore would be headed 'cost per kilogram,' 'cost per litre' or 'cost per metre'.

(e)   After the completion of the final process, the output is transferred to the finished goods store.

Work in Progress. In the example above, work in progress has been ignored, but of course the completion of work is not always going to occur simultaneously with the end of a costing period. Some items will only be partially complete. Consequently, not all the costs can be transferred to the next process, as some of the costs are appropriate to the uncompleted work. But how are the costs to be divided between the output transferred to the next process and the work still in progress? The solution is to calculate what are known as 'Equivalent Units'.

Equivalent Units. The term is defined by the I.C.M.A. Terminology as 'a notional quantity of completed units substituted for an actual quantity of incomplete physical units in progress, when the aggregate work content of the incomplete units is deemed to be equivalent to that of the substituted quantity (e.g. 150 units 50 per cent complete = 75 equivalent units). The principle applies when operation costs are being apportioned between work in progress and completed output.'

In order to convert incomplete units into complete units, it is necessary to estimate the extent to which the work in progress at the end of the period has been completed. The cost per unit can then be calculated.

Example. The manufacture of a certain product is carried out in two stages, process A and process B. The following information for a particular costing period applies to process A:

	£
Direct materials	6,000
Direct wages and expenses	2,000
Production overhead	2,000
Cost of production	10,000

Completed production amounted to 15,250 units but the following units were only partly complete:

1,000 units, 50 per cent complete;
1,000 units, 25 per cent complete.

Prepare an account for Process A.

It is necessary firstly to calculate the number of equivalent units produced, thus:

$$
\begin{array}{lcr}
100 \text{ per cent of } 15{,}250 \text{ units} & = & 15{,}250 \\
50 \text{ per cent of } 1{,}000 \text{ units} & = & 500 \\
25 \text{ per cent of } 1{,}000 \text{ units} & = & 250 \\
\hline
\text{Equivalent units} & & 16{,}000 \\
\hline
\end{array}
$$

The cost per completed unit is calculated therefore by dividing the costs of £10,000 by 16,000 equivalent units.

Process A Account

	Cost per unit £	Amount £		Cost per unit £	Amount £
Direct materials	0.375	6,000	Output transferred to Process B	0.625	9,531
Direct wages and expense	0.125	2,000	Work in progress c.d.	0.2345	469
Production overhead	0.125	2,000			
	0.625	10,000		-	10,000
Work in progress b.d.	0.2345	469			

Notes:

(a) The cost per completed unit is ascertained by using the formula:

$$\frac{\text{Costs incurred during the period}}{\text{Number of equivalent units produced during the period}}$$

(b) The output is valued by multiplying the number of units completed, i.e. 15,250, by the cost per completed unit

(c) The work in progress valuation is obtained by multiplying the number of equivalent units in progress by the cost per completed unit, i.e. 750 x £0.625.

(d) The process account is completed by calculating a cost per unit for work in progress, i.e. £469 divided by the 2,000 units which are uncompleted at the end of the period. The work in progress valuation is carried down to the beginning of the following costing period.

In the above example, the extent to which units are complete is the same for all items of cost. The units which are 50 per cent complete are half complete in respect of direct materials, direct wages, direct expenses and production overhead. However, it often happens that the degree of completion is different for each item of cost. For example, some units might be complete as far as direct materials are concerned, but only 75 per cent complete in respect of direct wages. In other words, all the material has been issued to a process but the article has not been completely fashioned or shaped. No further material needs to be added, but addition al labour has still to be expended. The extent to which units are com plete will therefore vary between the items of cost. In order to ascertain the total cost per unit it is necessary to calculate the cost per equivalent unit for each item of cost, i.e. for direct materials, direct wages, production overhead, etc.

Example. The cost information for process A is the same as the previous example, i.e.

	£
Direct materials	6,000
Direct wages and expenses	2,000
Production overhead	2,000
Cost of production	10,000

Again, 15,250 units have been completed, but the work in progress situation is as follows :

(a)   1,000 units are fully complete with regard to direct materials but only 50 per cent complete in respect of direct wages and expenses and production overhead.

(b)   The other 1,000 units are also fully complete with regard to direct materials, but only 25 per cent complete in respect of the other items of cost.

Prepare a process account for cost centre A

Process A Account

	Cost per unit £	Amount £		Cost per unit £	Amount £
Direct materials	0.3478	6,000	Output transfered to Process B	0.5978	9,116
Direct wages and expenses.	0.1250	2,000	Work in progress c.d.	0.4420	884
Production overhead	0.1250	2,000			
	0.5978	10,000		—	10,000

Notes:

(a)   The cost per unit of each item is obtained first, thus :

	Cost £	Equivalent units	Cost per unit £
Direct materials	6,000	17,250	0.3478
Direct wages and expenses	2,000	16,000	0.1250
Production overhead	2,000	16,000	0.1250

(b) The cost per complete unit is ascertained by adding together the costs per unit of the various items of expenditure.

(c) Work in progress is calculated for each item of cost, thus :

	£
Direct materials 2,000 units at £0.3478 per unit	696
Direct wages and expenses, 750 equivalent units at £0.125 per unit	94
Production overhead, 750 equivalent units x £0.125 per unit	94
	884

(d) A check on the calculation is obtained if the process account does in fact balance.

(e) The cost per unit of work in progress, i.e. £0.442, is obtained by dividing £884 by the number of uncompleted units, i.e. 2,000.

(f) Where the problem consists of ascertaining the cost per unit of the second or subsequent process, the output transferred from a previous process must be taken as an item of cost. However, the input will always be 100 per cent complete, as it is only completed units that are transferred from one process to another. It is particularly important to include the costs transferred from a previous process when calculating the value of work in progress.

It is convenient at this point to summarise the steps required in the preparation of a process account where work is incomplete at the end of a period and where the degree of completion of the various cost items is not the same.

(a) Calculate the equivalent production for each item of cost, e.g. direct materials, direct wages, etc. and ascertain the unit cost by dividing the cost of each item of cost by the equivalent units appropriate to each. Enter the cost per unit together with the total cost of each item on the debit side of the process account.

(b) Total the debit side, including the unit cost column. The total of the unit cost column represents the total cost per completed unit.

(c) Enter the unit cost total on the credit side against the completed output and calculate the amount transferred to the next process, or finished stock as the case may be, by multiplying the number of completed units by the unit cost per completed unit.

(d) Calculate the valuation of work in progress by taking the cost per unit of each item, including input received from a previous process, and multiplying individually by the appropriate equivalent units in progress.

(e) Calculate the unit cost of work in progress by dividing the valuation by the uncompleted units (not just equivalent units).

(f) Bring down the work in progress figure to the debit side of the process account, and debit the next process or finished stock with the output transferred.

The student can now check his grasp of the subject matter by attempting the following question. It is suggested that the solution is not referred to until the question has been attempted. The six steps above can be used as a guide.

Question. On March 1st, 1,000 units were transferred from process 1 to process 2 at a unit cost of £2.40. During March, the following costs were incurred in process 2.

	£
Direct materials	480
Direct wages	2,024
Production overhead	2,484

At March 31st, 800 units were complete. The position on the uncompleted units was as follows :

Direct materials	80% complete
Direct wages	60% complete
Production overhead	60% complete

All completed units are transferred to process 3. Prepare a Process 2 Account for March, showing the cost of the output to be transferred to process 3, and the value of work in progress at March 31st.

Solution. Equivalent units:

Direct materials = 800 + 80 per cent of 200 = 960
Direct wages   = 800 + 60 per cent of 200 = 920
Production
overhead   =   ditto   = 920

Process 2 Account

	Units	Cost per unit £	Amount £		Units	Cost per unit £	Amount £
Output transferred from Process 1	1000	2.40	2400	Output transferred to Process 3	800	7.80	6240
Direct materials		0.50	480	Work in progress c.d.	200	5.74	1148
Direct wages		2.20	2024				
Production overhead		2.70	2484				
	1000	7.80	7388		1000	-	7388
Work in progress b.d.	200	5.74	1148				

Notes:

Work in progress was calculated thus:

a) Output transferred from process 1 = 200 units x £2.40 per unit = £480
Direct materials = 160 equivalent units x £0.50 per unit   = £ 80
Direct wages = 120 equivalent units x £2.20 per unit   = £264
Production overhead = 120 equivalent units x £2.70 per unit = £324
                                                             £1148

b)Not only should the debit and credit sides agree in respect of total costs but in units also.

Opening Work in Progress. If a problem asks for opening work in progress to be calculated, this is ascertained in the same manner as closing work in progress, but is entered on the debit side at the commencement of the period.

Losses in Process. Some losses are bound to arise during the manufacturing process. These will be due to various causes, for example, evaporation damage to material and material failing to pass inspection. Losses of this nature cannot usually be avoided and it is because of the inevitability of such events that management seeks to estimate the average loss which is likely to occur at each stage of production.

Normal Losses. A prediction will be made of the loss that is likely to occur under normal conditions, and which is acceptable to management. It is termed the Normal Loss in Process. It is estimated on the basis of past results and is often expressed as a percentage of the input to the process. This has the effect of increasing the cost per unit of good production. For example, if the cost of producing 1,000 units is £1.89 per unit, the unit cost, given that there is a normal loss in process of 10 per cent would be £2.10, i.e. $\frac{£1,890}{900}$. Any further losses that occur are treated as abnormal losses and it is therfore necessary for control purposes to record the input and output of each particular process in order that the units lost are accounted for and, furthermore, segregated between normal and abnormal losses.

The entries relating to normal losses in the cost accounts depend on whether the discarded material does in fact have some recovery value. Before proceeding further it is necessary to introduce two more terms together with their I.C.M.A. definitions in order to avoid misunderstanding.

Waste - 'Discarded substances having no value'
Scrap - 'Discarded material, having some recovery value which is usually disposed of without further treatment(other than reclamation and handling), or re-introduced into the production process in place of raw material.'

All units lost are credited in the process account, but in the case of scrap, the saleable value is also credited, after deducting any handling costs.

Example. Assume that 10,000 litres of a particular liquid are introduced into the first process at a cost of 5 pence per litre. Other costs incurred in the process are :

	£
Direct wages	100
Production overhead	65

It is estimated that the normal loss is 5 per cent of input, and as it has no saleable value, it can be referred to as waste.

Process 1 Account

	Litres	Cost per litre £	Amount £		Litres	Cost per litre £	Amount £
Direct materials	10,000	0.05	500	Normal loss (waste)	500	-	-
Direct wages			100	Output transferred to Process 2	9,500	0.07	665
Production overhead			65				
	10,000	-	665		10,000	-	665

Note that the loss of 500 litres is carried by good production.

Example. Using the information above, it is now assumed that the liquid lost has a saleable value of one pence per litre.

Process 1 Account

	Litres	Cost per litre £	Amount £		Litres	Cost per litre £	Amount £
Direct materials	10,000	0.05	500	Normal loss (scrap)	500	0.01	5
Direct wages			100	Output transferred to Process 2	9,500	0.0695	660
Production overhead			65				
	10,000	-	665		10,000	-	665

The only difference between this example and the last is that the process account has been credited with the revenue expected from the sale of the scrap. This has had the effect of reducing the cost of the good production from 7 pence to 6.95 pence. It will be noted from the definition of scrap that 'recovery value' does not only include saleable value. If the material can be used in another process, the transfer will be effected in the cost accounts by debiting the process account that is to use the discarded material, and crediting the account that has no further use for the material. It is necessary to arrive at some valuation of the transferred mat erial and this can be done by placing a value on the material commensurate with the price that would have to be paid to obtain the same material elsewhere. The same principle applies if the material is transferred to stores pending use at a future date.

Abnormal Losses. It was stated above that where losses occur which exceed the estimated normal loss, then these losses must be separated. The benefit in treating the costs in this way is that the attention of management is directed to losses above normal. This gives management the opportunity to look into the possible causes and to take the necessary action to avoid such losses in the future. Alternatively, if the estimate of the normal loss were too optimistic, so causing repeated abnormal losses, management can revise the normal loss percentage figure.

A credit entry for abnormal loss is made in the process account and to do this the cost of the normal loss must be shared between good production and abnormal loss. Consequently the cost per unit of abnormal loss will be identical to the unit cost of good production.

Example. Using the figures above, it is assumed in this instance that the actual output amounted to 9,200 litres

Process 1 Account

	Litres	Cost per litre £	Amount £		Litres	Cost per litre £	Amount £
Direct materials	10,000	0.05	500	Normal loss	500	0.01	5
Direct wages			100	Output transferred to Process 2	9,200	0.0695	639
Production overhead			65	Abnormal loss	300	0.0695	21
	10,000	-	665		10,000	-	665

Note: The cost per litre of output and abnormal loss has been calculated thus:

$$\frac{£665 - £5}{9,500}$$

The losses recorded on the credit side of the process account are debited to the normal loss and abnormal loss accounts.

Normal Loss Account

	£		
Process 1	5		

Abnormal Loss Account

	£		
Process 1	21		

These accounts can now be credited with the revenue expected to be received from disposal, i.e.

Normal loss = 500 x £0.01 = £5
Abnormal loss = 300 x £0.01 = £3

The difference on abnormal loss account is then transferred to costing profit and loss account.

Normal Loss Account

	£		£
Process 1	5	Scrap sales	5

Abnormal Loss Account

	£		£
Process 1	21	Scrap sales	3
		Costing profit and loss	18
	21		21

Abnormal Gains. Where the quantity lost in process is less than expected, an abnormal gain arises. The treatment in the cost records is similar to the treatment of abnormal losses, except that there is a slight variation at the end.

Example. Taking the basic information again, it is assumed that the output this time was 9,700 litres.

Process 1 Account

	Litres	Cost per litre £	Amount £		Litre	Cost per litre £	Amount £
Direct material	10,000	0.05	500	Normal loss	500	0.01	5
Direct wages			100	Output transferred to	9,700	0.0695	674
Production overhead			65	Process 2			
Abnormal gain	200	0.0695	14				
	10,200	-	679		10,200	–	679

	£
Process 1	5

Abnormal Gain Account

	£
Process 1	14

It is at this point that the procedure deviates slightly. The normal loss account cannot be credited with £5 as, in this example, there are only 300 litres to sell, i.e. 10,000 less 9700. Consequently, only £3 can be credited. The difference is dealt with by the following entry:

Dr. Abnormal gain account
Cr. Normal loss account

Normal Loss Account

	£		£
Process 1	5	Scrap sales	3
		Abnormal gain	2
	5		5

Abnormal Gain Account

	£		£
Normal loss	2	Process 1	14
Costing profit and loss	12		
	14		14

Notes:

a) The cost per unit of output is calculated in the same manner as for abnormal losses. The cost per unit, i.e. 6.95 pence, is the same for the output in both examples, and for the abnormal loss in the first example and the abnormal gain in the second. In fact, whatever the output, the cost per unit would be the same. If only 6,000 litres were produced the cost per unit would still be calculated by using the formula $\dfrac{£665 - £5}{9,500}$

b) Scrap Sales account is debited with the amount expected to be received from the sale of scrap.

Scrap Sales Account
(First example)

	£
Normal loss	5
Abnormal loss	3

This account will be credited with the cash actually received for the scrap, any difference being transferred to costing profit and loss account.

c) A separate account must always be kept for abnormal gains. Abnormal losses in one process should not be offset against abnormal gains in another process.

The following question will test the student's grasp of the above material on losses in process.

Question. A product is manufactured after being passed through three separate processes, the output of each process being transferred immediately to the next process, except that the output of process 3 is transferred to finished stock. The normal loss for each process is estimated as :

Process A	15%
Process B	10%
Process C	5%

The costs for March were:

	Process A £	Process B £	Process C £
Direct material - Alpha (50,000kg)	26,000	-	-
Beta (20,000 kg)	-	15,800	-
Gamma(10,000kg)	-	-	10,800
Direct wages	1,200	700	1,500
Direct expenses	300	348	341

Production overhead, which is absorbed by using the direct wages percentage rate, is £8,500. The output from process A was 40,500 kg., from process B, 55,500 kg. and from process C 62,200 kg. The following prices can be obtained from scrap sales:

	£
Process A	0.10 per kg.
Process B	0.20 per kg.
Process C	0.24 per kg.

You are required to prepare the necessary accounts, ignoring work in progress.

Solution.

Process A Account

	kg.	Cost per kg. £	Amount £		kg	Cost per kg. £	Amount £
Direct material(Alpha)	50,000	0.52	26,000	Normal loss	7,500	0.10	750
Direct wages			1,200	Output transferred to Process B	40,500	0.70	28,350
Direct expenses			300	Abnormal	2,000	0.70	1,400
Production overhead			3,000				
	50,000		30,500		50,000		30,500

Process B Account

	kg.	Cost per kg. £	Amount £		kg.	Cost per kg. £	Amount £
Output transferred from Process A	40,500	0.70	28,350	Normal loss	6,050	0.20	1,210
Direct materials(Beta)	20,000	0.79	15,800	Output transferred to Process C	55.500	0.84	46,620
Direct wages			700				
Direct expenses			348				
Production			1,750				
Abnormal gain	1,050	0.84	882				
	61,550		47,830		61,550		47,830

Process C Account

	kg.	Cost per kg. £	Amount £		kg.	Cost per kg. £	Amount £
Output transferred from Process B	55,500	0.84	46,620	Normal loss	3,275	0.24	786
Direct material(Gamma)	10,000	1.08	10,800	Output transferred to Finished Stock	62,200	1.00	62,200
Direct wages			1,500	Abnormal loss	25	1.00	25
Direct expenses			341				
Production overhead			3,750				
	65,500		63,011		65,500		63,011

Normal Loss Account

	£		£
Process A	750	Scrap sales	750
Process B	1,210	Scrap sales	1,000
Process C	786	Abnormal gain	210
		Scrap sales	786
	2,746		2,746

Abnormal Loss Account

	£		£
Process A	1,400	Scrap sales	200
Process C	25	Scrap sales	6
		Costing profit and loss	1,219
	1,425		1,425

Abnormal Gain Account

	£		£
Normal loss	210	Process B	882
Costing profit and loss	672		
	882		882

Scrap Sales Account

	£
Normal loss	750
Abnormal loss	200
Normal loss	1,000
Normal loss	786
Abnormal loss	6

Costing Profit and Loss Account

	£		£
Abnormal loss	1,219	Abnormal gain	672

Notes:

(a) The scrap sales account will be credited with the amount actually received for the sale of scrap, the difference on this account being transferred to costing profit and loss account.

(b) Notice that the amount of money lost in processes B and C represents the total cost at that stage including costs incurred in previous processes. Consequently losses occuring in later processes will be more costly than those that arise in earlier processes. However, those losses in later processes can be reduced in cases where higher prices can be received for their sale, as in the question above.

(c) Where one is required to calculate the cost of a single item, the material added in the second and subsequent processes will not increase the total number of units being costed. But if, for example, the cost per kilogram or litre is asked for, additional material introduced at the various stages of production will increase the total weight or volume by which the costs are to be divided.

By-products. A by-product is defined by the I.C.M.A. Terminology as 'a product which is recovered incidentially from the material used in the manufacture of recognised main products, such by-product having either a net realisable value or a usable value, such value being relatively unimportant in comparison with the saleable value of the main products. By-products are usually subjected to further processing after separation from the main product.' Net realisable value is defined as 'the estimated selling price (net of trade discounts but before deducting settlement discounts), less all attributable costs incurred after separation from the main product

A by-product, then, can emanate from the manufacturing process, even though the main objective was to produce another product. However, it would be wasteful merely to dispose of it when, with perhaps further processing, a subsidiary product can be marketed.

For example, if coal is heated without air, coke is obtained which is used to make iron. But besides coke, other chemicals are obtained from the gaseous products of the roasting; these include benzene, naphthalene, creosote, pitch, bitumen and wax, all of which are saleable.

Alternatively, the by-product can be used instead of purchasing new material from outside the business. The value of the by-product will be relatively small when compared to the value of the main product. Where the volume of the secondary product is significant, it would then have the status of a joint product. What is significant is a matter of opinion,so it is not possible to distinguish accurately between by-products and joint products.

But how are by-products to be treated in the process costing accounts seeing that there is no way of distinguishing between the cost of producing the main product and the costs associated with by-products? How is the amount recovered from the sale of by-products to be treated in the cost accounts? The following are some of the methods which can be employed:

(a)   Aggregate the sales of major products and by-products and de duct the process costs to arrive at a profit or loss for the process. In this method no attempt is made to segregate the joint costs of the process.

(b)   Similarly, deduct the income from the sale of by-products from the joint costs. The income referred to is net income, that is after the deduction of any further costs occuring after separation in order to bring the by-product to a marketable condition. The assumption is that all the costs are incurred in producing the main product, but these costs are reduced by the income received from the sale of the by-product. The use of the sales value can reduce the benefit of the cost information, as if the sales value of by-products fluctuates from one period to the next, the joint costs would be similarly affected. Inefficiences could be hidden in those months where the costs are reduced by sizable sales values. In order to prevent this occurence, some advocate the use of standard values based on past experience for by-products, so that there is a consistency in the reduction of main product costs. The disadvantage of using standard values however would be apparent where future events did not conform to past experience, so requiring constant revaluation of the standard.

(c)   Omit the revenue received from the process account. Instead, treat it as other income and include in the costing profit and loss account

This method is particularly suitable where the income is very small.

(d) Apportion the costs. This method is more appropriate to joint products and will be dealt with later. It has been included here also because of the indistinct line that separates by-products and joint products.

Joint Products. These are 'two or more products separated in the cours course of processing, each having a sufficiently high saleable value to merit recognition as a main product.' (I.C.M.A. Terminology). As it was stated above, the line between by-products and joint products is somewhat blurred. When is a saleable value high enough to warrant being regarded as a joint product? Individual cost accountants must make their own decision.

A product can be defined as a joint product if it were the deliberate intention of management to produce it; it was part of the scheme of things; it did not happen incidentally. The object was to process material so that two or more products emerge, or, alternatively, two different grades of the same product. It is not of cource necessary for the products to be of equal value.

But how is each product to be costed? With by-products this was fairly straightforward because the amounts of money involved did not warrant serious consideration. But seeing that it is management's intention to manufacture a product, albeit in conjunction with another product, it is vital that cost information relating to each product is made available. The difficulty lies in segregating the costs up to the point of separation. Afterwards, each product may go its own way, being subject to different processes. Some method of apportionment needs to be found in order to gauge the profitability of each product and to provide a reasonable valuation of work in progress. An additional reason why apportionment is necessary is in order to provide meaningful information for fixing selling prices. The following methods can be used:

(a) Apportion the joint costs between the products in the ratio of the market value of production at the point of separation.

(b) Apportion the costs using sales value of production as a base. However, sales value has little relevance if further processing is to be undertaken, especially if there is a disparity between two products in the amount of further work to be carried out. In such a case, the market value mentioned above is more suitable. It is possible to convert sales value to market value by deducting the costs incurred after the point of separation.

(c) Apportion the costs at the point of separation using some physical unit of measurement, e.g. litres, kilograms, metres, number of units. The physical unit of measurement must be common to the joint product and this method cannot be used if, say, one product is measured by weight (kilograms) and another by volume (litres).

It must be emphasised that whichever method is used, apportionment is only necessary for joint costs. Costs which occur after the point of separation can be allocated directly to individual products.

Example. A single process is used to manufacture three products, R, S and T. The joint process costs for the month of June came to £12,500 and the production and sales statistics are as follows :

Product	Production (kg)	Sales kg.	£ per kg
R	4,000	3,500	1.50
S	3,000	2,250	2.00
T	5,400	3,900	1.25

Calculate for each product (a) the profit earned for June and (b) the value of work in progress at June 30th, apportioning the joint process costs between the products on the basis of (i) sales value and (ii) weight.

Sales value method.

Firstly, apportion joint costs using sales value of production as a basis.

Product	Production kg.	Selling price £	Sales value of production	Costs £
R	4,000	1.50	6,000	4,000
S	3,000	2.00	6,000	4,000
T	5,400	1.25	6.750	4,500
			18,750	12,500

Then, apportion costs of each product between work in progress and cost of sales.

Product	Costs £	Work in progress Kg.	Work in progress £	Cost of Sales Kg.	Cost of Sales £
R	4,000	500	500	3,500	3,500
S	4,000	750	1,000	2,250	3,000
T	4,500	1,500	1,250	3,900	3,250
			2,750		9,750

Lastly, calculate profit.

Product	Sales kg.	£	Sales value £	Cost of sales £	Profit £
R	3,500	1.50	5,250	3,500	1,750
S	2,250	2.00	4,500	3,000	1,500
T	3,900	1.25	4,875	3,250	1,625
			14,625	9,750	4,875

Physical measurement method.

Firstly, calculate the cost per kilogram, i.e. $\dfrac{£12,500}{12,400} = £1.0081$

Next, calculate the costs by applying the above unit cost.

Product	Work in progress		Cost of sales	
	kg.	£	kg	£
R	500	504	3,500	3,528
S	750	756	2,250	2,268
T	1,500	1,512	3,900	3,932
	2,750	2,772	9,650	9,728

Lastly, calculate profit.

Product	Sales value £	Cost of sales £	Profit £
R	5,250	3,528	1,722
S	4,500	2,268	2,232
T	4,875	3,932	943
	14,625	9,728	4,897

Summary of the two methods.

Product	Sales value method		Physical measurement method	
	W.I.P £	Profit £	W.I.P. £	Profit £
R	500	1,750	504	1,722
S	1,000	1,500	756	2,232
T	1,250	1,625	1,512	943
	2,750	4,875	2,772	4,897

Notes:
(a)   Under the sales value method, all the products have the same per centage profit, i.e. $33\frac{1}{3}$ of sales, as costs are apportioned to the various products in proportion to the sales value. It is feasible to assume that higher quality products will use a greater share of the joint costs.
(b)   Under the physical measurement method, the percentage profit on sales works out at :

R	32.8
S	49.6
T	19.3

The higher the selling price, the greater the profit margin.

Service Costing.
   The I.C.M.A. Terminology defines Service Costing as 'that form of operation costing which applies where standardised services are provided either by an undertaking or by a service cost centre within an under- taking.'
   Service costing is used by bus companies, road haulage firms, hospital and colleges, in fact by any organisation which provides a service rather than manufactured goods. The formula for calculating the cost per unit is as follows:

$$\frac{\text{Costs incurred during the period}}{\text{Number of units provided during the period}}$$

The problem here is to find a suitable cost unit to express the costs. Units used, depending on the service provided, are hours, tons, miles, ton-miles, passenger-miles, student-hours, patient-days, etc.

Where a two-part rate is used, for example ton-miles, the denominator in the formula is calculated by multiplying the two parts together. For example, if a vehicle carried a load which weighed 5 tons for a distance of 20 miles, the number of units would be 100 ton-miles.

The same principle is used when arriving at the costs of a service department, for the costs of service departments are often recovered by charging the user departments for the number of units used times the rate per unit. For example, the maintenance department could charge other cost centres in the factory an amount based on the number of hours spent on a particular job times the rate per hour.

EXAMINATION PRACTICE
Students are advised to attempt the questions under simulated examination conditions. Then check their answers with the suggested answers at the back of the book.

Question 30   Contract cost accounts   Answer page 273

On 3rd January, 1978 B Construction Limited started work on the construction of an office block for a contracted price of £750,000 with completion promised by 31st March 1979. Budgeted cost of the contract was £600,000. The construction company's financial year end was 31st October, 1978 and on that date the accounts appropriate to the contract contained the following balances.

	£000
Materials issued to site	161
Materials returned from site	14
Wages paid	68
Own plant is use on site at cost	96
Hire of plant and scaffolding	72
Supervisory staff: direct	11
indirect	12
Head office charges	63
Value of work certified to 31st October 1978	400

142

Cost of work completed but not yet
certified   40
Cash received related to work certified   330
Depreciation on own plant is to be provided at the rate of
12½% per annum on cost.
£2,000 is owing for wages
Estimated value of materials on site is £24,000
No difficulties are envisaged during the remaining time to complete
the contract.

You are required to:
(a)   prepare the contract account for the period ended 31st October,1978
showing the amount to be included in the construction company's profit
and loss account;
(b)   explain the reason(s) for including the amount of profit to be shown
in the profit and loss account;
(c)   show extracts from the construction company's balance sheet at 31st
October, 1978 so far as the information provided will allow.

(Institute of Cost & Management Accountants)

Question 31   Process costing   Answer page 275

A new process has been started and for the first month costs were
as follows:

Material (inserted at the start of the process)
    A   400 lbs at £1.25 per lb
    B   3,000 lbs at 40p per lb
Labour
    Supervision   £300
    Operators' wages 2,000 hours at £1.50 per hour
Overhead
    Charged at 100% of total labour cost.
During the first month, 3,000 lbs of the product was completed and
taken into stock. There was no gain or loss in the process. The work in
process at the end of the month was taken as 75% complete in relation
to labour and overhead, and 100% complete as far as material was concerned.
You are required to prepare the relevant process account for the month
showing:
a)   cost of completed product in the month;
b)   value of work in process at the end of the month.

(Institute of Accounting Staff)

F. Ltd. produces an item which passes through two processes before it can be sold. In a month, the relevant data was:

Process	1	2
Raw material input (5,000 units)	£7,500	-
Material added in process		£2,040
Direct Labour	£8,525	£7,920
Direct Expenses	£5,975	£4,665
Output (units)	4,500	4,000
Normal loss as a percentage of input	15	10
Scrap value of each lost unit	£1	£1.50

There was no stock at the start or end of either process.

You are required to show all the relevant process accounts.

(Institute of Accounting Staff)

(a)   Explain the fundamental differences between job costing and process costing and state three industries, other than the food industry, which use process costing.

(b)   A company within the food industry mixes powered ingredients in two different processes to produce one product. The output of process 1 becomes the input of process 2 and the output of process 2 is transferred to the packing department.

From the information given below, you are required to open accounts for process 1, process 2, abnormal scrap and packing department and to record the transactions for the week ended 11th November, 1978.

Process 1

Input: Material A	6,000 kilograms at £0.50 per kilogram
Material B	4,000 kilograms at £1.00 per kilogram
Mixing labour	430 hours at £2 per hour
Normal scrap	5% of weight input

Scrap was sold for £0.16 per kilogram

Output was   9,200 kilograms

There was no work in process at the beginning or end of the week.

Process 2

Input: Material C	6,600 kilograms at £1.25 per kilogram
Material D	4,200 kilograms at £0.75 per kilogram
Flavouring essence	£300

Mixing labour   370 hours at £2 per hour
Normal waste   5% of weight input
Output was   18,000 kilograms

There was no work in process at the beginning of the week but 1,000 kilograms were in process at the end of the week and were estimated to be only 50% complete so far as labour and overhead were concerned. Overhead of £3,200 incurred by the two processes was absorbed on the basis of mixing labour hours.

Within process 1, abnormal scrap arose because some batches failed to pass the quality control check at the end of each mix. However, no loss in weight occurred and all scrap was sold for cash on the last day of the week. Any resultant balance on the abnormal scrap account was transferred to profit and loss account.

(Institute of Cost & Management Accountants)

Question 34   Process costing   Answer page 280

Fastgro is an agricultural fertiliser which is produced by subjecting certain basic materials to chemical processes, the output of Process A being tras

being transferred to Process B from which the fertiliser emerges in sealed containers.

The normal scrap of Process A is 25% of input, and of Process B, 10% of input, all scrap is sold for 15p per kg.

Costs allocated to Batch No. 1234 were:

Process A
    Material X   40,000 kg, at 20p per kg.
    Labour   £258
    Overhead   £742

Process B
    Material Y   10,000 kg, at 50p per kg
    Labour   £128
    Overhead   £540

The output from Process A was 29,600 kg and from Process B 36,000 kg.

You are required to prepare accounts for each of the two processes and for the scrap.

(Association of Certified Accountants)

(a)MA Chemicals Limited process a range of products including a detergent 'Washo', which passes through three processes before completion and transfer to the finished goods warehouse. During April, data relating to this product were as shown :

	Process			
	1	2	3	Total
	£	£	£	£
Basic raw material (10,000 units)	6,000	-	-	6,000
Direct materials added in process	8,500	9,500	5,500	23,500
Direct wages	4,000	6,000	12,000	22,000
Direct expenses	1,200	930	1,340	3,470
Production overhead				16,500

(Production overhead is absorbed as a percentage of direct wages.)

	Units	Units	Units
Output	9,200	8,700	7,900
	%	%	%
Normal loss in process, of input	10	5	10
	£	£	£
All loss has a scrap value, per unit, of	0.20	0.50	1.00

There was no stock at start or at end in any process.

You are required to prepare the following accounts:

    (i)   process 1;
    (ii)   process 2;
    (iii) process 3;
    (iv) abnormal loss;
    (v)   abnormal gain.
b)   Define briefly the following :

    (i)   normal loss;
    (ii)   abnormal loss;
    (iii) abnormal gain;
    (iv) scrap;
    (v)   waste.

(Institute of Cost & Management Accountants)

(a)   The standard processing loss in refining certain basic materials into an industrial cleaning compound is 15%, this scrap being sold for 50p per kg. At the beginning of Period 6, 8,000 kg of basic material was put into a process, the output of which was 7,000 kg of cleaning compound. The basic material cost 80p per kg, wages of process operators amounted to £1,200 and overhead applied to the process was £480. Prepare the necessary accounts to show the results of the process.

(b)   The production of a product known as Tojo requires the treatment of input units through three distinct processes at each of which refining material is added and labour and overhead costs are incurred.

Work in progress at the beginning of Period 9 consisted of 8,000 input units which had passed through the first process, the cost to that point being £96,000. During period 9, refining material which cost £31,594 was put into the process and labour costs amounted to £23,940. Process Overhead is applied at the rate of 40% of process labour.

7,200 units were completed during the Period and transferred to Process 3. Of the remainder, the firm's Chief Chemist estimated that in respect of refining material, labour and overhead, half were 75% complete at the end of Period 9, and the other half, 40% complete.

You are required to write up Process 2 Account for Period 9 showing clearly the cost to be transferred to Process 3, and the value of the work in progress at the end of the period.

(Association of Certified Accountants)

(a)   In the context of process costing how would you distinguish a by product from a joint product?

(b)   Liquigas Ltd. produces the four products J, K, L and M through a process which for November, 1976 cost £1,500,000. Production and sales during the month were as follows :

	Production tonnes	Sales tonnes	per tonne
J	5,000	4,000	£100
K	8,000	6,000	125
L	5,000	4,500	80
M	3,000	2,700	200

There were no stocks on hand at the beginning of November.
You are required to prepare a statement showing the value of the stocks of the four products at the end of November and to state any assumptions you have made.

(Association of Certified Accountants)

6
Cost accounts

Introduction

The double entry system of book-keeping used in financial accounting is also employed in cost accounting. Every debit entry made in one cost account must have a corresponding entry in another cost account. In this chapter, the entries made in the cost accounts will be considered, as will the link between cost accounts and financial accounts. This topic will be examined in two sections, for there is a choice between two alternative systems, namely, Interlocking Accounts and Integral Accounts. The following definitions are given by the I.C.M.A. Terminology :

Interlocking Accounts. - 'A system in which the cost accounts are distinct from the financial accounts, the two sets of accounts being kept continuously in agreement or readily reconcilable'.

Integral Accounts. - 'A single set of accounts which provides both financial and management accounting information.'

Interlocking Accounts.

The entries in the cost accounts and the financial accounts are made from the same basic data. A double entry is made in the financial books, and a further double entry is made in the cost accounts to record the same transaction. There are, however, a few items of income and expenditure that are recorded in the financial accounts only; equally, there are a number of entries made in the cost accounts which do not appear in the financial books, for, as it was pointed out in chapter one, cost accounting is not only concerned with external transactions, but also with transfers that occur within the business.

The cost accounts are kept in the cost ledger which is the principal book of account in the costing system. There are also a number of subsidiary ledgers. These usually include:

(a) The Stores Ledger. The stock accounts are kept in this ledger and there is an account for each separately identifiable class of material handled by the stores. The entries are made from goods received notes, material requisitions, and so on. The stores ledger has been dealt with in chapter 2.

(b) Work in Progress Ledger. This ledger contains the accounts of jobs, contracts or processes, depending on the method of costing employed. Each account is debited with direct costs, and also a share of the overhead using an absorption rate.

(c) Finished Goods Ledger. When goods are transferred to finished goods store, a credit entry is made in the work in progress ledger and a corresponding entry made in the finished goods ledger. An account is kept for each identifiable class of saleable product. When goods are sold, the cost of production is transferred from the finished goods ledger to the cost of sales account.

(d) Overhead Ledger. This ledger contains a record of overhead costs and is often sub-divided by having a separate section for each of the major functions of the business. The overhead costs of each function are further sub-divided into the various items of expenditure, for example, electricity, telephone charges, stationery, and so on, a cost code number (or standing order number) being allocated to each individual item of expenditure.

Control Accounts. Each of the above ledgers has a control account. The transactions are recorded in detail in individual accounts and are also entered in summary form in the control account. For example, if £20 were posted to the debit side of each of five different job accounts, an amount of £100 would be debited to work in progress control account. The posting to control accounts is in addition to making the double entry and it provides a check on the accuracy of the postings to individual accounts. At the end of the costing period, the sum of the balances in the individual accounts should agree with the balance on the control (or summary) account.

Control accounts are not affected by transfers that occur within one ledger. For example, a transfer of material from one job to another affect affects the job accounts but not the work in progress control account. Entries are only made in control accounts where the corresponding entry affects a different ledger. The use of the work in progress control account has already been illustrated in the section on Job Costing in chapter 5.

Cost Ledger Contra Account. The purpose of this account, which is contained in the cost ledger, is to maintain the double entry principle. It is sometimes referred to as the General Ledger Adjustment Account or the Cost Ledger Control Account. It is usual for entries to be made in the financial books first for income and expenditure. Where an entry is made in the cost accounts, which has in the first place been made in the financial accounts, an entry must be made in the Cost Ledger Contra Account.

Cost Accounting Entries. Below are listed some typical transactions, together with the debit and credit entries necessary.

Transaction	Debit	Credit
a) MATERIALS		
Materials purchased from a supplier for:		
i) stock;	Stores ledger control account	Cost ledger contra account

ii) a specific job.	Work in progress ledger control account	Cost ledger

Materials issued from stores:

i) direct materials;	Work in progress ledger control account	Stores ledger control account
ii) indirect materials.	Production overhead (or marketing overhead etc.)	Stores ledger control account

b) WAGES

Direct wages	Work in progress ledger control	Cost ledger contra account
Idle time booked by direct workers	Production overhead	Cost ledger contra account
Maintenance time booked by direct workers	Production overhead	Cost ledger contra account
Indirect wages and salaries	Production overhead (or administration overhead etc.)	Cost ledger contra account

c) OVERHEAD

Overhead incurred	Production overhead (or marketing overhead etc.)	Cost ledger contra account
Production overhead absorbed	Work in progress ledger control account	Production overhead
Marketing overhead absorbed	Cost of sales account	Marketing overhead
Administration overhead absorbed	Cost of sales account	Administration overhead
Research and Development overhead absorbed	Cost of sales account	R & D overhead

It is suggested above that administration overhead absorbed should be debited to cost of sales account. An alternative procedure would be to debit finished goods account instrad, but many accountants are of the opinion that the valuation of finished goods stock should comprise only direct costs plus production overhead. This view was put forward in chapter 4 under the heading of Administration Overhead.

Under/over Absorption of Overhead. The various overhead accounts are balanced by transferring the difference to an overhead adjustment account, the difference representing the under/over absorption of overhead. The balance of overhead adjustment account is transferred to costing profit and loss account at the end of the costing period.

Sales. The value of the sales for the costing period is credited to costing profit and loss account, the debit entry being made in the cost ledger contra account.

Costing Profit and Loss Account. To this account are transferred the sales cost of sales and under/over absorption of overhead. The balance represents the profit or loss for the period, the opposite entry is made in the cost ledger contra account.

Example. The following balances appeared in the cost ledger at March 1st

	Dr.	Cr.
	£	£
Stores ledger control account	32,520	
Work in progress ledger control account	40,200	
Finished goods ledger control account	18,580	
Cost ledger contra account		91,300
	91,300	91,300

The information relative to the month of March is as follows :

	£
Purchases received from suppliers, requisitioned by	
(a) the storekeeper	29,510
(b) the production control department	76,420
(c) the financial accountant	170
Direct materials issued from stores to production	28,930
Indirect materials issued from stores to	
(a) production	1,390
(b) administration	720
(c) marketing	830
Payroll costs	
(a) direct labour	17,130
(b) idle time	150
(c) production salaries (indirect)	2,730
(d) administration salaries	1,910
(e) marketing salaries	2,420
Direct expenses	1,530
Indirect expenses	
(a) production	7,270
(b) administration	6,860
(c) marketing	3,540
Sales	165,000

Production cost of goods sold	137,500
Cost of work completed	140,000
Materials returned from stores to supplier	150
Production overhead absorbed	11,500
Administration overhead absorbed	9,900
Marketing overhead absorbed	6,500

It is the policy to value stock of finished goods at production cost only
Prepare the cost accounts, including a costing profit and loss account
for March, and extract a trial balance at March 31st.

Stores Ledger Control Account

	£		£
Balance b.d.	32,520	Work in progress	28,930
Cost ledger contra	29,510	Production overhead	1,390
		Administration overhead	720
		Marketing overhead	830
		Cost ledger contra	150
		Balance c.d.	30,010
	62,030		62,030
Balance b.d.	30,010		

Work in Progress Ledger Control Account

	£		£
Balance b.d.	40,200	Finished goods	140,000
Cost ledger contra	76,420	Balance c.d.	35,710
Stores ledger	28,930		
Cost ledger contra	17,130		
Cost ledger contra	1,530		
Production overhead	11,500		
	175,710		175,710
Balance b.d.	35,710		

Finished Goods Ledger Control Account

	£		£
Balance b.d.	18,580	Cost of sales	137,500
Work in progress	140,000	Balance c.d.	21,080
	158,580		158,580
Balance b.d.	21,080		

Cost Ledger Contra Account

	£		£
Stores ledger	150	Balance b.d.	91,300
Sales	165,000	Stores ledger	29,510
Balance c.d.	86,800	Work in progress	76,420
		Administration overhead	170
		Work in progress	17,130

	Production overhead	150
	Production overhead	2,730
	Administration overhead	1,910
	Marketing overhead	2,420
	Work in progress	1,530
	Production overhead	7,270
	Administration overhead	6,860
	Marketing overhead	3,540
	Costing profit and loss	11,010
251,950		251,950
	Balance b.d.	86,800

Production Overhead Account

	£		£
Stores ledger	1,390	Work in progress	11,500
Cost ledger contra	150	Overhead adjustment	
		account under-absorbed	40
Cost ledger contra	2,730		
Cost ledger contra	7,270		
	11,540		11,540

Marketing Overhead Account

	£		£
Stores ledger	830	Cost of sales	6,500
Cost ledger contra	2,420	Overhead adjustment	
		account under-absorbed	290
Cost ledger contra	3,540		
	6,790		6,790

Administration Overhead Account

	£		£
Cost ledger contra	170	Cost of sales	9,900
Stores ledger	720		
Cost ledger contra	1,910		
Cost ledger contra	6,860		
Overhead adjust-ment account - overhead over-absorbed	240		
	9,900		9,900

Cost of Sales Account

	£		£
Finished goods	137,500	Costing profit and loss account	153,900

	£		£
Administration overhead	9,900		
Marketing overhead	6,500		
	153,900		153,900

Overhead Adjustment Account

	£		£
Production overhead	40	Administration overhead	240
Marketing overhead	290	Costing profit and loss account	90
	330		330

Costing Profit and Loss Account

	£		£
Cost of sales	153,900	Sales	165,000
Overhead adjustment acct.	90		
Profit	11,010		
	165,000		165,000

Trial Balance
As at March 31st.

	Dr.	Cr.
	£	£
Stores ledger control account	30,010	
Work in progress ledger control account	35,710	
Finished goods control account	21,080	
Cost ledger contra account		86,800
	86,800	86,800

Notes:

(a) Notice that when a transaction affects the financial accounts, an entry is made in the cost ledger contra account. The student will recall that in chapter 1 it was stated that the cost accounts are also concerned with transfers within the business. In such cases, for example the transfer of direct materials from stores to the production department, the cost ledger contra account is not affected.

(b) Control accounts have been shown in order to illustrate the double entries. It will be appreciated that entries are also made to the individual accounts included in the various ledgers. For example, direct materials issued from stores to production are not only entered in the stores ledger and work in progress ledger control accounts, but as there is an account for each item of stock and each job, contract or process, entries are made in the individual accounts also. The same applies to the overhead accounts. Not only will production overhead be debited, but also individual accounts that make up the total production overhead, for example, stationery, consumable materials, etc.

(c)   In this example, under/over absorption of overhead has been transferred to overhead adjustment account and then to costing profit or loss account. However, because over/under absorption of overhead depends on the degree of production activity and the amount of expenditure which might vary from month to month, some cost accountants would carry forward the balances on overhead accounts at the end of each month and only transfer the under/over absorption at the end of the accounting year. In such cases, production overhead, marketing overhead, etc, would appear in the monthly trial balances.

A problem is sometimes set, in which the student is given opening and closing balances and is required to ascertain the movement that occurs during a costing period.

Example.   The following trial balances were produced for May 31st and June 30th.

	£	£
Stock ledger control account	30,157	32,342
Work in progress ledger control account	18,457	21,321
Finished goods ledger control account	25,421	23,730

The following information relating to the month of June is also available:

	£
Purchases for stock	42,100
Direct wages	23,700
Indirect wages (production)	3,270
Indirect materials issued from stores to production departments	725
Indirect production expenses	7,832

Production overhead is absorbed using a direct wages percentage rate of 50 per cent.

Prepare the cost accounts for June and show (a) the production cost of goods sold during the month and (b) the over/under absorption of production overhead. A cost ledger contra account can be ignored.

Stores Ledger Control Account

	£		£
Balance b.d.	30,157	Production overhead	725
Cost ledger contra	42,100	Work in progress	39,190
		Balance c.d.	32,342
	72,257		72.257
Balance b.d.	32,342		

Work in Progress Ledger Control Account

	£		£
Balance b.d.	18,457	Finished goods	71,876
Cost ledger contra wages	23,700	Balance c.d.	21,321
Production overhead	11,850		
Stores ledger	39,190		
	93,197		93,197
Balance b.d.	21,321		

Finished Goods Ledger Control Account

	£		£
Balance b.d.	25,421	Cost of sales	73,567
Work in progress	71,876	Balance c.d.	23,730
	97,297		97,297
Balance b.d.	23,730		

Production Overhead Account

	£		£
Cost ledger contra wages	3,270	Work in progress - overhead absorbed	11,850
Stores ledger	725		
Cost ledger contra expenses	7,832		
Overhead adjustment account - overhead over-absorbed	23		
	11,850		11,850

The steps required to complete the above accounts are as follows :

(a) Using the information given, make as many entries as possible.

(b) The deficiency in the stores ledger control account of £39,190 must represent the cost of materials issued to work in progress. Make the double entry.

(c) The missing figure in the work in progress ledger control account will be the production cost of goods sold transferred to finished stock. Enter £71,876 in both accounts.

(d) Similarly, the difference in the finished goods ledger control account of £73,567 is the cost of goods sold during the month; this amount can be entered.

(e) The balance on production overhead account is the extent to which overhead is over-absorbed, so this account can be completed.

Capital Orders. Situations often arise when workers who are normally engaged on production activities, undertake improvements to plant and machinery or other assets. All such work which is of a capital nature must be recorded and this is done by allocating a capital order number to each job and charging to it all the costs involved. The cost of production is entered in the cost accounts as follows :

> Dr. Capital order account .
> Cr. Work in progress ledger control account.

It is essential that at the end of the accounting year, the costs are transferred to the financial books by debiting cost ledger contra account and crediting the capital order account.

Reconciliation of Financial and Cost Accounts.

After ascertaining the costing profit and loss for the accounting year, it is necessary to reconcile this figure with the net profit or loss as revealed by the financial accounts. The management accountant uses the information provided by both sets of records and it is therefore important that any differences between the two are discovered if he is to present to management information that is consistent. Differences occur for a variety of reasons and these will now be examined.

(a)   Some items of income and expenditure are normally only included in financial accounts. Items which are purely financial in nature are omitted from the cost accounts; also costs which might be considered abnormal or exceptional. These are often excluded from the cost accounts on the grounds that their inclusion would mislead management. Examples of items which have solely affected the financial profit or loss are:

(i)   profits and losses on the sale of assets;
(ii)   expenditure incurred in raising capital, e.g. share issue expenses;
(iii)   interest paid or received;
(iv)   rent receivable;
(v)   dividends received;
(vi)   goodwill, preliminary expenses or debenture discount written off
(vii)   fines.

Although interest paid is listed above as not being included in the cost accounts, some cost accountants choose to include it. Not only do they include items like debenture interest and bank interest in the cost accounts, they also include notional interest based on the amount of capital employed used by each cost centre. For example, if one department requires a lot of plant and machinery, has a high investment in stocks and allows customers lengthy credit facilities, then that department is consuming a high proportion of the company's capital and capital has to be paid for, if not in terms of interest, then in dividends paid to shareholders.

However, it is generally accepted that both interest actually incurred and notional interest should be excluded from the cost accounts on the grounds that they have to do with finance and not costing. Although it is deducted before arriving at net profit and therefore not strictly an approportion, nevertheless it is similar to dividends in that it is a payment for capital. If dividends are excluded, then interest should also be excluded. However, it should be included in statements when it is necessary to compare one department with another, or when comparing the costs of manual operations with manufacture by machines, or to decide whether the company should perform certain operations or whether it would be less costly to sub-contract. In these latter two cases, in order to make a true comparison, notional interest charges for machinery need to be included, as the company has to obtain finance from shareholders or elsewhere to purchase the machinery.

(b)   There are some items which are included in the cost accounts but not in the financial accounts, the two main examples being notional interest on capital employed and notional rent. Where premises are owned by a business, there is no payment made for rent. However, it is thought by some cost accountants that a notional charge for rent should still be included in the cost accounts for the use of buildings. This is particularly appropriate where manufacture is undertaken in various factories some of which are owned whilst others are rented. In order to make proper comparisons it would be necessary to include a charge for notional rent for those factories which are owner-occupied.

(c)   Some items of expenditure are treated differently in the two sets of accounts. For example, it may be the policy of a cost accountant to include only overhead absorbed using a predetermined rate based on some prediction of future events, without making any adjustment for under/over absorption of overhead. In such a case, the financial accounts will show overhead incurred, whereas the cost accounts will show overhead absorbed.

Different bases are sometimes used in the valuation of work in progress In the cost accounts, it may be the practice to charge administration overhead to work in progress, but in the financial accounts, because of the need to adopt a degree of caution, the work in progress valuation may well exclude administration overhead.

Depreciation could also vary. A policy may be adopted where depreciation is charged to cost centres even after a fixed asset has been written off in the financial accounts, the reason for the charge being that the cost centre should be charged for, in effect, hiring the machine.

The profit figure to use in the financial accounts is 'Net profit before taxation.' However, some examiners, in order to test the students' understanding of principles, deliberately include a financial profit and loss account in which appropriations of profit, such as dividends paid, corporation tax and transfers to general reserve, are treated as costs. These appropriations should really be added back to the profit figure, but it is sufficient for the purposes of providing a reconciliation to treat then as costs which appear in the financial books only.

The procedure to adopt when submitting a reconciliation statement is to start with the profit as per the cost accounts and then to decide which adjustments must be made in order to deal with each item of income and expenditure in the same manner as they were dealt with in the financial accounts. If this is done successfully, the profit in the cost accounts plus and minus the necessary adjustments will give an answer that agrees with the profit as stated in the financial accounts.

It should be appreciated that the reconciliation is a statement and not part of the ledger. It is not necessary to make the adjustments in the cost accounts.

Example. The financial accounts for the year ended 31st March 19... show an amount of £30,000 for 'Profit after taxation'. The following iter items have been included in the accounts:

	£
Interest received	1,500
Interest paid	2,000
Fines	30
Loss on sale of plant	750
Audit fees	1,000
Dividends received	1,200
Taxation	20,000

The costing profit and loss account showed a profit of £53,280 after including notional rent of £1,500.

Opening and closing stocks were valued as follows :

	Financial accounts		Cost accounts	
	Opening £	Closing £	Opening £	Closing £
Raw materials	127,500	142,100	140,800	149,000
Work in progress	52,300	55,000	55,000	61,900
Finished goods	74,700	71,400	78,600	82,200

Prepare a statement reconciling the profit in the financial accounts with the profit in the cost accounts.

Reconciliation Statement

	£	£	£
Profit per cost accounts			53,280
Add Interest received		1,500	
Dividends received		1,200	
Notional rent		1,500	
			4,200
			57,480
Less Interest paid		2,000	
Fines		30	

Loss on sale of plant	750
Taxation	20,000
Difference in stock movement	4,700
	27,480
Profit per financial accounts	30,000

Notes:

(a) The difference in stock movement was calculated as follows :

Financial accounts

Opening stocks	£254,500
Closing stocks	£268,500
Therefore, increase	£ 14,000

Cost accounts

Opening stocks	£274,400
Closing stocks	£293,100
Therefore, increase	£ 18,700

The stock movement in the cost accounts shows an increase £4,700 greater than the increase in the financial accounts. This has the effect of giving a higher figure in the cost accounts, so it has to be deducted in the statement in order to bring the profit per the cost accounts into line with the financial profit.

(b) Taxation has been included in the statement, but as an alternative it could have been excluded and an adjustment made to the profit per financial accounts figure, i.e. £50,000 instead of £30,000.

(c) Audit fees should not appear in the statement as this expense is treated alike in the financial and cost accounts.

Although it was stated earlier that the reconciliation is not part of the ledger, nevertheless the adjustments can be made using the format of an account, thus:

Memorandum Reconciliation Statement

	£		£
Interest paid	2,000	Profit per cost accounts	53,280
Fines	30	Interest received	1,500
Loss on sale of plant	750	Dividends received	1,200
Taxation	20,000	Notional rent	1,500
Difference in stock movement	4,700		
Profit per financial accounts	30,000		
	57,480		57,480

It is important that co-operation exists between the financial and cost accounting sections and that documents used to record information in the financial books are passed to the costing section, otherwise the reconciliation procedure will be a lengthy one.

Integral Accounts.

Where the financial and cost accounts are integrated, a single set of accounts is in operation. Instead of some transactions giving rise to a double entry in the financial accounts and a further double entry in the cost accounts, one debit and one credit only are required. The separate systems are therefore combined into one system.

Internal transactions are dealt with in the same way as in interlocking accounts. For example, if materials are issued from stores to production, the entries under interlocking and integral accounts are:

> Dr. Work in progress ledger control account
> Cr. Stores ledger control account

Financial accounting is not concerned with movements of materials within the business, so the above transaction appears in the cost accounts only. It is therefore only those transactions which are recorded in both sets of books in the interlocking system that need to be looked at under the integral system.

The student should be able to see how four entries can be reduced to two by following a few examples.

(a)   Direct materials bought from an outside supplier and delivered to stores.

Interlocking accounts

Financial	Cost
Dr. Purchases account	Dr. Stores ledger control account
Cr. Creditors control account	Cr. Cost ledger contra account

Integral accounts

> Dr. Stores ledger control account
> Cr. Creditors control account

(b)   Special stationery ordered for the sales manager and paid for by cash

Interlocking accounts

Financial	Cost
Dr. Stationery account	Dr. Marketing overhead account
Cr. Cash account	Cr. Cost ledger contra account

Integral accounts

> Dr. Marketing overhead account
> Cr. Cash

The marketing overhead account will be sub-divided so as to allow the cost to be classified by nature of expense, i.e. stationery.

Advantages of Integral Accounts. There is a reduction in the number of entries and the reconciliation of the two sets of accounts is not necessary. This reduces the number of clerical assistants required.

EXAMINATION PRACTICE

Students are advised to attempt the questions under simulated examination conditions. Then check their answers with the suggested answers at the back of the book.

Question 38   Cost accounts   Answer page 287

Job number 707 was completed in three departments of a factory. Cost details for this job were:

Department	Direct Materials £	Direct Wages £	Direct Labour Hours
X	650	800	1,000
Y	940	300	400
Z	230	665	700

Works overhead is recovered on the basis of direct labour hours and administrative overhead as a percentage of works cost.
The figures for the last cost period for the three departments on which the current overhead recovery rates are based, were:

Departments	X	Y	Z
Direct Material	£6,125	£11,360	£25,780
Direct Wages	£9,375	£23,400	£54,400
Direct Labour Hours	12,500	36,000	64,000
Works Overhead	£5,000	£ 7,200	£ 9,600
Administrative Overhead	£2,870	£14,686	£ 8,978

You are required to draw up a cost ledger sheet showing the cost of job 707, and to show the price charged, assuming a profit margin of 20% on total cost.

(Institute of Accounting Staff)

Question 39   Cost accounts   Answer page 287

B. Ilder commenced business on 1 May, 1976 having obtained three orders for house extensions, the costs of which during his first month's trading were as follows :

	Job 1 £	Job 2 £	Job 3 £
Direct wages			
Direct wages	528	451	308
Materials issued from stores	2,752	2,341	1,473
Special materials bought in	215	-	46
Materials returned to stores	71	-	-

Ilder has estimated his overhead for the year ending 30 April, 1977 at £10,500 and the direct labour hours at 17,500. Under a trade union agreement dated 1 May all direct workers were paid 110p per hour from that date. For costing putposes overhead is absorbed on a direct labour hour basis; the overhead incurred in May was £800

Job No.1 was completed on 31 May and invoiced to the customer at the contracted amount of £4,500.

You are required to:

(a) Prepare (i) cost accounts for each of the three jobs;
        (ii) control accounts for overhead and work in progress for May;
        (iii) Profit and Loss Account for May.

(b) Given that the cost estimate for Job No.1 was as follows :

	£
Materials	2,850
Direct wages (500 hrs)	525
Overhead	300

prepare a reconciliation of estimated and actual costs and comment briefly on the possible causes of any differences.

(Association of Certified Accountants)

Question 40   Cost accounts   Answer page 289

The following balances were extracted from the records of CFL Ltd for the month of May 1976:

	May 1 £	May 31 £
Finished Goods Stock	7,298	16,732
Work-in-Progress : Materials	28,480	21,360
Work-in-Progress : Labour	44,500	49,840
Work-in-Progress : Factory Overhead	11,125	12,460
Raw Materials Stock	146,138	114,098

During the month raw materials costing £85,440 were purchased and the direct labour payroll amounted to £149,520.

Included in the issues from Raw Materials Stock were items valued £10,680 which were used for the maintenance of factory premises and plant and machinery.

Factory Overhead is absorbed on the direct labour cost basis, the rate for May 1976 being 25%.

From the foregoing data you are required to write up the accounts referred to above and to show the cost of goods sold during the month.

(Association of Certified Accountants)

Mr. T. Oymaker is in business as a manufacturer of children's toys. His involvement with the manufacturing and marketing operations of his business leave him no time to maintain a proper set of business records. He is aware, however, of the need for accounting information and to enable a practising accountant friend to prepare periodic accounts for him, he complies with a set of 'rules' prescribed for this purpose; these include:

(1)   Production overhead is absorbed by reference to direct labour cost, the rate being 80%.

(2)   Finished stock is valued at direct cost plus production overhead;

(3)   The amount added to production cost to arrive at selling price is 25%.

From the information set out below, you are required to :

(a)   write up the accounts for
    (i)   Work in progress,
    (ii)   Finished stock,
    (iii)   Raw materials in stock; and

(b)   prepare
    (i)   Profit and Loss Account for the month of October 1978,
    (ii)   Balance Sheet at 31 October 1978

	30 September 1978 £	31 October 1978 £
Work in Progress	9,600	7,200
Finished Stock	12,000	7,920
Raw Materials Stock	14,400	12,000
Debtors for Goods Sold	8,400	9,300
Creditors for raw materials	6,400	7,600
Fixed Assets	5,000	5,000

Summary of bank transactions for the month to 31 October 1978 :-

	£
Balance at Bank 30 September	2,000
Receipts from debtors	28,800
Payments:	
Direct labour	3,600
Creditors for raw materials	7,200
Production Overhead	3,200
Marketing Costs	1,200
Administration Costs	800

N.B. You are advised to submit details of your workings.

(Association of Certified Accountants)

A company operates a cost accounting system which is not integrated with the financial accounting system. Materials received are recorded at actual price; issues are charged at standard prices at which time price variances are calculated. The standard price for material 426 is £2.0 per unit and transactions relating to this material for the month of October 1975 are shown below.

You are required to record these transactions in the cost accounting system by means of journal entries, but narrations for each transaction are not required.

1975
October

1	Ordered 2,000 units @ £1.90 per unit
8	Received 1,000 units, which were invoiced
9	Issued to production 500 units
10	Returned to supplier 50 units which were faulty; full credit allowed
13	Issued to production maintenance department 100 units
15	Production department requisitioned 400 units
16	Issued to production department 350 units
16	Transferred 50 units from production maintenance to production department
17	Received 500 units, which were invoiced
20	Issued 50 units to production maintenance department
21	Issued to production, 300 units
24	Fire destroyed 100 units; claim submitted to insurance company
27	Paid supplier £1,900
28	Production department returned 50 units to store
30	Insurance company agreed claim in respect of fire
31	Cheque received from insurance company for £190
31	Physical inventory recorded of 80 units.

(Institute of Cost & Management Accountants)

A company operates a financial accounting system and a cost accounting system. Extracts from both final accounts for the year are shown below, from which you are required to prepare a reconciliation statement or account.

The final financial accounts included the following :

	£
Debenture interest	2,000
Interest received	1,000
Discount allowed	8,000
Discount received	3,000
Net profit	57,000

Stock valuation

	Opening stock £	Closing stock £
Raw materials	152,000	198,000
Work-in-progress	66,000	72,000
Finished goods	84,000	87,000

The final cost accounts included the following :

	£
Interest on capital	30,000
Notional rent	20,000
Administration overhead over-absorbed	10,000
Production overhead under-absorbed	15,000
Selling and distribution overhead over-absorbed	14,000

Stock valuations:

	Opening stock £	Closing stock £
Raw materials	164,000	187,000
Work-in-progress	61,000	68,000
Finished goods	90,000	94,000

(b) Explain the meaning of:

    (i)   interest on capital;
    (ii) notional rent.

Discuss briefly the reason why the cost accountant may choose to introduce these items into the cost accounts.

(Institute of Cost and Management Accountants)

7
Marginal costing

Introduction

It was stated in chapter 1 that costs can be classified in various ways. In Marginal Costing, costs are examined and classified according to behaviour. Items of cost are investigated to see how they respond to changes in the volume of output or sales. The I.C.M.A. Terminology defines Marginal Costing as 'a principle whereby marginal costs of cost units are ascertained. Only variable costs are charged to cost units, the fixed costs attributable to a relevant period being written off in full against the contribution for that period.'

Marginal costing is not a method of costing like job costing or process costing, but it can be superimposed on a costing method, the marginal costing principle and the method being coupled together and used conjointly to produce one complete system. The choice of costing method will depend upon the nature of the business activity, but marginal costing can be used in conjunction with job costing, process costing or some other method, in order to facilitate the provision of suitable information to assist management in planning, decision-making and control.

The definition of marginal costing mentions three types of cost, namely, marginal cost, variable cost and fixed cost. The following definitions are given by the I.C.M.A. Terminology :

Marginal cost. The variable cost of one unit of a product or a service; i.e. a cost which would be avoided if the unit was not produced or provided.

Variable cost. A cost which, in the aggregate, tends to vary in direct proportion to changes in the volume of output or turnover.

Fixed cost. A cost which accrues in relation to the passage of time and which, within certain output or turnover limits, tends to be unaffected by fluctuations in volume of output or turnover. Examples are rent, rates, insurance and executive salaries.

To ascertain the marginal cost of a product, it is necessary, then, to distinguish between variable costs and fixed costs, for the marginal cost is, for all practical purposes, equivalent to the variable cost of one unit. 'Marginal', then is synonymous with 'variable' when applied to the cost of a single unit.

Variable Costs.

Variable costs, in total, tend to vary in direct proportion to changes in the volume of production or sales. Notice the use of the word 'tends' in the definition of variable cost. It is unlikely that a cost varies exactly in direct proportion to increases or decreases in output or turnover. There is, rather, a tendency to vary. A cost is considered to be variable if it is inclined to move in sympathy with the volume of output; in other words, if there is a close proximity to direct variation.

Variable cost comprises direct cost and variable overhead. One additional unit produced gives rise to additional costs in respect of direct materials, direct wages and direct expenses. For example, if the direct materials cost to manufacture 1,000 units is £1,000, then the manufacture of 1,100 units would probably result in a direct materials cost of £1,100. However, it could be argued that, as the demand for materials increases, the opportunity to take advantage of quantity discount would also increa crease. Direct materials to produce 1,100 units may cost, say, £1,095. Consequently, the cost in this case does not vary absolutely in direct pro portion to the increase in output, but the modest difference of £5 is tolerable and direct materials therefore can be considered as a variable cost. The same is true for all direct costs.

Assuming that increases or decreases in output do not vary to a significant extent from one week to another, direct costs are prone to vary in proportion to output; a slight divergence is unlikely to disturb the genera principle. Moreover, costs which increase at a slightly lower rate than the increase in output will often be compensated for by costs which rise at a slightly higher rate than the increase in output.

Although variable production overhead varies with output, variable selling overhead, such as salesmen's commission, tends to vary with the volume of sales.

Fixed Costs.

Fixed costs are relatively unaffected by changes in the level of production or sales. Rates payable to the local authority do not increase simply because an additional 10 units have been produced. Executive salaries are similarly unaffected. The amount of fixed costs incurred during a costing period does not depend upon the degree of activity on the shop floor or among the sales force. Indeed, fixed costs would hardly deviate from normal even if, during a costing period, there was no production at all. Costs such as insurance premiums would still have to be met.

Because fixed costs do not, in total, respond to fluctuations in the level of activity, an increase in the volume of sales will result in a decrease in the fixed cost per unit. Therefore as it is only the total of variable costs, which increases in response to a rise in volume, the increase in total cost is proportionately less than the increase in volume.

Example. The variable cost of producing a certain article is £0.50 per unit. During the month of September, 5,000 units were produced, and in October the production rose to 6,000 units. Fixed costs amount to £1,500 per month.

	September	October
Output (units)	5,000	6,000
	£	£
Variable cost	2,500	3,000
Fixed cost	1,500	1,500
Total cost	4,000	4,500

It will be noted that the total variable cost has increased from £2,500 to £3,000, but the variable cost per unit has remained constant at £0.50. Conversely, the total fixed cost has stayed the same, whereas the fixed cost per unit has fallen as output has risen:

$$\text{Fixed cost per unit } - \text{ September } = \frac{£1,500}{5,000} = 30 \text{ pence per unit}$$

$$- \text{ October } = \frac{£1,500}{6,000} = 25 \text{ pence per unit}$$

The fixed element in the costs above has meant that the increase in production is not matched by an equivalent increase in costs. Output shows a rise of 20 per cent, but total costs have only gone up by 12½ per cent. The existence of fixed costs has had the effect of slowing down the upward movement in total costs. The first 5,000 units cost £4.000, whereas the nxt 5,000 units would only cost £2,500, i.e. 5,000 times the marginal cost of £0.50. The benefit which accrues from high volume can therefore be appreciated. Additional output causes a reduction in the cost per unit because fixed costs can be spread over a greater volume.

Example. Using the information given in the previous example, it is possible to ascertain the total cost and the cost per unit at various levels of output

Output (units)	Costs			Cost per unit		
	Variable	Fixed	Total	Variable	Fixed	Total
	£	£	£	£	£	£
5,000	2,500	1,500	4,000	0.50	0.30	0.80
6,000	3,000	1,500	4,500	0.50	0.25	0.75
7,000	3,500	1,500	5,000	0.50	0.21	0.71
8,000	4,000	1,500	5,500	0.50	0.19	0.69
9,000	4,500	1,500	6,000	0.50	0.17	0.67
10,000	5,000	1,500	6,500	0.50	0.15	0.65

At this point a word of warning must be given. To say merely that fixed costs do not vary is wrong. Such a statement is misleading. Note that the definition of fixed cost states that it is a cost which tends to be unaffected by fluctuations in volume of output or turnover only 'within certain output or turnover limits'. There is a point when even fixed costs become variable. If production increases substantially, additional accommodation would possibly be required. Therefore, rates paid to the local council would be affected. Furthermore, additional executive staff might be required, causing an increase in the remuneration paid to them. Extra accommodation and production stocks would result in higher insurance premiums. It is doubtful whether, in the above example, fixed costs would remain at £1,500 for an output of 10,000 units.

Therefore, the principle is that fixed costs will only remain fixed if the movement in production and selling activity does not deviate too greatly from the normal level.

What is more, there are other factors which cause so-called fixed costs to vary. Even if there is no variation in activity, rent, rates, insurance and the salaries of administration staff will not remain perpetually fixed. Inflation will have its effect. Also, a decision by management could cause a change in the level of fixed costs. A move to a more prestigious office block might be contemplated even though higher sales in the short term are unlikely.

The point is that fixed costs tend to remain static in response to changes in the level of output or turnover. This is the distinction that must be drawn between fixed costs and variable costs. It is the way they behave in response to changes in volume which is the key issue. Other factors like inflation and management decisions have their effect on both fixed costs and variable costs.

Another point to be made is that fixed costs vary in accordance with time. In the above example, the fixed cost for one month was £1,500, but for two months it was £3,000. Consequently, fixed costs are sometimes referred to as period costs because they are related to the length of the costing period and not to the volume of production or sales.

To sum up, fixed costs do fluctuate due to inflation, management decisions and in accordance with the passage of time. However, they are relatively unaffected by fluctuations in the volume of production or sales, in the short term especially, and as long as the production and sales do not vary considerably from month to month.

As all direct costs are assumed to be variable, fixed cost comprises only fixed overhead, but that includes the fixed overhead of all the major functions of the business, namely, production, marketing, administration and research and development.

Contribution.

Another term used in the definition of marginal costing is Contribution, which is the difference between sales value and variable cost. This difference is the contribution made to fixed cost and profit. In other words, after deducting the variable cost from the sales, the amount left over provides a fund from which fixed costs can be paid. After fixed costs have been met, the balance is profit. The term, Margin, is sometimes used instead of Contribution.

Example. With reference to the table above, let it be assumed that the selling price of each unit is £1.20. Using the data relating to 5,000 units, it is possible to present the information in the following manner :

Units sold	5,000
	£
Sales value	6,000
Variable cost	2,500
Contribution	3,500
Fixed cost	1,500
Profit	2,000

If the above statement is examined, it will be apparent that not only can the contribution be ascertained by deducting the variable cost from the sales value, but also by adding together the fixed cost and the profit, i.e. £1,500 + £2,000. Consequently, the following formula can often be used to solve marginal costing problems:

Sales – Variable cost = Fixed cost + Profit

The definition of marginal costing stated that only variable costs are charged to cost units, whereas fixed costs are written off against contribution for a costing period.

Example. The following information is given for products A, B and C.

	A	B	C
	£	£	£
Selling price per unit	2.00	1.50	1.30
Variable cost per unit	1.20	1.10	0.80

During the month of November, the number of units sold were: A, 4,00 B. 7,000 and C. 2,500. The fixed costs were £5,000. The information fo the month could be presented in the following way :

	A	B	C	Total
Number of units sold	4,000	7,000	2,500	13,500
	£	£	£	£
Sales value	8,000	10,500	3,250	21,750
Variable cost	4,800	7,700	2,000	14,500
Contribution	3,200	2,800	1,250	7,250
Fixed cost				5,000
Profit				2,250

Alternatively, the information could be shown as follows:

	A	B	C
Number of units sold	4,000	7,000	2,500
Contribution per unit	£0.80	£0.40	£0.50
Therefore, contribution	£3,200	£2,800	£1,250

	£
Total contribution	7,250
Fixed cost	5,000
Profit	2,250

The contribution is arrived at by finding the difference between the selling price of a unit and its marginal cost, and as the variable cost per unit is the same for each additional unit produced, the contribution per unit will also be unchanged. So, within certain output and turnover limits, the contribution will be the same for each unit produced.

It will be noticed that in the example no attempt is made to apportion the fixed costs to the various products. As fixed costs accrue in relation to the passage of time and are insensitive to changes in the level of output or sales, there is little point in arbitrarily alloting them to products A, B and C. Consequently, they are written off against the total contribution earned during the period in which they occur.

Profit/Volume Ratio.

This ratio, sometimes referred to as the P/V ratio, is something of a misnomer, for 'profit' in this context means contribution. As volume refers to the total sales value, the formula for calculating the ratio is :

$$\frac{\text{Contribution}}{\text{Sales}} \times 100$$

The profit/volume ratio, then, is contribution expressed as a percentage of sales.

As stated above, the contribution will be the same for each additional unit produced. The relationship between selling price, variable cost and contribution is the same at various levels of output. In the previous example, the selling price, variable cost and contribution for each unit of product A were £2.00, £1.20 and £0.80 respectively. For 2 units, the sales value will be £4.00, the variable cost £2.40 and the contribution £1.60, and so on. Therefore, if one is in a position to express contribution as a percentage of sales for a particular product, then one can calculate the contribution provided by different levels of output. The assumption is made that, in the short term, the selling price and the marginal cost of a product are the same for each unit produced.

Example. Referring again to product A in the previous example, the P/V ratio is 40 per cent, i.e. $\frac{£3,200}{£8,000} \times 100$. Now find the contribution made if sales were (a) £10,000 and (b) £11,500.

Contribution in (a) = 40 per cent of £10,000 = £4,000
(b) = 40 per cent of £11,500 = £4,600

It will be appreciated that variable cost must equal 60 per cent of sales seeing that Sales minus Variable cost equals Contribution.

Where a business is manufacturing a number of products, it is normally desirable to calculate a P/V ratio for each product in order to see the percentage contribution provided by each.

Management should always be trying to bring about an improvement in P/V ratio. The higher the percentage, the greater the contribution towards fixed costs and profit. An improvement in the percentage can be achieved by:

    (a)   an increase in the selling price;
    (b)   a reduction in the variable cost per unit;
    (c)   concentrating on those products which provide the highest contribution.

An increase in the selling price will cause an increase in the contribution of each unit, but there is the risk that the volume of sales might be affected. If competition from other companies is high, a rise in selling price might precipitate a switch in public demand to another company's product.

A reduction in the variable cost per unit could be achieved by purchasing the latest machinery, thereby cutting the number of direct hours required to complete each operation. However, this reduction might be offset by higher fixed costs such as depreciation and insurance.

The P/V ratio is just one statistic that management should consider and whilst an improvement in the percentage should be sought, the effect on other factors like the volume of sales and fixed costs should not be overlooked.

Limitations of P/V Ratio. The P/V ratio must be used with care. There are occasions when it can be used to advantage, even when a number of products are manufactured. One overall percentage can be employed in order to forecast the contribution provided at various output levels.

Nevertheless, if the products manufactured are dissimilar, the widespread use of the P/V ratio will produce misleading conclusions, especially if the combination of products sold fluctuates from month to month.

Break-even Point.

The break-even point is the level of sales volume at which neither a profit nor a loss is made. At this point the business 'breaks-even'. The break-even point can be expressed in terms of sales value or, alternatively, as the number of units sold.

Earlier in the chapter it was stated that:

    Sales - Variable cost = Fixed cost + Profit.

As at the break-even point profit equals nil, then it follows that :

    Sales at the break-even point — Variable cost = Fixed cost.

Put another way, at the breakeven point, fixed cost equals contribution. Consequently, it is necessary to earn enough to support the fixed costs before any profit can be earned. After the break-even point has been reached, all contribution will result in additional profit, seeing that fixed costs have already been covered. However, where the contribution from sales does not reach the level of fixed costs, a loss is incurred.

The break-even point (BEP) can be calculated by the formula :

$$\frac{\text{Fixed cost}}{\text{Contribution}} \times \text{Sales}$$

The result expresses the BEP in terms of sales value.

To express the break-even point for one particular product in terms of the number of units, the following formula can be used :

$$\frac{\text{Fixed cost}}{\text{Contribution per unit}}$$

It is also possible to find the break-even point by dividing the fixed cost by the P/V ratio.

Example. The following information is available for a certain costing period:

Units sold	=	5,000
Selling price per unit	=	£2
Variable cost per unit	=	£1.50
Fixed cost	=	£2,000

Calculate the level of sales required to break-even.

From the above information, it is apparent that sales are £10,000, variable costs are £7,500, and the contribution to fixed costs and profit is £2,500. Using the first formula above :

$$\text{BEP} = \frac{£2,000}{£2,500} \times £10,000 = £8,000$$

Using the second formula :

$$\text{BEP} = \frac{£2,000}{£0.50} = 4,000 \text{ units}$$

Hence, if 4,000 units, having a sales value of £8,000 were sold, neither a profit nor a loss would be made. The contribution made by the sale of 4,000 units is £2,000, i.e. 4,000 x £0.50, which is only sufficient to cover the fixed costs and no more.

The P/V ratio, using the information provided in the example, is :

$$\frac{£2,500}{£10,000} \times 100 = 25 \text{ per cent}$$

Notice that the break-even point in terms of sales value can also be found by the formula $\frac{\text{Fixed cost}}{\text{P/V ratio}}$, i.e. $\frac{£2,000}{25 \text{ per cent}}$ or $\frac{£2,000}{0.25} = \underline{\underline{£8,000}}$

Break-even Charts.

The relationship between sales, costs and profit at different levels of activity can be displayed diagramatically by using a break-even chart. It is possible to see at a glance the approximate profit or loss that is likely to be earned at a specific level of activity. The chart also shows quite clearly the break-even point itself.

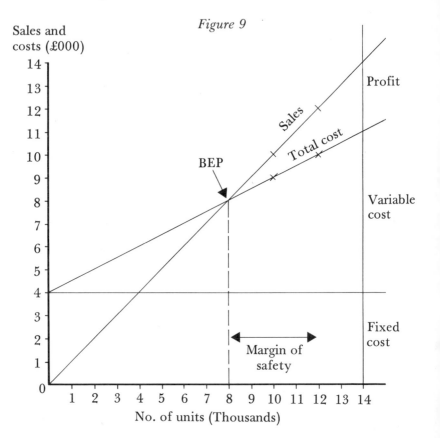

Figure 9

In a break-even chart (see *Figure 9*), the horizontal axis is used for the activity (or capacity) and the vertical axis for costs and sales. Alternatively, if the activity is not expressed in terms of the number of units, or is not relevant as in cases where the break-even chart summarises the details of a number of products, the horizontal axis is used for sales and the vertica axis is used only for costs. It is necessary to draw three lines on the chart as follows:

1. A fixed cost line, parallel to the horizontal axis, which will cut the vertical axis at the fixed cost level. The line runs parallel to the horizonta axis because the fixed cost is the same for all levels of activity.

2. The total cost line. The total costs at various levels of output can be

plotted on the graph and a line drawn, which must meet the fixed cost line on the vertical axis, seeing that when the activity is nil, the total cost is the same as the fixed cost.

3. The sales values at various levels of activity are plotted on the graph and a line drawn. The sales line must start at the point where the vertical and horizontal axes meet, as nil activity produces nil sales.

The point at which the sales and total cost lines intersect is the break-even point and by dropping a vertical line from the BEP to the horizontal axis it is possible to read off the number of units which must be sold in order to break even.

It is also possible to forecast the profit to be made at specific levels of sales by referring to a particular quantity of units along the horizontal axis and drawing an imaginary vertical line at ninety degrees. The profit or loss is represented by the gap between the total cost line and the sales line.

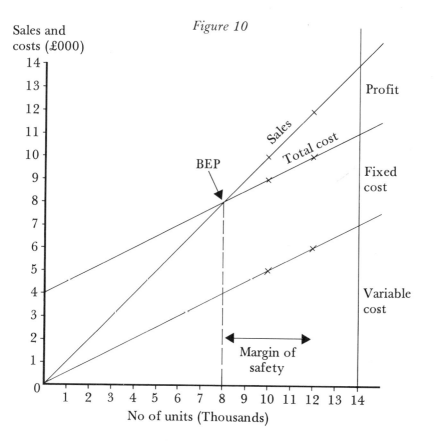

Figure 10

There is another form of break-even chart (*Figure 10*), the difference being that a variable cost line is inserted first and then the fixed costs are placed on top of the vertical costs. This method is an improvement on the previous one, for by placing the fixed cost and profit together, it is possible to read off the contribution provided at different levels of activity. The contribution is represented by the gap between the sales line and the variable cost line.

Example. The break-even charts illustrated in *Figures 9* and *10* are based on the following information :

Selling price per unit	£1
Variable cost per unit	£0.50
Fixed costs per month	£4,000
Number of units sold : January	10,000
- February	12,000

The point at which the total cost line intersects the sales line is the point where the business breaks even. A glance at the charts indicates that the break even point is 8,000 units. In other words, the contribution provided by the sale of 8,000 units will be sufficient only to cover the fixed costs.

It is also possible by referring to the charts to estimate the profit that will be achieved at various levels of sales.

Example. State the profit or loss that will be achieved on the sale of (a) 13,000 units and (b) 7,000 units.

By referring to 13,000 units on the horizontal axis and drawing an imaginary vertical line at 90 degrees it will be seen that the profit would be £2,500. Note that sales is £13,000 and total cost is £10,500. When only 7,000 units are sold, the sales line is positioned beneath the cost line indicating a loss. A look at the charts will reveal that the gap between the two lines is £500. Sales are £7,000, whereas costs are £7,500.

Margin of Safety.

The term is defined by the I.C.M.A. Terminology as 'the excess of normal or actual sales over sales at break-even point. It may be expressed as a percentage of either normal sales or actual sales, whichever is selected for consideration.' The details in the previous example give no indication as to the normal level of sales, but the margin of safety for February is £4,000. The actual sales have exceeded the sales at break-even point by £4,000, i.e. £12,000 − £8,000. Expressed as a percentage of actual sales, this represents a safety margin of 33.33 per cent.

This percentage indicates whether the business is susceptible to a drop in demand. A narrow margin of safety would mean that a slight decline in volume might have a significant effect on profits. A 33 per cent margin on the other hand, is wide enough for a company to be relatively unaffected by a small reduction in demand for its products. A substantial fall in sales would have to take place before break-even point is reached, so the business will still be making profits even if output does fall. The nearer the position to the BEP, the nearer one is to making a loss. A wide margin of safety is therefore hightly desirable. The margin of safety is indicated on the break-even charts.

Limitations of Break-even Charts.

A number of objections have been raised against the use of break-even charts. It has been said that their use is limited, and misleading conclusions can be drawn by those using them. The following are some of the objections raised.

1. As variable costs do not vary exactly in direct proportion to the volume of production or sales, it is false to show total cost as a straight line. It was pointed out earlier in the chapter that the cost of additional direct materials may increase at a rate which is somewhat less than the increase in output or turnover. On the other hand, direct materials, to meet a sudden increase in demand for the company's products, may have to be purchased at short notice from another supplier whose prices are higher. Similarly, the working of overtime is often necessary to produce more goods, and because overtime rates are higher than basic rates, the variable cost may be higher on additional production. Although increases in variable costs above the normal rate will, to some extent, be cancelled by increases below the normal rate, the straight line on the graph does not accurately indicate the real situation.

2. Likewise, to show sales as a straight line does not express the true position. Revenue from sales does not increase absolutely in direct proportion to output. Additional sales may only be achieved if a quantity discount is given to those customers who buy large quantities. The top of the sales line should, therefore, curve down slightly.

3. Where an organisation manufactures a variety of products, a single break-even chart has its limitations because the contribution per unit will be different for each product. Any major change in the product mix from from one month to the next will completely invalidate the information provided by the chart. A way round this would be to prepare a break-even chart for each individual product, but the problem would be how to apportion the fixed costs.

4. As fixed costs only remain fixed within certain output or turnover limits, the break-even chart cannot be used to provide information over a wide range of output. At higher activity levels, there may well be an increase in fixed costs.

5. Inflation affects fixed costs as well as variable costs. Costs are changing all the time. Again, a decision on the part of management might bring about a change in the distribution of costs between fixed and variable. A break-even chart is like a photograph; it reveals the position at a particular moment. Inflation and management decisions can mean that the chart is soon out of date.

In spite of all these objections, break-even charts are still widely used and have a useful role to play. They can provide useful information to management so long as managers are made aware of their limitations. Complete accuracy is not always essential, and it is often sufficient to obtain an indication of the likely results to be achieved by following a particular course of action. In the break-even chart shown above, nobody would suggest that if 8,000 units were sold, the costing profit and loss statement would show exactly a nil profit figure. The technique is not invalidated by the approximations. It is sufficient for management to know that if sales dropped to around 8,000 units the profit, at best, would be negligible, and the likelihood of a loss occurring is strong.

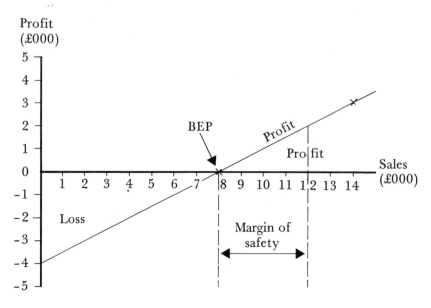

Figure 11 – Profit Graph

The Profit Graph

This is similar to a break-even chart and by eliminating the fixed cost and total cost lines, attention is directed specifically to profit. The horizontal axis, representing sales or activity, is drawn in the centre of the graph; the vertical axis represents profit, but that part of the line below the horizontal axis is the loss area. The information from previous break-even charts has been used to plot the various points on the profit graph (*Figure 11*). Sales of £14,000 provide a profit of £3,000 and sales amounting to £7,000 produce a loss of £500. The profit line cuts the horizontal axis at the break-even point and intersects the vertical axis at -£4,000, the amount of the fixed cost, for at nil sales the loss incurred equates to the total fixed costs. It is an easy matter to read off the profit earned at other sales levels; for example, sales of £13,000 would provide a profit of £2,500.

It is not necessary, of course, to draw break-even charts in order to solve marginal costing problems. Solutions are easily found by using the various formulae, for instance, the P/V ratio, the formula for the break-even point and the marginal cost equation. The advantage of the break-even chart is that it conveniently summarises the position over a range of activity and as such it is suitable for managers who require a quick grasp of the situation. The main points are highlighted on the chart and the attention of management is drawn to them.

Marginal Costing and Absorption Costing Compared

Absorption costing is defined by the I.C.M.A. Terminology as 'a principle whereby fixed as well as variable costs are alloted to cost units. The term may be applied where (a) production costs only, or (b) costs of all functions are so alloted.' Although the term Absorption Costing has not been previously mentioned in this book, all theory up to the end of chapter six has been based on absorption costing principles. Direct costs were allocated to cost units and absorption rates were calculated in order that all overhead was alloted to cost units. Production overhead costs, fixed and variable, were absorbed at the point of manufacture so that work in progress was valued at cost of production, which comprises direct costs, variable production overhead and fixed production overhead

Under marginal costing, only variable costs are charged to cost units. There is no attempt to find suitable bases of apportionment for fixed costs. They are merely written off in full against the contribution provided by various cost units. Consequently, the work in progress valuation under marginal costing will exclude the fixed element of production overhead. This cannot be done under the absorption costing principle as no analysis of fixed and variable costs is carried out. If the valuation of work in progress using marginal costing principles excludes fixed production overhead, then the valuation must be less than under absorption costing. A lower stock valuation produces a lower profit figure in the costing profit and loss account.

Example. The selling price of a particular product is £10 and the marginal cost is £6.50. During the month of April, 800 units were produced of which 500 were sold. There was no opening stock at the commencement of the month. Fixed costs amounted to £1,800. Provide a statement using (a) marginal costing and (b) absorption costing, showing the closing stock valuation and the profit earned under each principle. ciple.

	Absorption £	Absorption £	Marginal £	Marginal £
Sales (500 units)		5,000		5,000
Opening stock				
Cost of production:				
Variable cost	5,200		5,200	
Fixed cost	1,800		1,800	
	7,000		7,000	

less closing stock:

$$£7,000 \times \frac{300}{800} \qquad 2,625$$

$$£5,200 \times \frac{300}{800} \qquad\qquad\qquad 1,950$$

Cost of sales	4,375	5,050
Profit/(loss)	625	(50)

The difference of £675 in the two results arises because under the absorption costing principle a proportion of fixed cost has been included in the closing stock and will be charged against future sales. The fixed costs treated in this way can be calculated as follows:

$$£1,800 \times \frac{300}{800} = £675$$

Those who advocate the use of marginal costing principles would argue that fixed costs occur independently of production and should be written off in full against the contribution of the period. Notice that under marginal costing, fixed costs have been excluded when closing stock is valued. The closing stock could more easily have been computed as follows:

No. of units in stock x variable cost per unit

$$= 300 \times £6.50 = £1,950$$

Now let it be assumed that in the following month, May, 750 units were produced and 600 were sold.

	Absorption		Marginal	
	£	£	£	£
Sales (600 units)		6,000		6,000
Opening stock	2,625		1,950	
Cost of production:				
Variable cost	4,875		4,875	
Fixed cost	1,800		1,800	
	9,300		8,625	
less closing stock:				
$£9,300 \times \frac{450}{1,050}$	3,986			
$£6.50 \times 450$			2,925	
Cost of sales		5,314		5,700
Profit		686		300

When production for a particular month exceeds sales, absorption cost-ing will always provide a higher profit figure than marginal costing. The reverse will occur in those months when sales exceeds production. A much simpler statement could be prepared for marginal costing, thus:

	April £	May £
Contribution per unit = £3.50		
Therefore contribution is:		
April (500 x £3.50)	1,750	
May (600 x £3.50)		2.100
less Fixed costs	1,800	1,800
Profit/(loss)	(50)	300
Closing stock:		
April 300 x £6.50	1,950	
May 450 x £6.50		2,925

Semi-variable Costs.

A semi-variable cost, sometimes referred to as a semi-fixed cost, is one which contains both fixed and variable elements. It is a cost which is only partly affected by changes in the volume of production or sales.

It was seen earlier in the chapter that it is unlikely that an item of ex-penditure will vary exactly in direct proportion to fluctuations in the level of output or sales, but where there is a tendency to vary, the cost is treated as being completely variable. However, semi-variable costs are costs which are either mainly variable with a significant fixed element, or mainly fixed with a large variable content.

What is variable, fixed or semi-variable will depend on the organisation in question, but in many businesses the cost of maintenance of plant and machinery is a semi-variable cost. A maintenance agreement is often in existence which provides that the supplier of a machine will undertake to service the machine periodically. Clearly, the routine maintenance is a fixed cost. The machine will be serviced, say, every three months, irres-pective of the quantity of production processed. On the other hand, if during a particular period a high volume of production necessitated using the machine more often than normal, the chances of breakdown would increase; more attention would be required and parts replaced more fre-quently. These costs are variable. The amount spent depends upon the volume of output. Many items of expenditure, therefore, have a fixed component and a variable component.

The task is, then, to segregate these two components and include them in the two main categories of fixed and variable, so eliminating semi-vari-able costs. But how is this to be achieved? It is possible to investigate the make-up of each item of cost by examining invoices, petty cash vouchers and other documents, noting separately the fixed costs and the variable costs. However, this is time consuming and costly, and there is no guarantee that the split between the two would be exactly repeated in future costing periods. In marginal costing, complete accuracy is not essential, even if it could be achieved. It is sufficient, therefore, to employ a method of segregating the fixed and variable elements of semi-variable costs which gives an approximate division between the two. Two methods are suggested here, namely, the 'High-Low' method and the use of Scattergraphs.

Both methods involve the examination of previous results. For example, take the cost of a particular item of expenditure, say maintenance of plant and machinery, for each of the past six costing periods. Eliminate, as far as possible, the effect of inflation. In other words, convert each period's cost to the level of prices existing currently. Also, remove those costs that have altered due to reasons not connected with changes in output. In addition to ascertaining the cost details for each period, ascertain the activity level for each period, this can be expressed in terms of the number of units produced, or the number of direct hours worked, or the number of machine hours, and so on. Having done this, it is now possible to separate the fixed and variable elements using one of the two methods previously mentioned. The procedures outlined below would have to be undertaken for each item of expense that is semi-variable in nature.

The 'high-low' method. In this method, the periods which contain the highest and lowest costs are taken and compared. The difference between the two figures is related to the difference between the two activity levels. As fixed costs are relatively unaffected by changes in output, the increase or decrease in the costs over the two periods must be due to variable costs. By dividing the difference in costs by the difference in activity, the variable cost per unit (or hour) can be computed.

Example. Information relating to the last six costing periods was ascertained. After adjusting the costs to bring them into line with current price levels, the adjusted figures, together with the activity levels, were as follows:

Costing period	Cost £	Output (units)
1	21,000	22,000
2	22,000	24,000
3	26,000	30,000
4	27,000	32,000
5	22,000	25,000
6	25,000	27,000

The high and low cost periods are 1 and 4. There has been an increase in costs amounting to £6,000 and a rise in output of 10,000 units. The £6,000 must consist entirely of variable costs, so the variable cost per unit can be computed thus:

$$\frac{£6,000}{10,000} = £0.60 \text{ per unit}$$

The costs for the two periods can be summarised as follows:

	£
Period 1, variable cost = 22,000 units x £0.60 per unit =	13,200
therefore, fixed cost =	7,800
	21,000
Period 4, variable cost = 32,000 units x £0.60 per unit =	19,200
therefore, fixed cost =	7,800
	27,000

If another period is observed, say period 6, it will be apparent that the fixed cost component comes out at a figure that is different from £7,800. The reason for this is that variable costs rarely vary absolutely in direct proportion to output. All that can be said is that the variable cost per unit is approximately £0.60.

Period 6, variable cost = 27,000 units x £0.60 per unit =	£16,200
therefore, fixed cost =	£ 8,800
	£25,000

Nevertheless, it is possible to arrive at fairly accurate figures by taking any two costing periods. The reason for taking high and low months is in order to include as wide a range of activity as possible so that the change in output is significant enough to measure the variable cost.

The Scattergraph. In this method, the following steps are necessary after obtaining the costs and activity levels for past costing periods:

1. Construct a graph, the horizontal axis of which is for activity and the vertical axis being used for costs.

2. For each period, plot the costs at the various levels on the graph.

3. Draw a line which links as many points as possible, and which has an equal number of points to either side of the line, ignoring those points which indicate abnormal results. This line is called the 'line of best fit' and should reach the vertical axis.

4. The point at which the line of best fit, i.e. the total cost line, cuts the vertical axis, indicates the fixed cost element, and a line representing the fixed cost can then be drawn parallel to the horizontal axis.

5. The variable cost element for a particular level of activity is indicated by the gap between the total cost and fixed cost lines.

6. Divide the variable cost for a certain level of activity by the number of units to obtain the variable cost per unit.

Example. The figures given in the example illustrating the hig-low method have been used to illustrate the scattergraph (*Figure 12*). The total cost line, i.e. the line of best fit, cuts the vertical axis at £8,000. Therefore, at nil activity the cost is £8,000. This, then, represents the fixed

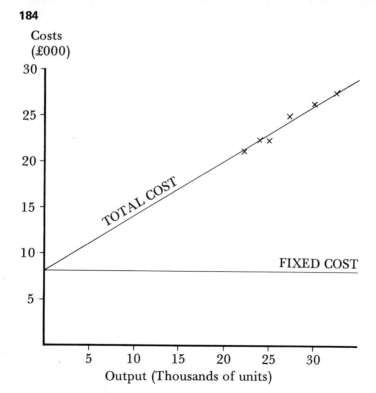

Costs
(£000)

TOTAL COST

FIXED COST

Output (Thousands of units)

Figure 12 — Scattergraph (used for segregating the fixed and variable elements of semi-variable costs)

cost element and a horizontal line is drawn across the graph to indicate fixed costs. If one refers to 20,000 units along the horizontal axis, it is apparent that the total cost for this level of activity is £20,000. The variable cost, indicated by the gap between the total cost and fixed cost lines is £12,000. The variable cost per unit, therefore, is £0.60, i.e. $\dfrac{£12,000}{20,000}$

Contribution and the Limiting Factor.

It was stated above that the business will tend to concentrate on those products which make the highest contribution to fixed overhead and profit. However, the decision of management will also be based on factors which, at times, limit the activities of a business. The volume of output or sales will depend on this limiting factor, which could be the availability of raw materials or skilled labour, although the limiting factor is usually the level of demand for the company's products. The decision of management to proceed with the production of those products with the highest contribution may have to be reconsidered in the light of the limiting factor. In such circumstances, it is necessary to calculate the contribution per unit of the limiting factor.

Example. The following details have been extracted from the budget of a manufacturing company which produces two products, A and B.

	A	B
Maximum possible output (units)	10,000	10,000
	£	£
Variable costs:		
Direct materials	10	20
Direct wages	7	10
Overhead	3	6
Selling price per unit	25	45

Due to an unexpected shortage in the supply of essential raw materials, the company can no longer produce 10,000 units of each product. Only £275,000 of direct materials will be available and the managing director has suggested that in view of the higher contribution provided by Product B, the company should concentrate on the manufacture of that product. The fixed costs are budgeted at £80,000. You are required to calculate:

(a)   the original budgeted profit;
(b)   the profit that will be achieved if manufacture is concentrated on B;
(c)   the profit that will be achieved from any alternative suggestion you may wish to make.

	A	B
	£	£
(a) Sales	250,000	450,000
Direct materials cost	100,000	200,000
Direct wages cost	70,000	100,000
Variable overhead	30,000	60,000
Variable cost	200,000	360,000
Contribution	50,000	90,000

	140,000
less fixed costs	80,000
Profit	60,000

	£
(b) Contribution from product B (as above)	90,000

After using £200,000 of direct materials, only £75,000 in value is left to manufacture product A. Therefore only 75 per cent of the maximum output can take place, i.e. 7,500 units. Contribution from product A is, then :

7,500 units x £5 per unit	37,500
	127,500

	£
less fixed costs	80,000
Profit	47,500

(c)   However, calculate the contribution per unit of the limiting factor (materials) for A and B.

$$A = \frac{£\ 50,000}{£100,000} = £0.50 \text{ per £ of direct materials}$$

$$B = \frac{£\ 90,000}{£200,000} = £0.45 \text{ per £ of direct materials}$$

Note that the contribution per £ of the scarce resource of materials is higher for product A. Therefore, concentrate on the product which produces the highest contribution per unit of the limiting factor.

	£
Contribution for product A	50,000

After using £100,000 of direct materials only £175,000 in value is left to manufacture product B. Therefore, only 87.5 per cent of the maximum output can take place, i.e. 8,750 units. Contribution from product B, then is:

	£
8,750 x £9	78,750
	128,750
less fixed costs	80,000
Profit	48,750

Note: this produces a higher profit than in (b).

Treatment of Direct Wages.

Earlier in the chapter it was stated that all direct costs vary more or less in direct proportion to output. However, some would argue that direct wages should be treated as a fixed cost. If, due to a decline in the demand for a company's product, there is a corresponding fall in the volume of production, it is not possible nowadays to dismiss operators and re-engage them when demand picks up again. Various statutes have been passed in recent years to make it more difficult to make employees redundant. Moreover, it is unwise to release skilled workers every time there is a short term slack period, for when the time comes to increase output again, the skilled workers previously laid off might no longer be available. In many instances, therefore, they will be retained and paid a guaranteed minimum wage. This may be somewhat less than their wages during times of full production but nevertheless there is often an amount beyond which their remuneration will not be allowed to fall.

Even though the proportion of direct wages that is appropriate to idle time will be transferred to production overhead, this does not alter the fact that the basic wage is in reality a fixed cost. It could be argued that direct wages is a semi-variable cost; the guaranteed wage represents the fixed element, whereas any payment above this is regarded as variable.

Where production is largely mechanised, the amount produced may depend on the speed of the machine and not on the efforts of the direct workers. Also, if output is affected by machine breakdown and other factors outside the control of the machine operators, in such circumstances direct wages are often treated as totally fixed.

In examination questions, however, the student should treat direct wages and all direct costs as variable, unless the wording of the question indicates that they should be treated otherwise.

Marginal Costing and Decision-making.
One of the most important activities of management is decision - making. Various courses of action will from time to time present themselves to a manager and he must often make a choice from a number of alternatives. This will involve making predictions on the possible outcome of each option open to him. Plans will be drawn up and forecasts prepared of costs to be incurred.

It is therefore essential for a manager to have an understanding of the manner in which costs behave and their effect on alternative courses of action. Uncertainty is an element in most business decisions, but an appreciation of cost behaviour will help to reduce the uncertainty.

The use of marginal costing principles will enable informed predictions to be made on the outcome of each alternative examined. The scope for making decisions based on marginal costing are considered below.

Reducing the selling price to increase volume. A proposal is sometimes put forward to lower the selling price of a particular product if there is evidence that in so doing the demand is likely to increase.

Example. The following details were extracted from the budget for the forthcoming year:

	£	£
Sales (48,750 units)		438,750
Direct materials cost	117,000	
Direct wages cost	70,200	
Variable overhead	46,800	
Fixed overhead	110,000	
		344,000
Net profit		94,750

In order to improve the amount of net profit budgeted, it is proposed to reduce the selling price from £9 to £8 per unit. It is anticipated that if this reduction is made, the volume of sales would increase by 30,000 units.

Assuming the selling price were reduced as suggested, calculate:

(a)   the net profit that will be achieved;
(b)   the sales required in order to break even;
(c)   the sales required to yield a profit of £100,000

Before answering (a), the following calculations can be made:

1.   The variable cost, using the budgeted information provided abo
above, is £234,000 (£117,000 + £70,200 + £46,800). The marginal cos
can be calculated, therefore by dividing £234,000 by 48,750: £4.80.

2.   The contribution, then, if the selling price were to be reduced t
£8, would be £3.20.

It is now possible to answer part (a), thus:

	£
Contribution, 78,750 x £3.20	252,000
less fixed overhead	110,000
Net profit	142,000

(b)   The break even point   =   Fixed costs x $\dfrac{\text{Sales}}{\text{Contribution}}$

$$=\quad £110,000 \quad \text{x} \quad \dfrac{£630,000}{£252,000}$$

$$=\quad \underline{£275,000}$$

Note that the figure for Sales was obtained by multiplying 78,750 by
The break even point can also be expressed in terms of units, i.e. 34,37
units. So, if 34,375 units, having a contribution of £3.20 per unit, wer
sold, the total contribution would be £110,000, sufficient to cover the
fixed cost and no more.

(c)   Note that the Profit/volume ratio is 40 per cent, i.e. $\dfrac{£3.20}{£8.00}$ x 100

After the break-even point has been reached, all contribution will resul
in additional profit. As contribution is 40 per cent of sales, £100,000
profit will be earned by achieving the following level of sales:

$$\text{Sales at BEP} + (£100,000 \text{ x } \dfrac{100}{40})$$

$$=\ £275,000 + £250,000$$

$$=\ \underline{£525,000}\ (\text{or } 65,625 \text{ units})$$

Testing the accuracy of the above calculation, the contribution provided by the sale of 65,625 units is £210,000. After deducting £110,00
for fixed cost, one is left with £100,000 profit.

Selling below normal selling price. It is sometimes worthwhile to allow
customer a special discount if he agrees to place a large order. Whether
this is done or not will depend on whether surplus capacity is available.

If it is, as long as the marginal cost is below the proposed selling price, the available capacity can be utilised in earning additional contribution. On the other hand, if demand for the company's products is already greater than the capacity available to produce them, then clearly a reduction in the selling price will not be contemplated, seeing that the company working at full capacity can meet all orders without the need to bring down selling prices.

Example. A company manufactures a single product which sells for £10. The variable cost is £6 and over the next 12 months, it is expected that 60,000 units will be produced and sold. Fixed costs over that period are estimated at £80,000. However the company is only working at 75 per cent of capacity and a prospective customer is prepared to place an order for 20,000 units if the price per unit can be reduced. Other sales will not be affected. The company has a profit objective of £190,000 and is looking for ways to achieve this end whilst at the same time utilising some of its surplus capacity. What is the lowest price which can be quoted for the special order?

The offer made by the enquirer is certainly worthy of consideration, for the company must be responsive to any suggestion that will entail the utilisation of its surplus capacity. The shortfall in profit at present is £30,000:

	£
Contribution, 60,000 x £4	240,000
less fixed costs	80,000
Budgeted profit	160,000
Profit objective £190,000	

If the order were accepted it would need to provide £30,000 seeing that it would take up all the spare capacity. A contribution of £1.50 per unit is therefore required, i.e. $\frac{£30,000}{20,000}$. As the marginal cost is £6, the minimum selling price for the special order would have to be £7.50 per unit.

Assessing the profitability of products. The following cost statement has been prepared for the previous financial year :

	Product A £	Product B £	Product C £	Total £
Direct materials cost	16,800	12,500	18,200	47,500
Direct wages cost	8,900	7,400	9,700	26,000
Production overhead	2,100	1,800	3,100	7,000
Cost of production	27,800	21,700	31,000	80,500
Administration overhead	1,800	1,800	1,800	5,400

Marketing overhead	2,900	2,000	2,700	7,600
Total cost	32,500	25,500	35,500	93,500
Sales	40,500	23,000	42,000	105,500
Profit/(loss)	8,000	(2,500)	6,500	12,000

Because of the loss incurred by product B, the management is considering stopping production of that product, However, when analysing the costs between fixed and variable, the following information emerges with regard to variable costs.

	A £	B £	C £	Total £
Production overhead	1,500	1,200	2,500	5,200
Marketing overhead	1,100	700	1,200	3,000

All other overhead costs are fixed. Prepare a suitable statement for management that will assist in the decision on whether to abandon production of product B.

	A £	B £	C £	Total £
Sales	40,500	23,000	42,000	105,500
Variable costs (including direct costs)	28,300	21,800	31,600	81,700
Contribution	12,200	1,200	10,400	23,800
Fixed costs				11,800
Net profit				12,000

The failure to differentiate between variable and fixed costs in the first statement has led management to draw erroneous conclusions. Once costs have been classified by behaviour, it becomes apparent that product B is making a useful contribution and its production should therefore be continued. If it were abandoned, profit would be reduced by 1,200, the amount of the contribution lost.

However, there are other factors to consider. As the other two products make a more valuable contribution, consideration should be given to the possibility of running down production of product B in favour of expanding the production of A and C. But is there the demand for additional units of A and C? Are they coming to the end of their life cycle? In the long term, will product B turn out to be more profitable? Are there possibilities for reducing its marginal cost?

While the second statement provides more meaningful information than the first, decisions cannot be based entirely on information revealed by cost statements. Even marginal cost statements are for the guidance of management and should be used with care.

Planning the product mix that will achieve the highest possible profit.
Marginal costing can be used in order to decide on the products to be

sold, and the quantity of each, during a forthcoming period. If the marginal cost of producing and selling each product is known, the business can concentrate on those products which make the highest contribution to fixed cost and profit. It is possible to compare the results to be achieved from a number of alternative courses of action.

Example. The following three alternative plans are being considered for the next accounting year:

Plan A - Sell 1,000 units of product X and 500 units of product Y
Plan B - Sell   800 units of product X and 740 units of product Y
Plan C - Sell   760 units of each product.

The budget figures are:

	X £	Y £
Selling price	8	7
Direct materials cost	3	3
Direct wages cost	2	2
Variable overhead	0.50	0.25

Calculate the budgeted profit that would result from each of the three alternatives. The budgeted fixed costs are £1,500.

Workings.

	X £	Y £
Selling price	8	7
Marginal cost	5.50	5.25
Contribution per unit	2.50	1.75

Plan A

	£
Contribution provided by product X = 1,000 x £2.50 =	2,500
Y = 500 x £1.75 =	875
Total contribution	3,375
less Fixed costs	1,500
Net profit	1,875

Plan B

	£
Contribution provided by product X = 800 x £2.50 =	2,000
Y = 740 x £1.75 =	1,295
Total contribution	3,295
less Fixed cost	1,500
Net profit	1,795

Plan C

	£
Contribution provided by product X = 760 x £2.50 =	1,900
Y = 760 x £1.75 =	1,330
Total contribution	3,230
less Fixed costs	1,500
Net profit	1,730

However, other factors may influence the decision, e.g. availability of skilled labour, availability of materials, capacity, working capital, consumer demand.

EXAMINATION PRACTICE
Students are advised to attempt the questions under simulated examination conditions. Then check their answers with the suggested answers at the back of the book.

Question 44   Break even calculations   **Answer page 293**

Last year A Ltd. sold 13,000 units for £65,000 and made a loss of £5,000. The variable cost was £4 per unit.

For the current year, you are informed that fixed costs will increase by £3,000 over those of last year, the sale price will be increased by 20% per unit, and variable cost will be £5.50 per unit up to the 10,000 unit level, but will decrease to £5 per unit for units above the 10,000 unit level.

You are required:
(a)   to find the break even point of sales value for the current year
(b)   to find the profit if 30,000 units are sold in the current year.

(Institute of Accounting Staff)

Question 45   Break even calculations   **Answer page 294**

In a firm, a detailed budget of costs and sales at various levels has been prepared, but due to a typist's error, most of the information has been destroyed. The remaining information is as follows :

Sales Level (units)	6,000	8,000
Material Cost	£18,000	£24,000
Labour Cost	£15,000	£19,000
Overhead Cost	£11,700	£14,700

The sale price is £8 per unit at all levels.
You are required to find:
(a)   the fixed element, if any, of each component cost:
(b)   the breakeven point.

The following is the standard specification for ten 'Bedford' coffee tables:

Materials	Standard Quantity	Standard Price
Heywood	40 square feet	£5.75 per 100 square feet
Helix	¼ gallon	£1.40 per gallon
Fibre Glass Packing	24 rolls	£4.50 per gross
Container	1	£7.20 per dozen

Labour	Standard Time	Standard Rate
Fitters	30 minutes	90p per hour
Polishers	6 minutes	50p per hour

Annual Overheads: Fixed £14,400; Variable £8.640. Allocated on basis of Direct Labour Hours.

Budget Activity Level: Effective weekly working hours 40; working weeks per annum 48; employees 5.

You are required to calculate the sale price of one coffee table, on the basis of a gross profit of $33\frac{1}{3}\%$ on sale price.

(Institute of Accounting Staff)

A company of which you are cost accountant manufactures goods in three separate factories. The projected figures for the next year are as follows:

Factory	Edinburgh £	York £	Gloucester £
Sales	440,000	400,000	700,000
Branch Expenses			
Salaries	42,000	38,000	62,000
Advertising	8,000	15,000	10,000
Other	10,000	8,000	11,000

There is a central office in London which is estimated to cost £154,000 and this is to be apportioned to the three factories on the basis of the sales figures. Variable costs amount to 75% of the sales of each factory. You are required to a) prepare a comparative Profit and Loss account for the next year; b) advise on whether the York factory should be closed if that would save all the York branch expenses and reduce the central office expenses from £154,000 to £124,000.

(Institute of Accounting Staff)

The AB Company operates a chain of franchise operators in a country-wide group of supermarkets and has approached you for advice. The manager is proposing to market a new pack consisting of a shirt, with matching tie, socks and handkerchief. He wishes the financial potential to be assessed in relation to two methods of promoting sales - firstly by paying commission and secondly by a salary bonus.

The details are: sale price of pack   £9.80
                  Variable cost of pack   £8.40
   Fixed cost, including staff salaries   £12,600

You are required to calculate a) the breakeven point in units if a sales commission of 60p per pack is paid to the sales staff; b) the breakeven point in value if no sales commission is paid, but staff salaries are increased by a total of £9.800; c) the margin of safety in units in a) and b) if sales reach 18,000 packs.

(Institute of Accounting Staff)

(a)   Explain the term 'cost behaviour' and comment on its relevance to business decision making.

(b)   The following table shows the production quantities and related total costs of a company manufacturing a single product.

Period	Production Units	Total cost
1	1,500	£2,600
2	1,800	3,256
3	2,500	4,560
4	3,200	5,800

Using the index 100 to represent cost levels in Period 1, the following indices apply to succeeding periods

Period 2	110
3	120
4	125

On the basis of the foregoing you are required to calculate the total costs to be expected in Period 5 during which production of 4,000 units is planned and the cost level index is expected to be 135.

(Association of Certified Accountants)

The budget of S Ltd. provides for the manufacture and sale of 10,000 spodgets per month, the unit standard cost being £6, made up as follows:

Direct material	£3.5
Direct labour	£0.5
Fixed overhead	£2.0
the selling price of the spodget being	£8.0

Production and sales quantities for Periods I and II were as follows:

	Period I	Period II
Production	10,000	10,000
Sales	8,000	12,000

You are required to:
(a) prepare operating statements for each of the two periods;
    (i)   assuming the company uses marginal costing
    (ii) assuming absorption costing is used, and
(b) comment on the differences of the two systems as regards:
    (i)   stock valuations
    (ii) period profit

(Association of Certified Accountants)

Industrial Fitments Ltd produce three types of shelving viz 'Factory', 'Stores' and 'Office', which are made from the same basic material, viz. mild steel, which costs £1 per square metre. The standard unit cost of the three products are as follows :

	'Factory'	'Stores'	'Office'
	p	p	p
Direct material:			
Mild steel	84	78	75
Attachments	14	25	30
Direct labour:			
Machining	10	15	19
Spraying	4	7	6
Unit selling prices are:	175	186	190

Sales expectations for the forthcoming month are:

	Units
'Factory'	2,000
'Stores'	2,400
'Office'	1,600

Owing to an industrial dispute, suppliers of mild steel have intimated

that they will be able to supply only 2,500 square metres during the month.
You are required to:
(a)   prepare a statement which will enable you to advise management on the most profitable production pattern to pursue;
(b)   mention briefly the matters which should receive the attention of management when confronted with the type of situation described above

(Association of Certified Accountants)

Question 52   Margin of safety and contribution   Answer page 299

(a) Define and illustrate by means of simple arithmetical examples:
   (i)   contribution/sales ratio
   (ii)   margin of safety
(b) Demonstrate the relationship between a firm's contribution/sales ratio, its percentage margin of safety, and its profit/sales ratio.
(c) What is the significance of a firm's margin of safety?
(d) The following details relate to product X

	£	£
Selling Price		120
Costs:		
Material	60	
Labour	15	
Variable overhead	5	
Fixed overhead	10	
		90
Profit		£30

During the forthcoming year it is expected that material costs will increase by 10%, wages by $33\frac{1}{3}$% and other costs by 20%.
You are required to calculate the percentage increase in the selling price of X which would maintain the firm's contribution/sales ratio.

(Association of Certified Accountants)

Question 53   Marginal costing and decision-making   Answer page 300

    The variable cost of the power drill manufactured by Hometools Limited is £4 and the selling price £10. The company expects its net profit for the year just ending to be £275,000 after charging fixed costs amounting to £85,000.
The company's production capacity is not fully utilised and market research suggests three alternative strategies for the forthcoming year, viz.:

Strategy	Reduce selling price by	Sales volume expected to increase by
1	5%	10%
2	7%	20%
3	10%	25%

(a) Assuming the same cost structure as the current year, evaluate the alternative strategies available to the company and state which is the most profitable.
(b) Suggest other considerations which management would probably have in mind in making its decision.

(Association of Certified Accountants)

Question 54   Marginal costing   Answer page 300

Summarised profit and loss statements of DC Electrical Company Limited for the two years ended 31st December, 1974 and 1975 are shown below:

	1974 £000s	1975 £000s
Sales	650	720
Marginal cost of sales	390	340
Contribution	260	380
Fixed overhead	240	260
Net profit	20	120

As a result of the poor performance of the company in 1974, management decided to implement a reorganisation of production methods and to increase selling prices by 20% from 1st January, 1975.
You are required to calculate how much increase in net profit in 1975 was due to the change in:
(a) marginal cost;
(b) sales price;
(c) sales volume;
(d) total fixed overhead.
State any assumptions you may have made in your calculations.

(Institute of Cost & Management Accountants)

Question 55   Marginal costing   Answer page 301

A company manufactures three products, X, Y and Z. The budgets are currently being prepared for 1977 and estimates have been submitted for sales, costs and output.

From the data provided below you are required to prepare two statements to show:

(i)   the expected profit if the original budget is pursued;
(ii) the expected profit at maximum sales demand.

The standard cost per unit is as follows:

	Product		
	X	Y	Z
	£	£	£
Direct materials: Aye	8	6	6
Bee	2	4	2
Cee	6	2	4
Direct wages	8	10	12
Variable overhead	6	8	8
Fixed overhead	12	15	18

Fixed overhead is absorbed as a percentage of direct wages and is based on the original budget

	Units	Units	Units
Budgeted output for 1977	8,000	6,000	10,000
Maximum sales demand (estimated)	10,000	7,500	12,500

	£	£	£
Sales price	40	50	60

(Institute of Cost & Management Accountants)

Question 56   Marginal costing   Answer page 301

The trading results for the year ending 30th June, 1978 of D. Limited, a face cream manufacturer, are expected to be as follows:

	£000	£000
Sales (100,000 jars)		400
Costs:		
Material	50	
Wages: direct	82	
indirect, fixed	19	
Production expenses:		
variable	25	
fixed	30	
Administration expenses		
fixed	24	
Selling expenses:		
variable	20	
fixed	22	
Distribution expenses:		
variable	18	
fixed	10	300
Profit		100

Forecasts for year ending 30th June, 1979 are given below:
1. A sales price reduction to £3 per jar will increase sales volume by 50%
2. Material prices will remain unchanged except that, because of increased quantities purchased, a 5% quantity discount will be obtained.
3. Direct wage rates will increase by 10%.
4. Variable selling costs will increase proportionately with sales value.
5. Inflation will increase variable production and distribution expenses by 10%.
6. All fixed costs will increase by 20%.
7. There will be no stocks or work-in-progress at the beginning or end of the year.
You are required, using the information, to:
(a) prepare a statement showing the profit forecast for the year ending 30th June, 1979 on a marginal costing basis;
(b) comment on the result forecast in your answer to (a) above;
(c) prepare an alternative profit statement for the year ending 30th June, 1979 based on a sales price increase of 10% on 1977/78 price and a sales volume of 100,000 jars;
(d) state the price increase per jar (and as a percentage to three decimal places) needed, above the current sales price, for year ending 30th June, 1979 to achieve a profit of £110,000.

(Institute of Cost & Management Accountants)

Question 57   Marginal and absorption costing   **Answer page 302**

Using the information given below, prepare profit statements for the months of March and April 1978 using:
(a) marginal costing;
(b) absorption costing.

	£
Per unit:	
Sales price	50
Direct material cost	18
Direct wages	4
Variable production overhead	3
Per month:	
Fixed production overhead	99,000
Fixed selling expenses	14,000
Fixed administration expenses	26,000
Variable selling expenses,	
10% of sales value	

Normal capacity was 11,000 units per month.

	March units	April units
Sales	10,000	12,000
Production	12,000	10,000

(Institute of Cost & Management Accountants)

Question 58   Marginal costing and decision-making   Answer page 304

Your company is considering a trade union claim for an increase of 10% on the hourly wage rates of all direct workers. As an alternative the management would prefer to negotiate a productivity deal whereby a bonus to direct workers of £0.08 for every unit produced is paid. The work study department has estimated that production could be increased by 12½% without any additional hours being worked, if the productivity bonus were paid. The sales director is confident of selling the increased output if the price for all sales were to be reduced by £0.10 per unit.

Budgeted results for the forthcoming year, excluding the above possible wage or sales increases, are as follows:

	£000	£000
Sales, 1,200,000 units		2,400
Direct materials	480	
Direct wages	720	
Variable production overhead	108	
Fixed production overhead	200	
Variable selling cost (5% of sales value)	120	
Fixed selling cost	80	
Variable distribution cost	96	
Fixed distribution cost	74	
Fixed administration cost	202	
		2,080
Profit		320

You are required, in the form of a report to the managing director to:
(a) set out the budgeted results for each alternative and recommend the course of action to be followed; and
(b) indicate three of the uncertainties which have to be taken into consideration when making the decision.

(Institute of Cost & Management Accountants)

8
Budgetary control

Introduction

Discussion of costing principles and techniques commenced in chapter 7 with an examination of the Marginal Costing principle, which was later compared with another costing principle, Absorption Costing.

At this point, the technique of Variance Accounting is considered and the term is given the following definition in the I.C.M.A. Terminology:

'A technique whereby the planned activities of an undertaking are expressed in budgets, standard costs, standard selling prices and standard profit margins, and the differences between these and the comparable actual results are accounted for. Management is periodically presented with an analysis of differences by causes and responsibility centres, such analysis usually commencing with the operating profit variance. The technique also includes the establishment of a suitable arrangement of accounts in the principal ledger.'

Variance Accounting embraces both Budgetary Control and Standard Costing, and it is the former which will be considered in this chapter. Before proceeding further, it is as well to define Budgetary Control. The following definition is included in the I.C.M.A. Terminology:

'The establishment of budgets relating the responsibilities of executives to the requirements of a policy, and the continuous comparison of actual with budgeted results, either to secure by individual action the objective of that policy or to provide a basis for its revision.'

The term Variance Accounting is more appropriate where the two techniques of Budgetary Control and Standard Costing are used together and included in one complete system. However, it will be seen that each technique involves accounting for variances between actual results and some predetermined standard or budget, so even if one technique is used without the other, variance accounting is still in operation.

In passing, it is worth noting that while budgetary control can be successfully employed without the addition of standard costing, the reverse seldom occurs, for it is difficult to operate standard costing without the aid of budgetary control.

Concentrating for the moment on budgetary control, the operation of the technique involves the following steps:

(a)   defining and specifying the objectives to be achieved by the business;

(b)   preparing business plans in order to ensure that the desired objectives are accomplished;

(c)   translating the plans into budgets, and relating the responsibilities of individual executives and managers to particular sections of the budget;

(d)   continuous comparison of actual results with the budget, and the calculation of differences between budgeted and actual performance;

(e)   investigating major differences in order to establish the causes;

(f)   prompt presentation of the information to management in a suitable form, relating the variances to individual responsibility;

(g)   corrective action by management in order to avoid a repetition of any wastage, excess and over-expenditure so that, although a temporary setback has occurred, the budget plan can still be achieved; alternatively, where events have occurred that make it impossible to achieve the budgeted targets, the revision of the budget so that the objective can be attained by the implementation of an amended plan.

Objectives of Budgetary Control.

The introduction of the technique of budgetary control would seek to achieve:

(a)   the systematic and detailed planning of the activities of the business over a specified period of time;

(b)   the co-ordination of activities and the direction of the actions of all employees towards a common goal;

(c)   a proper system of control by ascertaining divergences from plan establishing who is responsible, and taking the necessary action to correct the situation.

One of the main purposes of budgetary control is to provide a mechanism whereby control can be exercised over the activities of the business. It would be difficult for the chief executive to supervise personally the day to day operation of a business, especially in a large company comprising a number of factories spread over a wide area. A suitable system of control must be implemented; nothing will be achieved by just hoping that the desired objectives will be accomplished. It is necessary to review performance continuously to ensure that the business is meeting the targets laid down.

Budgetary control places the responsibility of accomplishing certain targets on the shoulders of individual executives and managers. The performance of departments for which they are responsible is continually being measured against predetermined targets, and any variations are subject to investigation. Managers, therefore, are given an incentive to achieve good results. The need to keep a tight rein on costs is impressed upon each manager. He must become cost conscious and he is continually being supplied with information which tells him whether he is meeting his targets; and if he receives the information speedily, there is the opportunity to take corrective action before it is too late. In this way, proper control can be exercised over expenditure.

However, it is easy to emphasise the control aspect of budgetary control simply because the word 'control' is included in the title. The technique has another main purpose. By planning the activities for a forthcoming period and translating the plan into monetary terms, the management is forced to think about the business. If this quantitative aspect were absent, the tendency would be to make grandiose plans, to be excessively optimistic and to live in a dream world. By quantifying the plans, management is brought back to reality. When expressed in financial terms the plans may not be worth very much. Planning is therefore a necessary ingredient of budgetary control.

Furthermore, by relating the budget to individual responsibility, further realism is brought into the situation. It is important that managers have a say in the preparation of their part of the budget and in some cases they may well challenge the results expected of them.

Co-ordination of the various activities is also achieved by operating the technique of budgetary control. A budget is prepared for the business as a whole; the various line and functional managers do not prepare budgets in isolation. The marketing manager must be aware of the volume of production that the production department is capable of producing. Equally, the production manager must base his budgeting on the probable demand for individual products. Similarly, the cash budget must take into account the amount and timing of the revenues to be received from sales, and so on. The various departmental budgets must be integrated to form one master budget which expresses the company plans in monetary terms.

To achieve the budgeted targets, co-operation between executives is essential. Each executive must direct the activities under his control in such a way that the overall objectives are reached.

The introduction of budgetary control, then, will achieve an improvement in planning, co-ordination and control, and present an appropriate alternative to relying on good fortune.

Preparation of the Budget.

The technique of budgetary control includes the task of preparing the budget, and the I.C.M.A. Terminology defines Budgets as:

'Financial and/or quantitative statements, prepared and approved prior to a defined period of time, of the policy to be pursued during that period for the purpose of attaining a given objective. They may include income, expenditure and the employment of capital.'

The preparation of budgets is normally the responsibility of a budget committee, which comprises the chief executive and, to ensure co-ordination, the various functional heads of department or their representatives. The committee will also include a budget officer, or budget controller, who is responsible for the administration of the budget programme. This is usually someone from the accounting function, but may not be a full-time appointment if the volume of work is insufficient to consume the whole of one person's time. The cost accountant will often act as budget officer.

It should not be thought that the budget officer is responsible for preparing the entire budget package from beginning to end. It is the responsibility of the various functional heads to prepare the budget for their particular function. The responsibilities of the budget officer usually consist of the following:

(a)   preparing and distributing a time table for the completion of each stage of the budget process and ensuring adherence to the dates stated;

(b)   providing information to functional executives and line managers on past results and probable future trends;

(c)   offering advice to executives and managers on the best method of carrying out the budget programme and maintaining frequent contact with them in order to clarify any difficulties that arise;

(d)   encouraging co-operation so that when the functional budgets are prepared, they can be integrated easily into a master budget;

(e)   bringing to the attention of the chief executive those matters which cannot be resolved by discussion with individual executives, for example, where co-ordination of sectional budgets is unlikely to be achieved;

(f)   checking sectional budgets for consistency and compatability;

(g)   reporting to the budget committee periodically on the progress of the budget preparation and any problems which arise;

(h)   preparing the master budget in time for it to be submitted to the Board for approval prior to the commencement of the budget period.

The Budget Period.

It is necessary at the outset of budget preparation to specify the length of the budget period, i.e. the period for which the budget is prepared and used. A decision on the matter will hinge on the type of business, but, generally, the most suitable period is one which lasts for one year and coincides with the financial year of the business.

Problems could arise if the period chosen is longer than a year. The budget is a fairly detailed document and it is difficult to predict with any degree of accuracy the conditions which are likely to exist after the expiration of a year. Furthermore, the budget exercise often commences at least six months before the start of the period to which it relates, so if the budget were longer than a year, one would be obliged to make predictions for at least eighteen months ahead. In many industries it is not possible to gauge the extent of demand so far in the future. Also, recent experience has shown that it is difficult to estimate accurately the proable rise in the annual rate of inflation over long periods. In short, the conditions which will exist in eighteen months time are likely to differ significantly from the conditions prevalent at the time the budget is being prepared. However, it is reasonable to make fairly detailed forecasts for up to a year.

To control the activities of a business effectively, the budget must be sub-divided into a number of shorter periods, for example, calendar months or four-week control periods. It was stated earlier that one of the reasons for adopting budgetary control is to make it possible to measure actual performance against some predetermined standard so that, after adverse variances have been investigated, corrective action can be taken to steer the business back on its intended course. This measurement, then, must take place at frequent intervals to give management the opportunity to take the necessary steps to put right any deviations from plan before the end of the financial year.

Many companies nowadays are engaged in long term planning; that is, expressing the company objectives in a five year plan. Because of the difficulty in making accurate predictions for periods of longer than a year, long term plans are much less detailed than annual budgets; they show the general direction in which the company is going. Where this technique is used, the annual budget should be based on the first year of the long term plan. It should show in detail what the long term plan states in summary form.

The Budget Manual.

In order to formalise the budget procedure and to avoid misunderstanding, some large sompanies produce a budget manual which specifies in detail the procedures to be followed, the forms to be used, and the responsibilities of various job-holders and the part they should play in the budgeting process.

Principal Budget Factor.

This term, which is also known as the Key Factor or Limiting Factor, is defined as follows in the I.C.M.A. Terminology:

'The factor which, at a particular time, or over a period, will limit the activities of an undertaking. The limiting factor is usually the level of demand for the products or services of the undertaking but it could be a shortage of one of the productive resources, e.g. skilled labour, raw material, or machine capacity. In order to ensure that the functional budgets are reasonably capable of fulfilment, the extent of the influence of this factor must first be assessed.'

It was stated earlier that the integration of the functional budgets is an important part of the budgeting process. This is especially true of the marketing and production budgets which must be in accord. But which budget is to be prepared first? Is the production budget to be based on the marketing budget or vice versa? In order to provide an answer, the principal budget factor must first be established. The marketing function may want to expand rapidly due to an upsurge in demand for the organisation's products, but if there is insufficient working capital to finance the expansion, it would be unwise to try to meet the additional demand. The availability of capital, then, is the limiting factor. Its low level places a restriction on the activities of the business. Similarly, a shortage of suitable accommodation and production facilities may place constraints on the marketing function.

However, it is possible, by management action, to minimise the effect of the limiting factor. If, for example, the level of demand is the key factor, a reduction in the selling price or an advertising campaign might stimulate demand. Also, if a shortage of skilled labour limits the amount of business, consideration might be given to the following:

(a) overtime working;
(b) the introduction of an incentive scheme to stimulate increased effort;
(c) an increase in wage rates to attract more skilled workers;
(d) sub-contracting part of the load to another organisation.

Another point worthy of mention is that the key factor may change. The principal factor at one time may be succeeded by another key factor

Having established the principal budget factor and the limit it imposes on other functions, the budget preparation can proceed. If the main factor is the level of demand, it is recommended that the sales budget should be prepared before the preparation of other functional budgets. The production budget and the other budgets will be based on the volume of goods that the business can sell.

Subsidiary Budgets.

The details of the budgets are built up in subsidiary budgets which include the following:

(a) Sales budget (including the marketing cost budget);
(b) Production budget;
(c) Plant Utilisation budget;
(d) Capital Expenditure budget;
(e) Other functional budgets, e.g. research and development, administration, personnel, purchasing;
(f) Cash budget.

There must be a subsidiary, or sectional, budget for every part of the business so that a budget exists for all the likely sources of income and expenditure.

Sales budget. The preparation of the sales budget is the responsibility of the marketing executive, although he will receive considerable assistance from the budget officer. As the budget officer represents the accounting function, he is able to provide the marketing executive with a great deal of historical cost and financial data on which the marketing executive can base his forecasts. In forecasting the probable demand for each individual product, an examination of past sales statistics may reveal certain underlying trends; sales of certain products may be increasing, whereas other products may be experiencing a decline.

In addition to looking at what has gone before, the marketing executive must consider future trends; the political, economic, social and technological events likely to occur and the probable effect on consumer demand. He should try and determine the extent to which existing business conditions will remain unchanged, and make an assessment of the future environment in which the business has to operate. Can he assume that the present level of sales will be repeated in the coming budget period, or can he foresee some event, some trend, which will disturb the existing pattern? The sales budget must be based on a realistic appraisal of business conditions. Although it is not possible to predict exactly what will happen in the future, this appraisal should be carried out before preparation begins on the details of the sales budget. It is essential that the activities of the marketing function are planned in a systematic manner if the objectives of the business are to be reached.

There are a number of external factors which influence the level of sales, some of which are listed below.

(a) Government policies, e.g. the decision to set up a Price Commission to which applications must be made to raise selling prices.

(b) Re-distribution of income, the effect of which is the transfer of spending power from one section of the community to another.

(c) Hire purchase restrictions; increasing or decreasing the amount of the deposit to be laid down on purchase, or extending or reducing the period over which the loan is to be repaid.

(d) Import restrictions introduced by the government of foreign customers.

(e) The prevailing affluence of the section of society at which the company's products are directed.

(f) Movements in population from one region to another.

(g) Changes in fashion, taste and custom.

(h) Competition from other organisations.

Account has to be taken of the influence that these and other external factors will have on customer demand. The marketing executive and the budget officer, indeed, the entire budget committee, must think about the probable outcome of future predicted events. Estimates must be made of the likely share of the market. A study of the future trends which are likely to affect sales will result in a more sensible forecast.

The effect of external influences can be mitigated by internal management action. Sales can be revitalised by making improvements or alterations to existing products. Demand can be stimulated by additional publicity, or by increasing incentives to salesmen. It may be possible to increase sales by exploiting a gap in the market; maybe a new territory can be opened, previously untried, where additional sales can be reaped.

Some difficulty will be experienced in budgeting the sales of new products. Past results are not available as a guide and the marketing executive will try to gauge the effect of introducing new products by carrying out a programme of market research and by soliciting the opinions of area sales managers and salesmen in the field. However, caution may be necessary as salesmen are notoriously optimistic.

Sales should be expressed in quantities, although this will not be possible for businesses which undertake work to customers' special requirements. Selling prices will be determined bearing in mind the extent of the competition in the area. After quantities and selling prices have been established, the sales values of the various products can be calculated.

The sales budget should be analysed by product, area, salesman, major customer, and by control period, which should take into account seasonal fluctuations.

After determining the sales value of each product, the marketing executive can then decide on the number of salesmen required to fulfil the sales budget, the salaries and commission payable, the support staff necessary, and so on. He must forecast the selling and distribution costs, analysing each cost by area. Again past results will act as a guide, but the potential increase in salaries and the rate of commission must be taken into consideration. Distribution costs will consist of the cost of operating the finished goods warehouse, packing, and transporting the products to customers.

Somes sales department costs are not related to the volume of sales budgeted for the forthcoming period. An advertising campaign, for example, may be proposed in order to influence the level of sales in future years.

Production Budget. The production executive, or production manager, is responsible for the preparation of the production budget, but, like the marketing executive, he will be looking to the budget officer to provide data and advice.

The production budget is based on the details of the sales budget and the proposed movement in the level of finished goods stock. The budget preparation will begin with a statement of the quantity of each product to be manufactured. The quantity will be costed by reference to production estimates or standard costs for each element of cost. The direct wages cost of producing each individual product will be ascertained by taking into account the number of direct hours required, an estimate of the wage rates to be paid during the budget period, and the various grade of workers employed in the factory.

Variable production overhead costs will depend on the volume of production, but the fixed costs of the production department must also be budgeted. Another factor which influences the total of production overhead is the allotment of service department costs. It will not therefore be possible to compute predetermined overhead absorption rates until budgeted costs from service departments have been notified to production departments.

The production budget should be analysed by product, production department and individual responsibility, and divided into control periods. It is important that the production executive is informed of the phasing of the sales budget, so that sufficient finished stock is available to satisfy seasonal fluctuations. It is assumed that the business wishes to keep an even flow of production, which means that stocks of finished goods will have to be built up in order to satisfy peak demand periods. However, the advantages of even production have to be balanced with the need to keep stocks to a minimum.

Once the production budget has been prepared, direct labour requirements can be budgeted in order to establish manpower levels for the forthcoming budget period. It is necessary to compare the hours required to fulfil the production programme with the hours available. A shortage of hours available can be remedied by overtime working, additional training, or the recruitment of more direct workers.

The materials content of the production budget is of interest to the buyer, for he will be able to plan the purchase of direct materials for the budget period. However, the purchase of materials will not necessarily correspond with the production budget, for the future policy with regard to stock and work in progress levels has to be taken into consideration.

Plant Utilisation budget. The production budget is the basis for the preparation of the plant utilisation budget. It is necessary to ascertain the number of hours that each machine (or groups of similar machines) will be in use. This is referred to as the 'machine loading'; it is the load, in terms of hours, that each machine will bear. The outcome could be that the existing machines will be overloaded. In order that the production and plant utilisation budgets can be successfully integrated, it may be necessary to plan for overtime working, or, if there is a substantial deficiency in the machinery available, the introduction of an extra shift. Other alternatives include the purchase of additional plant and machinery or the use of sub-contractors.

However, because of lack of capital, the purchase of capital equipment may not be a suitable alternative. If the plant utilisation budget cannot be amended, the production or sales budgets may need revision. This may not entail a reduction in the level of sales, but a different emphasis in favour of, perhaps, less profitable products. It may not mean that, over the budget period, less profit will be made, if the loss of profit incurred in switching from one product to another is compensated for by a saving in depreciation by postponing the acquisition of new plant.

When budgeting for the utilisation of plant, it must be remembered that provision should be made for the time spent in cleaning machinery, setting-up between operations, and repairs and maintenance.

Capital Expenditure budget. The plant utilisation budget will reveal where additional plant and machinery is needed. It is also necessary to consider the replacement of existing plant which is either worn out or obsolete. In addition to the inclusion of fixed assets to satisfy the requirements of the planned programme of production, other items of a capital nature should be listed in the capital expenditure budget, such as company cars for salesmen, transport lorries for the distribution of finished products, test equipment for research and development laboratories, and office equipment.

Other Functional budgets. In addition to the sales and production budgets, it is also necessary to prepare budgets for Administration, and Research and Development.

Cash budget. This budget summarises the anticipated cash receipts and payments for the budget period. It starts with the forecast cash balance at the commencement of the budget period, and, by adding the budgeted receipts for each month and subtracting the budgeted payments, the expected cash balance at the end of each month is ascertained. Cash, in this context, refers to cash in hand and cash at bank. The responsibility of preparing the cash budget rests with the accounting function.

It is essential to maintain the liquidity position of the business. Adequate liquid resources must be available when needed to discharge expenditure commitments. Wages and salaries must be paid on time; cash must be available to meet the tax liability and divident payments; and if suppliers are kept waiting for the settlement of their accounts, they may decide to suspend supplies, which might jeopardise the long-term interests of the business.

It is the purpose therefore of the cash budget to give advance warning of those months in the year when a deficiency of cash is most likely to occur. If sufficient warning is given, the necessary funds can be made available by negotiating a bank overdraft or obtaining finance from some other source. On the other hand, there may exist an excess of cash at some points during the year. Advance notice of such a situation could enable management to make suitable prior arrangements for investment outside the business.

The cash budget is based on the budgets that have already been prepared. It will reveal the extent to which the planned operations of the business can be financed. It must be appreciated that the cash budget is composed of receipts and payments, and not income and expenditure. An interval often occurs between the moment when a sale is made (income) and the time when the cash due on the sale is received (receipt). Consequently, when a company sells goods on credit, the sales will produce cash receipts in a later month. The same applies to the purchase of goods (expenditure) and the settlement of a supplier's account (payment). Accordingly, before preparation of the cash budget can begin, it is necessary to establish the average credit period taken by debtors and the average length of time taken to settle the accounts of creditors.

Other sources of funds consist of rent received, interest and dividends received, the sale of fixed assets, progress payments on long-term contracts, the issue of shares and debentures and other loan finance. Payments, in addition to the payment for purchases, include capital expenditure, overhead expenditure, wages and salaries, tax and dividend payments, repayment of a loan and redemption of debentures. It is necessary to forecast the month in which the various receipts and payments are to be made. It should be noted that depreciation does not involve the outlow of cash. It represents the loss in value of a fixed asset, but no cash changes hands.

The integration of the various budgets is an essential feature of the budgeting process, and if a shortage of cash cannot be overcome by short-term borrowing, it might be necessary to amend some or all of the other budgets. Although it was not appreciated by management at the outset of the budgeting exercise, the availability of cash may at this stage become the principal budget factor. However, other remedies must be considered before implementing wholesale changes to the existing budgets. Can the collection of outstanding debts be improved? Is it possible for capital expenditure to be postponed? Is there scope for a reduction in stock levels without endangering the flow of production? These options must be considered, but whatever action is taken, it is important that all the budgets are co-ordinated.

Example. From the following details, prepare a cash budget for the six months ending 30th September, 19-- showing the balance at the end of each month:

(a) The balance of cash and at bank at 1st April is forecast as £5,400
(b) Budgeted revenue income and expenditure is:

	Cash sales	Credit sales	Purchases	Direct wages	Overhead (excluding sales commission)
	£	£	£	£	£
an	800	10,500	5,500	2,000	1,200
Feb	750	11,000	5,800	2,000	1,300
March	780	14,000	7,200	2,200	1,200
April	920	13,200	8,900	2,400	1,500
May	600	14,300	8,200	2,400	1,400
June	680	16,400	6,400	2,600	1,300
July	840	11,900	5,500	2,500	1,400
Aug	820	15,600	4,900	2,700	1,400
Sept	950	17,000	7,400	3,000	1,500

(c) Salesmen receive a commission of 5% on all sales, to be paid during the month following the actual sales.
(d) Approximately 75% of debts are collected in the month following the sale, and the remaining debtors will normally settle their accounts two months after sales.
(e) On average, about one quarter of the direct wages are outstanding at the end of each month.
(f) Suppliers will normally allow one month's credit.
(g) It is assumed that overhead costs are paid in the month in which they are incurred.
(h) The capital expenditure budget shows that plant and machinery

costing £8,000 will be purchased during May and paid for two
months later.

Workings

	April £	May £	June £	July £	Aug £	Sept £
Sales						
Cash	920	600	680	840	820	950
Debtors (75 per cent)	10,500	9,900	10,725	12,300	8,925	11,700
Debtors (25 per cent)	2,750	3,500	3,300	3,575	4,100	2,975
Total	14,170	14,000	14,705	16,715	13,845	15,625
Sales Commission						
Sales of previous month	14,780	14,120	14,900	17,080	12,740	16,420
Commission - 5 per cent	739	706	745	854	637	821
Wages						
Same month (75 per cent)	1,800	1,800	1,950	1,875	2,025	2,250
Prev. month (25 per cent)	550	600	600	650	625	675
Total	2,350	2,400	2,550	2,525	2,650	2,925

The student should note that the increase in cash of £11,558 does not
represent profit. Sometimes profit earned by the business is used up by
increasing stock levels or allowing debtors to go beyond the period of
credit allowed. Also, the cash budget is influenced by capital expenditur
and it ignores depreciation.

The Master Budget
After the preparation of the subsidiary budgets has been completed,
the budget officer can proceed with the preparation of the master budg
This is a budget which summarises the details of the various subsidiary
budgets. All inter-departmental sales and purchases should cancel out so
that the budget officer can prepare a statement which reveals the planne
profit for the budget period. Cash, debtors and creditors budgets, to
gether with planned levels of stock, will enable him to prepare a forecas
balance sheet for the end of the budget period.

Cash Budget
for six months ending September 30th 19--

	April £	May £	June £	July £	Aug £	Sept £	April - Sept £
Balance at beginning of month	5,400	7,781	8,375	10,285	7,821	11,479	5,400
Receipts - Sales	14,170	14,000	14,705	16,715	13,845	15,625	89,060
Payments -							
Purchases	7,200	8,900	8,200	6,400	5,500	4,900	41,100
Direct wages	2,350	2,400	2,550	2,525	2,650	2,925	15,400
Overhead	1,500	1,400	1,300	1,400	1,400	1,500	8,500
Sales commission	739	706	745	854	637	821	4,502
Capital expenditure	—	—	—	8,000	—	—	8,000
	11,789	13,406	12,795	19,179	10,187	10,146	77,502
Balance at end of month	7,781	8,375	10,285	7,821	11,479	16,958	16,958
Net inflow/(outflow) of cash each month	2,381	594	1,910	(2,464)	3,658	5,479	11,558

Sometimes you are required to show the movement in cash during each month and this can be inserted in the cash budget above the balance at the end of the month. The movement is calculated by deducting the total payments for the month from the total receipts. In the example above, the movement would be shown as follows:

On completion, the budget officer will present the master budget to the Board of Directors, or top management, for approval.

The Control Aspect of Budgetary Control

At the commencement of the budget year, each manager will receive a copy of the budget appropriate to his sphere of responsibility. The budget will be phased by months or four-weekly periods so that each manager knows the limit of his allowed expenditure for each period.

At the end of each control period, the cost accountant will issue a cost statement to the various managers showing a comparison of actual results with budget for each item of income and expenditure. The variances from budget will be indicated and special attention should be paid to those which are unfavourable. A separate statement will be issued for each budget centre.

It is important that the statement is issued as soon as possible after the end of each month, and seeing that a manager will wish to take speedy corrective action on significant items, his attention should be directed towards the major adverse variances; these should be highlighted in some way on the statement. The larger variances should be analysed by cause wherever possible, and in some cases it may be necessary for the cost accountant to interpret some of the results to the manager.

However, too much detail should be avoided and the 'management by exception' principle should be adopted. Simply, the use of this principle means that managers concentrate only on those items which do not conform to budget, i.e. the exceptions.

Fixed and Flexible Budgets

Under the previous heading, the operation of the budgetary control technique was considered. Monthly reports which contrast the actual performance with the predetermined budget are of assistance to managers in that they highlight those areas where corrective action is necessary. Where there arises a significant adverse variance from budget, it would seem to indicate that the performance of the manager responsible has been below expectation.

However, this may not always be the case. Although an adverse variance might indicate inefficiency, a closer examination of the actual costs and the budgeted costs might well reveal that the reverse is true. In this context, it is sometimes necessary to distinguish between fixed and flexible budgets and to show that fixed budgets are inadequate for the purpose of cost control.

Fixed budgets. A fixed budget, as defined by the I.C.M.A. Terminology, is 'a budget which is designed to remain unchanged irrespective of the volume of output or turnover attained.' Once the budget has been approved by the Board of Directors, it is used as the criterion by which actual results are measured.

A moment's thought will show that this is an inadequate way to measure performance, for it is unlikely that the actual level of activity will correspond exactly with the planned level. Because the level of activity influences the variable costs, then an increase in activity, i.e. output, direct labour hours or machine hours, is likely to push a cost to a higher level than budget. Because of the probable difference in the level of activity between the budgeted level and the actual level, performance cannot be accurately assessed by comparing actual results with a fixed budget.

Example. In order to meet the budgeted output targets, it is necessary to utilise the plant and machinery for 40,000 hours during each quarter. The budgeted cost of the maintenance of plant and machinery is based on the above activity level, as it is considered to be a semi-variable cost. The fixed element, arrived at by costing the maintenance agreements in existence, was £800. The variable element, based on the estimated usage of the machinery, was £1,200. The actual cost of maintaining plant and machinery during a three-month period was £2,200. During the quarter the plant and machinery was actually utilised for 48,000 hours on production work. Show how the performance of the manager controlling the item of expenditure can be measured.

Cost Statement

for 3 months ended ....

	Budget	Actual	Variance Favourable/(Adverse)
	£	£	£
Maintenance of plant and machinery	2,000	2,200	(200)

Stated as above, the manager controlling this cost has apparently been guilty of inefficiency. However, the adverse variance has to be considered in the light of the additional number of machine hours, as the higher activity affects the variable component of the cost. This portion of the cost is dependent upon the extent to which the plant and machinery is used.

The converse is true also. A favourable variance might lead a manager to assume that he has performed well, but if activity is less than budget and the cost in question has a variable element, he may be under a misapprehension. Clearly, statements such as the above, which take no account of the level of activity, are misleading. Fixed budgets therefore have weaknesses for the purpose of cost control. To take an extreme case, if the budgeted cost of direct materials were £10,000 for a control period and the actual costs were nil, the buyer is unlikely to be congratulated on saving £10,000, for the underspending does not indicate extreme efficiency on his part. Seeing that direct materials cost is variable in nature, the indications are that the factory has been completely inactive during the costing period.

Flexible budgets. The I.C.M.A. Terminology defines a flexible budget as 'a budget which, by recognising the difference in behaviour between fix fixed and variable costs in relation to fluctuations in output or turnover, is designed to change appropriately with such fluctuations.' The budget is therefore amended each month in line with the level of activity so tha actual performance can be measured against budget for the same level of activity. If the activity is higher than budget, the budgeted allowance als increases. If less, the budgeted allowance is lowered. The fixed budget n longer represents the criterion for measuring expenditure.

Returning to the example above, it is necessary to compute how muc would be allowed for 48,000 machine hours in order to make an effective comparison. The performance will then be measured against the amended figure. It will be noted that the variable cost is 3 pence per machine hour, i.e. $\frac{£1,200}{40,000}$. The budgeted allowance for 48,000 machin hours is, therefore, £1,440 plus the fixed element of £800, i.e. £2,240. The following cost statement reflects the amended budget and provides an improved basis for comparison.

Cost Statement

for 3 months ended ....

	Fixed budget £	Flexible budget £	Actual £	Variance Fav/(Adverse) £
Maintenance of plant and machinery	2,000	2,240	2,200	40

By flexing the budget in this manner, the cost control information is more appropriate. Rather than overspending, the manager has brought about a small saving.

No adjustment to the fixed budget can be made unless the budget is built up by analysing fixed and variable costs. By segregating the fixed and variable costs it is possible to flex the budget to fall in line with any level of activity. The setting of flexible budgets is therefore dependent upon the ability to distinguish between fixed and variable costs.

EXAMINATION PRACTICE
Students are advised to attempt the questions under simulated examination conditions. Then check their answers with the suggested answers at the back of the book.

Question 59   Definitions   Answer page 305

The following terms are widely used in Cost Accountancy:
(a) Direct Cost; (b) Indirect Cost; (c) Overhead Absorption Rate; (d) Budget Period.
You are required to define and give examples of each.

(Institute of Accounting Staff)

Question 60   Budgeting and marginal costing   Answer page 305

The accountant of a company has prepared a draft budget for the coming year based on the three items produced. Details are as follows:

Product	A	B	C
Budget Sales (units)	20,000	15,000	8,000
Sale price per unit	£30	£40	£50
Variable cost per unit			
Material	£10	£20	£ 5
Labour	12	6	30
Sales	3	6	5
Fixed Labour Costs		£110,000	

Three members of the Board have each put forward their own recommendations to improve profitability. These are:
a)   Sales Director A special advertising campaign costing an additional £65,000, which would increase sales of all products by 25% for the year.
b)   Personnel Director. A labour incentive scheme which would increase variable labour cost by one sixth, but would eliminate the fixed labour costs for the year.
c)   Chief Accountant. Introduce a sales commission scheme which would increase the sales volume by 50% for a year, but would also increase variable selling cost by £2 per unit.

You are required to evaluate these three unrelated possibilities, showing the effect of each on the budget profit, and to state, with reasons, which you would recommend.

(Institute of Accounting Staff)

A manufacturing company is reviewing its product range as the basic material used in all its products has suddenly increased in price. The managing director wishes to make the best use of the company's capacity and resources and has come to you, the cost accountant, for advice.

On inspection, the budget figures for the next period are as follows:

Product	A	B	C	D
Maximum production (units)	5,000	5,000	5,000	5,000
Selling price per unit	£25	£33	£43	£56
Variable cost - material	9	12	17	20
labour	8	10	12	18
overhead	4	5	6	9

The total amount of material available to the company is limited by the supplier's production capacity to £200,000. The budgeted fixed costs total to £80,000.

You are required to calculate the product mix that would produce the maximum profit.

(Institute of Accounting Staff)

Fancitoys Limited is preparing its budgets for the quarter beginning 1 July. Stock on hand at the end of June is expected to be £72,000 and the balance at bank £10,000. In view of the pressure on liquid resources the directors have decided to reduce the stock level at the end of each month to an amount sufficient to cover the following two months' sales. Purchases are paid for by the end of the following month; the amount payable for June's purchases is £36,000.

Budgeted sales (which provide a gross profit of $33\frac{1}{3}\%$ on cost) are:

	£		£
July	40,000	October	48,000
August	42,000	November	52,000
September	46,000	December	44,000

Ten per cent of the sales are for cash and of the credit sales two-thirds are paid for during the month after the sale and the remainder during the following month. Credit sales during May amounted to £24,600 and during June £26,100.

The annual rental for the company's premises is £18,000 payable monthly. Other payments to be made are:

	July £	August £	September £
Salaries, wages and commission	4,800	5,100	5,500
Rates	800		
Other expenses	1,600	1,800	2,000

You are required to prepare the company's cash budget for the quarter beginning 1 July showing the balance at the end of each month.

(Association of Certified Accountants)

Question 63   Subsidiary budgets Answer page 307

C Limited makes two products, A and B, and is preparing an annual budget for 1976. You are required, using the information given below, to prepare:
(a) production budget;
(b) direct materials cost budget;
(c) purchases budget;
(d) direct wages budget.

Standard data, per unit of product:

Direct material	Standard price per kilo £	Product A kilos	Product B kilos
M 1	0.5	10	4
M 2	1.0	5	6
Direct wages	Standard rate per hour £	hours	hours
W 1	1.5	8	10
W2	1.0	12	5

Fixed production overhead is absorbed on a direct labour hour basis. There is no variable overhead. Administration, selling and distribution costs are absorbed on a budgeted basis of 20% of production cost. Profit is budgeted at 20% of selling price.

Budgeted data:

	Product A £000's	Product B £000's
Sales, for year:		
Division: North	750	600
South	1,250	1,800
East	950	800
West	800	1,600

Finished goods stock, valued
at standard production cost:

1st January, 1976	250	600
31st December, 1976	750	1,000

Direct material stocks, valued	Material M1	Material M2
at standard prices:	£000's	£000's
1st January, 1976	160	150
31st January, 1976	80	210

Fixed production overhead, per annum	£2,040,000
Direct labour hours, per annum	2,550,000

It is expected that there will be no work-in-progress at the beginning or end of the year.

(Institute of Cost & Management Accountants

Question 64   Budgetary control   Answer page 308

The Victoria Hospital is located in a holiday resort which attract vistors to such an extent that the population of the area is trebled for th summer months of June, July and August. From past experience this influx of visitors doubles the activity of the hospital during these month The annual budget for the hospital's laundry department is broken dowr into four quarters, i.e. April/June, July/September, October/December and January/March by dividing the annual budgeted figures by four. Thi budgeting work has been done for the current year by the secretary of the hospital using the previous year's figures and adding 16%. It is realise by the Hospital Authority that management information for control pur poses needs to be improved and you have been recruited to help to intro duce a system of responsibility accounting.

You are required, from the information given, to:

(a) comment on the way in which the quarterly budgets have been prepared and to suggest improvements which could be introduced when preparing the budgets for 1979/80;

(b) state what information you would like to flow from the actual against budget comparison (NB: calculated figures are *not* required).

(c) state the amendments that would be needed to the current practice of budgeting and reporting to enable the report shown on the following page to be used as a measure of the efficiency of the laundry manager.

Victoria Hospital - Laundry Department Report for quarter ended 30th September, 1978	Budget	Actual
Patient days	9,000	12,000
Weight processed, in lbs	180,000	240,000
Costs:	£	£
Wages	8,800	12,320
Overtime premium	1,400	2,100
Detergents and other supplies	1,800	2,700
Water, water softening and heating	2,000	2,500
Maintenance	1,000	1,500
Depreciation of plant	2,000	2,000
Manager's salary	1,250	1,500
Overhead, apportioned:		
for Occupancy	4,000	4,250
for Administration	5,000	5,750

(Institute of Cost & Management Accountants)

9
Standard costing

Introduction

In the previous chapter, it was stated that Variance Accounting embraces the separate techniques of Budgetary Control and Standard Costing the chapter then went on to deal in detail with Budgetary Control. Now it is the turn of Standard Costing to come under scrutiny. It is defined simply as 'the preparation of standard costs of products and services.' (I.C.M.A. Terminology). As in budgetary control, costs are firstly predetermined, and later compared with the actual costs incurred in order to ascertain the variance from the original plan.

Although similarities exist between budgetary control and standard costing, it is as well at this point to mention the differences. As the definition above indicates, standard costing involves estimating the costs of products and services. Budgetary control, on the other hand, is concerned with estimating the costs of all areas of the business, including overhead expenditure and capital expenditure. Under budgetary control, all the activities of the business are studied and translated into a financial plan for the ensuing budget period.

Another difference between the two techniques is the amount of detail involved in the preparation of predetermined costs. When preparing a budget the cost accountant will seek to arrive at predetermined costs for whole items of expenditure without attempting to go into very much detail in the case of certain items. For example, the budgeted cost of entertaining might be based on previous years' results, the rate of inflation expected in the coming year, and the probable increase or decrease in the volume of sales. No attempt will be made to estimate the number of customers to be entertained, the quantity of meals provided and the cost of each meal. In standard costing, the process of predetermining costs is more exact and requires the preparation of more detailed information. A standard is calculated for each operation that makes up the manufacture of each individual product and to do this it is necessary to estimate the cost of each component and sub-assembly invloved in each operation. The reader will see as the chapter develops that this is a painstaking task.

The technique of standard costing is particularly suitable in organisations which are involved in the large-scale manufacture of standardised products. Goods in these factories are produced as the result of a sequence of repetitive and continuous operations. Consequently, standard costing can be usefully employed in conjunction with process costing.

But standard costing can also be used by businesses which undertake jobbing work; this is especially so where a large number of jobs are undertaken using basic parts and sub-assemblies.

Purpose of Standard Costing

The main purpose of adopting standard costing is to provide management with information regarding deviations from plan; to indicate firstly what is attainable by efficient working, and subsequently to highlight those areas where attainable efficiency is not being achieved. This provides a basis for cost control. Standard costing compares what a product or service has cost with what it ought to cost. The results of the business can therefore be measured against some yardstick in order to ascertain the extent to which the actual performance is related to achievable efficiency. Furthermore, significant adverse variances are highlighted so that management can concentrate its efforts on correcting areas of excessive waste by adopting the 'management by exception' principle. The reporting in detail of deviations from standard means that inefficiencies do not remain hidden even if they happen to be offset by efficient operating in another area. If the performance as a whole were slightly better than expected, then there might be a temptation to be complacent, to be satisfied with the slight improvement. However, standard costing avoids this complacency by examining the performance in a number of areas so that, even though there may be only one area in which an adverse variance arises, nevertheless it is revealed and management is made aware of it. Because of this, there is the opportunity to take speedy, corrective action

Not only does standard costing provide a basis for cost control, it can also be used to arrive at closing valuations of stock and work in progress. In some instances, standard costs can form the basis of estimates prepared for potential customers and for fixing selling prices.

The following steps are involved in the operation of the technique of standard costing:

(a) determine standard costs for each product;
(b) calculate and record actual costs incurred;
(c) periodically, compare actual costs with the predetermined standards in order to ascertain the deviation from the standard; this difference is known as the cost variance;
(d) investigate the reasons for the differences and bring to the attention of management in the form of a variance analysis;

(e) action by management where appropriate to ensure that adverse variances are not repeated in the future and company objectives are achieved.

Standard Cost

This term is defined by the I.C.M.A. Terminology as:

'A predetermined cost calculated in relation to a prescribed set of working conditions, correlating technical specifications and scientific measurements of materials and labour to the prices and wage rates expected to apply during the period to which the standard cost is intended to relate, with an addition of an appropriate share of budgeted overhead.'

A standard cost, then, is a planned cost, estimated in advance of production or supply, and related to a particular product or service. It cannot be computed until a technical specification has been written up for the manufacture of the product, for it is on this document that the cost estimates are based. It is also necessary to establish the conditions under which the products are to be manufactured, e.g. the resources available and the volume of output; the cost of materials and labour will depend on such factors.

The comparison of actual costs with standard costs can be contrasted with other instances in which comparisons take place. It is possible, for instance, to compare actual results in one period with those of a previous period, but this practice is less than satisfactory because conditions existing currently may differ from those existing in a previous period. In the interim there could have occurred improvements in working conditions, changes in production methods, a changeover to a substitute material, the introduction of a productivity scheme or the purchase of more efficient plant and machinery. Also, current costs are affected by price rises beyond the control of management, and the previous period may have included exceptional expenditure which occurred in that period alone and is unlikely to arrise again. Costs of a previous period cannot be treated as a kind of norm on which future costs can be predicted.

Previous costs may include inefficiencies; to use those costs as a basis for guaging the efficiency of current working would result in perpetuating the same inefficiencies. Prior costs are therefore an inadequate means of measuring current performance.

If large differences do arise in a comparison of this year's costs with last year's, it may not be readily apparent why the difference has arisen. Is it due to a single factor, or a number of factors? Are some inefficiencies offset by efficient working in another area? For example, has an increase in the price of material hidden the better use of materials?

On the other hand, standard costs are the result of detailed preparation; it should be possible to explain why a difference has occurred by comparing current actual results with the detailed plan.

Types of Standard

Standards can be divided into two main groups, namely basic standards and current standards.

Basic standards. This is 'an underlying standard from which a current standard can be developed.' (I.C.M.A. Terminology). When a basic standard is established, the intention is that it shall remain unchanged for a number of years, it is not updated by changes in the level of material prices or wage rates. Therefore, it has the advantage of indicating long term trends and operates in a similar way to index numbers.

However, if a change occurs in the conditions under which an operation is carried out, then one is obliged to update the standard otherwise the effect of changed conditions will render ineffective the long term trend information. Conditions which are likely to change are:

(a) an alteration in the method of manufacture;
(b) the introduction of new materials;
(c) an improvement in labour efficiency;
(d) a change in the design of the product;
(e) new plant and machinery.

To be effective, the basic standard must be updated to take these factors into account, Although it might have been the intention to create a standard that would be in use for a number of years, because of a change in circumstances as indicated above, frequent revisions become necessary. Consequently, basic standards are rarely used except as a basis for preparing current standards.

Current standards. The I.C.M.A. Terminology defines a current standard as 'a standard established for use over a short period of time, related to current conditions.' The period covered by current standards is normally one year and the 'current condition' referred to in the definition takes into account the price and wage-rate levels expected to occur during the period to which the standard is intended to relate as well as latest anticipated efficiency levels, current materials and equipment, and methods of manufacture. When comparing actual costs with standards, current standard costs provide a more adequate measure, and the difference between the standard and actual results is more likely to be due to controllable factors. The disadvantage of current standards lies in the amount of clerical work involved in updating standard costs every year. However, even **basic** standards must be brought up to date to reflect the latest methods of manufacture, new materials and equipment, and so on. Why not therefore carry out this task annually and at the same time estimate the prices and wage rates that are likely to exist in the ensuing accounting year!

Standards can also be divided into ideal standards and expected standards.

Ideal standard. This term is defined by the I.C.M.A. Terminology as 'the standard which can be attained under the most favourable conditions possible.' A standard computed on such a basis assumes the absence of spoiled work, breakdown of plant and machinery, faulty materials; in fact, any wastage or inefficiency whatsoever. It supposes that nothing less than absolute efficiency will be achieved. This is tantamount to living in cloud-cuckoo-land. Such levels of performance are seldom reached.

It might be argued that to set the highest possible goals would stimulate management and workers to achieve a high level of performance. On the other hand, to set targets which cannot possibly be attained would dishearten people as soon as they realise that their best efforts still fall short of the mark. Consequently, they are likely to become dispirited, which might bring about a situation where their performance deteriorates significantly, lower than if more realistic targets had been set. Ideal standards can therefore be counter-productive; for some people there is nothing more debilitating than lack of success.

An advantage of standard costing is that variances from standard can be related to individual responsibility; but if ideal standards are used as a basis for measuring performance, managers would be less accountable for failing to achieve the standard. They could argue that it is impossible to achieve perfection. Ideal standards, therefore, are not recommended.

Expected standard. This is 'the standard which it is anticipated can be attained during a future specified budget period.' (I.C.M.A. Terminology) Expected standards are more realistic. They recognise that some wastage and inefficiency are inevitable. This is not to say that inefficiency is condoned; a high level of efficiency is still required. But the complete elimination of error, machine failure and so on is unlikely to occur and consequently targets will be set which accept this fact, but at the same time seek to minimise the extent of inefficient operating.

Standards based on conditions which are expected to exist are more likely to produce a response from the work force. Managers and workers will endeavour to reach realistic targets. Variances will indicate the extent to which efficient operating has been achieved; and managers can be held accountable for adverse variances if the standards are attainable. Also, managers will strive to attain them.

The above discussion on types of standards can be summarised by stating that current, expected standards are the ones which are most commonly used.

There is, however, one other type of standard which is worth a mention, namely the *normal standard*. This is defined as 'the average standard which it is anticipated can be attained over a future period of time, preferably long enough to cover one trade cycle.' (I.C.M.A. Terminology). This type of standard is not often used as it is difficult to estimate the length of the trade cycle with any degree of certainty.

Setting Standard Costs.

The setting of standard costs involves the endeavours and co-operation of various members of the organisation. The production control department will provide the technical specifications which state how each item is to be manufactured. Rates of pay will be supplied by the personnel department, material prices by the buyer, overhead absorption rates by the budget officer and so on. All this information will be fed through to the cost accountant who will be responsible for compiling the standard cost cards on which this information is recorded. There will be one card for each component and each sub-assembly. Standard costs must be prepared for the following:

(a) direct materials cost;
(b) direct wages cost;
(c) direct expenses;
(d) variable production overhead;
(e) variable marketing overhead;
(f) fixed overhead (if absorption costing is used).

Direct materials cost. The standard cost of direct materials is made up of two separate components, namely, price and usage, and it is necessary to compute the amount of each for every item of material used in the manufacturing process. With regard to usage, unless ideal standards are used, an allowance will have to be made for any unavoidable losses, e.g. defective material, breaking of bulk, and wastage during the production process. The technical specification, or bill of materials, will provide details of quantity per unit of output, quality, dimensions, part numbers, sizes and description of material.

The purchasing department will supply material prices, but these may have to be subject to the approval of higher management or a standards committee in order to avoid estimates which include price rises above what is reasonable for the coming budget period. The prices established must take into account existing price levels and the estimated movement in prices for the period under consideration. Where long-term contracts have been placed with suppliers for particular items of material, the relevant prices must form the basis of material price standards. Another factor which will influence material standards is the amount of stock in hand at the commencement of the budget period. The price of this stock will be the price obtaining during the period immediately prior to the budget period. In a period of rising prices this will have the effect of reducing the average price of materials consumed during the budget year. Standard costs must reflect this.

Standard costs can also be set for materials used in packing the finished products.

Direct wages cost. Like materials cost, the standard direct wages cost is based on information contained in the technical specification, or operations list, which should state the various operations required in order to manufacture each product. Against the description of each operation should be noted the machines to be used to fulfil the task; also, the departments in which the manufacturing process is to be carried out and the category of labour employed, for example, fitter, assembly worker, inspector, etc. It is also necessary to study closely each operation in the manufacturing process and determine the grade of worker appropriate for carrying out the operation. In this connection, there must be some correlation between the amount of work to be undertaken by each grade of worker and the availability of workers in particular grades to execute the quantity of work planned for the ensuing period. Such an analysis might reveal a surfeit of labour in one grade and shortages in other grades. A programme of training may have to be implemented in order to rectify the situation. Alternatively, the planned programme of work may have to be modified in the short term to bring planned production into line with the labour available.

The setting of standard costs for labour is closely related to the technique of work study, especially where the volume of work is high and many of the operations are repetitive in nature. The student might recall from his reading of chapter 3 that this technique comprised the separate techniques of method study and work measurement. Method study is concerned with the detailed examination of the way in which the manufacturing process is carried on, whilst in work measurement, time engineers seek to establish a time for each task to be carried out. Before standard times are set, it is worthwhile to use the technique of method study to make sure that the work is being carried out in the most effective manner. For example, does the description given to each operation in the technical specification represent the most effective method of manufacture? Would the introduction of new equipment greatly facilitate the work? Is the layout of the factory conducive to efficient operating? The task of work measurement can only proceed when the work study engineers are convinced that only the best methods for executing each task are being adopted. Any changes recommended and introduced must be incorporated in the technical specification.

A standard is fixed for each operation after allowing for rest periods and personal requirements. Standard labour costs can then be calculated by multiplying the standard time by the rate of pay expected to be in operation during the budget period. The estimated rate of pay will depend on existing wage rates, claims in the pipeline and the timing and amount of expected settlement, and it is the responsibility of the personnel department to compute the standard rates for each grade of labour, giving consideration to the various methods of remuneration that might be used to calculate actual wages. The time allowed to complete a task under an incentive scheme will also be the standard time under Standard Costing.

Production overhead. Standard costs for production overhead are established in the same manner as predetermined overhead absorption rates. Using the procedure which has already been explained in chapter 5, and assuming that the technique of budgetary control is being employed in conjunction with standard costing, the method for setting overhead standards is as follows:

(a)   For each cost centre, separate the fixed overhead and the variable overhead for the budgeted level of output;

(b) Choose a base by which the overhead is to be recovered, and express the budgeted output in these terms, for example, standard direct labour hours;

(c) Ascertain the standard variable overhead rate by dividing the bud-geted variable overhead for the budgeted level of output by the base chosen, e.g. the standard direct labour hours required to execute the level of output budgeted;

(d) Compute the standard fixed overhead rate in the same manner as the standard variable overhead rate.

The Standard Hour

This term is defined by the I.C.M.A. Terminology as ' a hypothetical unit pre-established to represent the amount of work which should be performed in one hour at standard performance.' It should be noted that the standard hour is a measurement of 'work' not of time. The advantage of using standard hours as a means of expressing the quantity of product-ion occurs when a department is producing a variety of products the total production of which could not be stated by using a common measu-rement, for example, one product is expressed in kilograms whilst anoth-er is measured in litres. By using the standard hour it is possible to quan-tify the total production of the department by using a term, i.e. the standard hour, which is common to both products.

Variance Analysis.

Standard costs must be set prior to the commencement of the budget period in order to provide a basis for the measurement of actual perform-ance. Periodically, the actual performance is compared with the pre-determined standard cost and the cost variance established; but if man-agement is to act upon the variance so that deviations from standard are not repeated in the future, it is essential that the information should be accompanied by as much detail as possible. The cost variance should, therefore, be suitably analysed.

Variance Analysis, then, is 'that part of variance accounting which relates to the analysis into constituent parts of variances between plan-ned and actual performance.' (I.C.M.A. Terminology). The purpose of such an analysis is to bring to the attention of management the reasons why actual operating profit and budgeted operating profit do not corres-pond. A breakdown of the differences into the various constituent parts will enable managers to concentrate on remedying areas of weakness; in consequence, cost control will be greatly facilitated.

Cost variances can be either favourable (F) or adverse (A). In operat-ing statements, where actual performance is better than standard, the extent of the achievement is expressed in financial terms and the letter F is appended. For example, if the direct materials used during a month's production were purchased at prices which were less than anticipated when standards were set, the information might be passed on to management thus: 'Direct materials price variance - £250 F.' Naturally, the letter A would be placed after amounts which indicated that performance was below standard.

The sum of all the variances should total the difference between budgeted and actual profit. There is a wide assortment of variances, but by far the most significant are the production cost variances; these can be divided into the following main categories:

(a) direct materials cost variance;
(b) direct wages cost variance;
(c) variable production overhead variance;
(d) fixed production overhead variance.

Direct materials cost variance. This is the difference between the standard cost of direct materials specified for the production achieved and the actual cost of direct materials used. It is especially important to note that the actual cost must be compared with the standard cost of *actual* production, not budgeted production. In other words, first determine the actual production for the period under review; then, calculate the standard cost of the actual production; and, lastly, compare the standard cost of actual production with the actual cost of production in order to ascertain the direct materials cost variance.

The direct materials cost variance can be divided into two parts,namely the direct materials price variance and the direct materials usage variance. The price variance is ascertained by comparing the standard prices specified with the actual prices paid for the direct materials used; the usage variance is the difference between the standard quantity specified for the production achieved and the actual quantity used, both valued at standard prices.

To simplify the above, the variances can be computed by using the following formulae:

Direct materials price variance = (SP − AP) x AQ
Direct materials usage variance = (SQ − AQ) x SP

The abbreviation SP refers to standard price; AP = actual price; AQ = actual quantity; SQ = standard quantity.

Example. The standard cost card includes the following information in respect of one unit of product A:

£

Direct materials cost - 5 kilograms of material Y at £0.60 per kg.   3.00

During a certain cost period, 4,000 units of A were manufactured and the material used in production was 20,200 kilograms of Y at a cost of £11,716. Calculate the material cost variance and separate the result into the component parts, price and usage.

	£	£
Standard direct materials cost of actual production -		
4,000 x £3		12.000
Actual cost		11,716
Therefore, direct materials cost variance		284 F

$$\text{Direct materials price variance} = (SP - AP) \times AQ$$
$$= (\pounds 0.60 - \pounds 0.58) \times 20,200$$
$$= \underline{\pounds 404} \text{ F}$$
$$\text{Direct materials usage variance} = \overline{(SQ - AQ)} \times SP$$
$$= (20,000 - 20,200) \times \pounds 0.60$$
$$= \underline{\pounds 120} \text{ A}$$

To obtain the actual price in the above example, it was necessary to divide the actual cost of £11,716 by the actual quantity used in production, i.e. 20,200 kilograms. In this instance the actual price that resulted was exactly £0.58. However, where the actual price does not work out at an exact figure, sometimes six places of decimals are required in order to achieve an accurate answer. Because of this, the student may prefer to use an alternative method of arriving at the price and usage variances.

In this method, the student should calculate the following:

(a)   standard cost (of actual production);
(b)   actual quantity at standard price;
(c)   actual cost.

The usage variance is (a) − (b); the price variance (b) − (c); and the direct materials cost variance is the sum of the two constituent parts, i.e. (a) − (c).

The standard cost and actual cost are given above; the actual quantity, 20,200, at the standard price, £0.60, equals £12,120. The usage variance is therefore £12,000 − £12,120, i.e. £120 A; and the price variance is £12,120 − £11,716, i.e. £404 F.

Wherever possible, the cause of price and usage variances should be established and related to individual responsibility. The aim should be to identify those managers who are accountable for adverse variances. However, this is often a difficult task, for a number of individuals could be responsible for a single variance. For example, it might be thought that an adverse materials price variance is entirely the responsibility of the buyer; that such a variance is an indication of his failure to meet the organisation's purchasing standards. The following is a list of some of the reasons why material price variances arise,and although the cause may be due to a failure on the part of the buyer, nevertheless it must not be assumed that this is always the case. In some cases, events are completely outside the buyer's control.

(a)   Price movements, either generally or in connection with specific materials, which are greater or less than anticipated when the original standards were fixed. Corrective action may not be possible; to a great extent, purchasers are not in a position to control prices charged to them. Naturally, the buyer will do all in his power to minimise the effects of price rises by trying to locate alternative sources of supply. Alternatively, it might be possible to acquire a cheaper substitute material which will perform the same task as the more expensive item. Often, though, the only remedial action that management can take to offset significant price rises is to pass the increase on to the consumer by way of increased selling prices.

(b) The use of materials which have a superior or lower quality than those stated in the technical specification. In many organisations, the buyer merely orders what the production control department requisitions and if the quality of materials stated in the technical specifications is not of sufficient standard to enable the finished product to pass a rigorous test and inspection programme, the production controller may be left with no alternative but to requisition a higher grade of material. The buyer simply translates this request into a purchase order for the materials requested.

(c) The termination of a source of supply which in the past provided inexpensive materials.

(d) A reduction in the volume of production so that the opportunity to take advantage of quantity discount is lost.

(e) The need to acquire emergency supplies. This could indicate that the stock levels require adjusting or that the re-order levels are being ignored. Where materials are needed urgently, the buyer has no time to seek out the cheapest source of supply. Moreover, it often means that the cost of delivery is much higher if the goods are to be delivered or collected immediately.

(f) Efficient or inefficient purchasing.

Like price variances, usage variances cannot necessarily be levelled against the most obvious person. It is usual to hold the production manager responsible for material usage variances, but there may be circumstances which are not within his control. Some of the causes of usage variances are given below.

(a) Inefficiency by the operator who has misused the material issued to him, so that a partly finished product has had to be scrapped.

(b) Spoiled work which is the result of insufficient maintenance of plant and machinery.

(c) Poor quality materials which resulted in the finished product failing inspection, or the use of a substitute material not really suited for the purpose. This could be the responsibility of the buyer if he has wrongly thought that a cheaper substitute was as good as the materials requisitioned by the production control department.

(d) A change in the method of production so that the standard for the current budget period is now out of date.

(e) The actual mix of materials not being the same as the standard mix. For example, whereas the standard mix to process a product was 3 parts of material Y to 2 parts of material Z, the actual combination used was, say, 2 parts of Y to 3 parts of Z.

One method of isolating the cause of adverse material usage variances is to issue to production only the standard materials required to execute a particular job or order. If additional materials are required during the course of production, these can then only be obtained by making out a document known as an Excess Materials Requisition or Excess Note which should state the reason for the need to requisition further supplies and be signed by the foreman responsible. Again, if materials are to be scrapped, a scrap docket should be completed, the valuation representing the work in progress to date at standard cost.

Direct wages cost variance. This is calculated by ascertaining the difference between the standard direct wages specified for the production achieved and the actual direct wages incurred. As with materials, the direct wages cost variance consists of a price element and a quantity element, although different terms are used, namely, the direct wages rate variance and the direct labour efficiency variance.

The student should not imagine that the introduction of these terms brings with them the need to commit to memory two additional formulae. The cost variances for wages are ascertained in the same way as for materials; the price component must be separated from the usage component. The direct wages rate variance is that portion of the direct wages cost variance which is the difference between the standard rates of pay specified and the actual rates paid, whereas the direct labour effic. iency variance is the difference between the standard direct wages cost for the production achieved, and the actual hours at standard rates. The formulae are:

Direct wages rate variance   = (SR − AR) x AH
Direct wages efficiency variance = (SH − AH) x SR

SR relates to standard rate; AR = actual rate; SH = standard hours; AH = actual hours. Note that the formulae above resemble the formulae for the materials price and usage variance; the only difference is that the words 'rate' and 'hours' are substituted for 'price' and 'usage'.

Example. Using the information in the previous example, the standard cost card also includes the following information:

	£
Direct wages cost - 3 hours at £2 per hour	6.00

During the same period, the 4,000 units were produced in 11,750 hours at a labour cost of £24,675. Calculate the labour cost variances.

	£
Standard direct wages cost of production achieved - 4,000 x £6	24,000
Actual cost	24,675
Therefore, direct wages cost variance	675 A

Direct wages rate variance = (SR − AR) x AH
= (£2 − £2.10) x 11,750
= £1,175 A

Direct labour efficiency variance = (SH − AH) x SR
= (12,000 − 11,750) x £2
= £500 F

In this example, the actual rate works out conveniently at exactly £2.10, i.e. £24,675 divided by 11,750. This may not always occur in problems; the alternative method is again shown, as no doubt some students will find this method much more to their liking.

		£
(a)	Standard cost of actual production	24,000
(b)	Actual hours at standard rate, 11,750 x £2	23,500
(c)	Actual cost	24,675

The efficiency variance is (a) − (b), £500 F; the rate variance is (b) − (c), £1,175 A.

Some of the reasons for wage rate variances are:

(a)   Difference in the amounts paid to particular grades of labour. As standards are normally prepared in advance of the budget period, some forecasting of wage settlements during the ensuing budget period is necessary. It often occurs that the timing and amount of wage awards differ from those predicted by the personnel department. This situation results from negotiations between management and trade unions, the supply and demand position in the industry or in a particular trade, or because of a change in the Government's incomes policy.

(b)   Using different grades of labour from those in the technical specification. The situation could arise where there is a shortage of, say, unskilled workers, and in order to complete a particular order it is necessary to use skilled or semi-skilled workers. In such a case, the average rate of pay will be higher than the rate envisaged when the standards were set.

Labour efficiency variances could arise because of:

(a)   a change in the methods of production;
(b)   purchase of more efficient machinery;
(c)   machine breakdown;
(d)   correcting spoiled work;
(e)   non-availability of materials and suitable machines;
(f)   efficiency or inefficiency of the direct workers engaged on production.

It is the job of the cost accountant to provide as much information as possible to management as to the cause of the variances reported; but the extent of the analysis will depend on the benefit likely to be obtained and the cost of providing more and more detail.

Care must be exercised in the interpretation of variances. There is a danger in concentrating too much on individual variances and losing sight of the overall position. The buyer, in order to obtain favourable materials price variances, may purchase a low-cost substitute which might result in an adverse labour efficiency variance because of the need to spend a lot of time putting the job right. Also the lower quality of the item purchased might result in the failure of the finished product when tested, so that a significant amount of re-work has to be undertaken. Some manager with overall authority must give guidance so that it is realised that the sum of the variances is more important than whether a single variance is favourable or adverse. An adverse variance is acceptable if a favourable variance results which more than compensates for the adverse variance.

Variable production overhead variance. This is the difference between the standard variable production overhead absorbed in the production achieved and the actual variable production overhead. This variance is not normally sub-divided; the reason for this is that the standard and the actual are measured using the same level of output for both; there can therefore be no quantity variance.

Example. The budgeted variable production overhead for the month of June is £15,000 and this is related to the production of 12,000 units. It transpired that during the month of June the actual figures were: variable overhead expenditure - £14,600; production - 12,500 units. Calculate the variable production overhead variance.

		£
Standard cost of actual production £15,000 x $\frac{12,500}{12,000}$		15,625
Actual cost		14,600
Variable production overhead variance		1,025 F

Fixed production overhead variance. The I.C.M.A. Terminology defines this as 'the difference between the standard cost of fixed overhead absorbed in the production achieved, whether completed or not, and the fixed overhead attributed and charged to that period.' Like direct material and direct wages, this variance consists of two elements: the fixed production overhead volume variance and the fixed production overhead expenditure variance.

The volume variance is calculated by ascertaining the difference between the budgeted output and the actual output and multiplying the result by the budgeted absorption rate. The variance represents the amount of overhead under/over absorbed due to the difference between budgeted and actual activity. The formula for calculating this variance is similar to the direct materials usage variance and the direct labour efficiency variance, for like the other variances, it too is a variance related to quantity. The formula is:

(Actual hours − Budgeted hours) x Budgeted absorption rate.

The expenditure variance is the difference between the budgeted and actual fixed overhead for a specified period. It is simply :

Budgeted fixed overhead − Actual fixed overhead.

Example. The budgeted fixed overhead for a specific period was £12,000 and the budgeted output in terms of standard hours was 5,000. The corresponding actual results were £12,300 and 5,500 standard hours. Compute the overhead variances.

£

Fixed production overhead absorbed – 5,500 x £2.40   13,200

(Note - overhead absorption rate of £2.40 calculated

thus $\dfrac{£12,000}{5,000}$)

Actual fixed overhead   12,300

Therefore, fixed production overhead variance   900 F

Fixed production overhead volume variance = (AH–BH) x £2.40

= (5,500–5,000)x £2.40

= £1,200 F

Fixed production overhead expenditure variance= £12,000–£12,300

= £300 A

It should be noted that it is not necessary to know the actual overhead incurred in order to calculate the volume variance; similarly, the expenditure variance does not depend on the number of standard hours budgeted or actually completed.

If the alternative layout were used, the solution to the above problem would be shown as follows:

£

(a) Fixed production overhead absorbed   13,200
(b) Budgeted overhead   12,000
(c) Actual overhead   12,300

The volume variance is (a)–(b), £1,200 F; the expenditure variance is (b)–(c), £300 A.

It might be advisable for the student to refer back to chapter 4 and th section on under/over absorption of overhead in order to note the similarity with this section.

Variances due to sales. The foregoing pages have dealt with production cost variances; cost variances will also occur in the administration and marketing functions. However, failure to achieve the standard profit for a particular period may be due as much to sales as to shortcomings with regard to cost control.

It was stated earlier in the chapter that the purpose of variance analysis is to direct management's attention to the reasons why budgeted profit and actual profit differ; it is therefore necessary to examine the effec on profit of any divergencies from the sales plan.

The main sales variance is the 'operating profit variance due to sales,' which is the difference between (a) the budgeted operating profit and (b) the margin between the actual sales and the standard cost of those sales.

Example. A business manufactures a single product. The budget for the month of June gives the following information appertaining to sales

Quantity	5,000 units
Selling price	£10 per unit
Standard cost	£ 7 per unit

During the month of June, 4,800 units were sold, having a total sales value of £49,200. Calculate the operating profit variance due to sales.

		£
(a)	Budgeted operating profit, 5,000 x £3	15,000
(b)	Actual sales	49,200
(c)	Standard cost of actual sales, 4,800 x £7	33,600
(d)	Margin between actual sales and the standard cost of those sales, (b) — (c)	15,600
(e)	Operating profit variance due to sales (d) — (a)	600 F

The variance is favourable because the margin which is based on actual sales, i.e. £15,600, is greater than the budgeted operating profit, £15,000 It will be noted that it is not necessary to know the actual variable costs as any disparity between standard and actual will be analysed under cost variances, not sales variances.

The operating profit variance due to sales can be divided into two subsidiary variances as the following diagram indicates:

Operating profit variance
due to sales

Due to selling prices   Due to sales volume.

As in many of the cost variances, there are both price and quantity components. The operating profit due to selling prices is the difference between the standard and actual prices of the sales effected. The formula would therefore be:

(Actual selling price - Standard selling price) x Actual quantity sold.

In the above example, the actual selling price is £10.25, i.e. $\dfrac{£49,200}{4,800}$

The selling price variance is therefore calculated thus:

(£10.25 — £10) x 4,800 = £1,200 F

Clearly, the variance must be favourable seeing that the actual selling price is 25 pence higher than the standard selling price.

The operating profit due to sales volume is the difference between budgeted and actual sales quantities, both being valued at standard unit operating profit margins.

The formula for calculating the sales volume variance is:

(Actual quantity - Budgeted quantity) x Standard unit operating profit.

Using again the foregoing example the sales volume variance is ascertained as follows:

(4,800 — 5,000) x £3 = £600 A

An adverse variance arises because the volume of sales is 200 units less than budget.

The sales variances will normally be the responsibility of the marketing executive or sales manager, but it will be necessary to investigate the causes of these variances before holding a marketing department accountable. The sales manager may not think it advisable to increase selling prices in line with budget. A situation could arise where a projected increase in price has been preceded by a fall in demand, perhaps as a result of a falling off in quality which is outside the responsibility of the marketing manager. Before raising selling prices, consideration will have to be given to the effect on volume. A potentially favourable price variance may be more than offset by an adverse volume variance; the state of the market may deter the sales manager from taking any action on prices. Alternatively, a reduction in prices by competitors may force the sales manager to reduce prices for a period.

At first sight, the responsibility for an adverse sales volume variance would lie with the marketing manager. But the failure to reach budgeted targets may not be due to any deficiencies on the part of the sales force; their ability to sell the requisite quantity of products may be frustrated by the inability of the production department to fulfil the production programme. It is therefore important to investigate thoroughly the reasons why the variances have arisen in order that appropriate management action can be taken to remedy the situation.

Operating profit variances. This is the difference between budgeted and actual operating profit related to a specific period. At the end of each costing period, the cost accountant will ascertain this figure, and it is his responsibility to undertake the variance analysis that has been outlined in the preceding pages.

The operating profit variance is the sum of all the subsidiary variances as shown by the following diagram.

Operating profit variance

Operating profit variance due to sales	General administration cost variance	Marketing cost variance	Production cost variance

Although this chapter has dealt with a number of variances, there are many more. Each business must make its own decision on the number and type of variances to include in its analysis, and the decision must be made on the basis of whether the information revealed is of benefit. Can performance be improved upon by the dissemination of the information made available by the analysis?

The manner in which the variances are to be reported to management must be considered. It is usual to issue a statement, but the form of the statement should be such that the attention of management is directed towards the disparity existing between budgeted and actual profit. One method of achieving this is to commence the statement with the budgeted profit for the period, and to add to it the favourable variances; adverse variances should then be deducted and the statement should conclude with the actual profit earned for the period in question.

Example. The standard selling price for a certain product is £12 and the budgeted sales for the month of July is 7,500 units. The standard cost card reveals the following details which concern the manufacture of one unit of the product:

	£
Direct materials - 2 kilograms of material A at £1.50 per kg.	3
Direct wages: 1½ hours at £2 per hour	3
Variable overhead	1
Fixed overhead (absorbed on the cost unit rate basis)	2
Standard cost	9

During the month of July, 7,600 units were sold, the sales value of which was £89,680. The cost of 15,160 kg of material A purchased during the month was £25,014. The direct wages cost amounted to £23,575 for 11,500 hours. The overhead costs for the month were: variable £7,900; fixed £15,600. There were no stocks or work in progress at either the beginning or the end of the month.

Present a statement to management which shows clearly:

(a) the budgeted profit for the month;

(b) the actual profit earned;

(c) why the budgeted profit has not been achieved.

Workings:	£	£
Budgeted sales, 7,500 x £12		90,000
Budgeted costs, 7,500 x £9		67,500
Therefore, budgeted profit		22,500
Actual sales		89,680
Actual costs — direct materials	25,014	
— direct wages	23,575	
— variable overhead	7,900	
— fixed overhead	15,600	
		72,089
Actual profit		17,591

Variances

Direct materials

	£
(a) Standard cost of actual production, 7,600 x £3	22,800
(b) Actual quantity at standard price, 15,160 kg x £1.50	22,740
(c) Actual cost	25,014
Direct materials usage variance = (a)−(b)	60 F
Direct materials price variance = (b)−(c)	2,274 A
Direct materials cost variance = (a)−(c)	2,214 A

Direct wages

	£
(a) Standard cost of actual production, 7,600 x £3	22,800

(b) Actual hours at standard rate, 11,500 x £2   23,000
(c) Actual cost   23,575
    Direct labour efficiency variance = (a)—(b)   200 A
    Direct wages rate variance = (b)—(c)   575 A
    Direct wages cost variance = (a)—(c)   775 A

Variable overhead
Standard cost of actual production, 7,600 x £1   7,600
Actual cost   7,900
Therefore, variable overhead variance   300 A

Fixed overhead
(a) Fixed overhead absorbed, 7,600 x £2   15,200
(b) Budgeted fixed overhead, 7,500 x £2   15,000
(c) Actual fixed overhead   15,600
    Fixed overhead volume variance = (a)—(b)   200 F
    Fixed overhead expenditure variance = (b)—(c)   600 A
    Fixed overhead variance = (a)—(c)   400 A

Sales variances
(a) Budgeted operating profit   22,500
(b) Actual sales   89,680
(c) Standard cost of actual sales, 7,600 x £9   68,400
(d) Margin between actual sales and the standard
    cost of those sales, (b)—(c)   21,280
(e) Operating profit variance due to sales, (d)—(a)   1,220 A

Sales variance due to selling prices
Actual selling price $\frac{£89,680}{7,600}$ 11.80
Standard selling price   12.00
Difference x actual quantity sold = £0.20 x 7,600   1,520 A

Sales variance due to sales volume
Difference between actual and budgeted sales
   quantities x standard unit operating profit,
   i.e. 100 units x £3 =   300 F

Operating Profit Statement for the month of July

	£	£
Budgeted profit		22,500
Add Favourable variances:		
Direct materials usage variance	60	
Fixed overhead volume variance	200	
Sales volume variance	300	
		560
		23,060
Less Adverse variances:		
Direct materials price variance	2,274	

Direct labour efficiency variance	200	
Direct wages rate variance	575	
Variable overhead variance	300	
Fixed overhead expenditure variance	600	
Selling price variance	1,520	
		5,469
Actual profit		17,591

Accounting for Standard Costs

The procedure for recording standard costs in the cost accounts is similar to that stated in Chapter 6, except that the standard cost of an item is more likely to be used than the actual cost.

With regard to materials, there is a choice between two methods. In chapter 2, the entries affecting the stores ledger account were briefly covered; receipts were entered using the actual cost, whereas issues were recorded at standard, any difference being written off to a materials price variance account at the end of the costing period in which the materials were issued to production. Consequently, under this method, work in progress is debited with the standard cost of materials issued from stores; but only the standard quantities which are required to manufacture the particular products. Any excess requirements are debited to materials usage variance account.

An alternative method of dealing with materials in the cost accounts is to debit stores ledger account at standard, so that the price variance is recorded in the cost accounts at the point of receipt rather than when the materials are issued to production. This is done by comparing the actual price as recorded on the supplier's invoice with the standard price, and multiplying the difference by the quantity received. A point in favour of adopting this particular method is that information on price variances is recorded and published at the earliest possible moment.

If the latter method is employed, i.c. both receipts and issues being recorded at standard, there is no need to record monetary values each time an entry is made in the stores ledger account. When the valuation of stock is required, it is an easy matter merely to multiply the quantity in hand by the standard price. Thus, this method does have the advantage of reducing the clerical effort required to maintain the stores ledger accounts.

However, where receipts are recorded at actual, this is more in line with accounting principles and the balance on stores ledger control account can be used for balance sheet purposes.

Example. During the month of April, 100 units of material A were received into stores. The supplier charged £1.30 per unit and the standard price was £1.20 per unit. During the month 65 units were issued to production in order to execute a job in which only 60 units were required. There was no stock in hand at the commencement of April.

Write up the stores ledger control account, using both methods.

Method 1.   Materials recorded at actual price in stores ledger on receipt.

Stores Ledger Control Account

	£		£
Creditors	130.00	Work in progress account	72.00
		Materials price variance account	
		65 x £0.10	6.50
		Materials usage variance account	
		5 x £1.20	6.00
		Stock c.d.35 x £1.30	45.50
	130.00		130.00

Method 2.   Materials recorded at standard price in stores ledger on receipt.

Stores Ledger Control Account

	£		£
Creditors	120.00	Work in progress account	72.00
		Materials usage variance account	6.00
		Stock c.d. 35 x £1.20	42.00
	120.00		120.00

Note: The Creditors Control Account would be credited with £130 and Materials Price Variance Account debited with £10, i.e. 100 x £0.10 per unit.

Work in Progress Account and Finished Goods Account are normally valued at standard cost.

Labour is usually debited to Work in Progress Account at standard, with differences between standard and actual being debited or credited to Direct Wages Rate Variance Account or Direct Labour Efficiency Variance Account, as the case may be.

Ratios used in Standard Costing

The following ratios can be used to measure performance in relation to production; in each case, the definition is taken from the ICMA Terminology.

Production volume ratio. The number of standard hours equivalent to the production achieved, whether completed or not, divided by (or expressed as a percentage of) the budgeted number of standard hours.

Note: the term 'activity ratio' is synonymous but it is not recommended.

Capacity ratio. The actual number of direct working hours divided by (or expressed as a percentage of) the budgeted number of standard hours

Productivity (or efficiency) ratio. The standard hours equivalent to the production achieved, whether completed or not, divided by (or expressed as a percentage of) the actual number of direct working hours.

Example. You are given the following information relating to the month of June:

	Budget	Actual
Units produced	6,000	6,300
Hours worked	12,000	13,200

Calculate (a) the production volume ratio, (b) the capacity ratio and (c) the efficiency ratio.

Production volume ratio

$$\frac{\text{Actual production in standard hours}}{\text{Budgeted production in standard hours}} \times 100$$

$$= \frac{12,600}{12,000} \times 100 \qquad = \qquad 105 \text{ per cent}$$

Note: actual production in standard hours is calculated by taking the units produced and multiplying them by 2 hours, i.e. the standard time to produce one unit.

Capacity ratio

$$\frac{\text{Actual hours}}{\text{Budgeted hours}} = \frac{13,200}{12,000} = 110 \text{ per cent}$$

Efficiency ratio

$$\frac{\text{Actual production in standard hours}}{\text{Actual hours}}$$

$$= \frac{12,600}{13,200} = 95.45 \text{ per cent}$$

EXAMINATION PRACTICE
Students are advised to attempt the questions under simulated examination conditions. Then check their answers with the suggested answers at the back of the book.

Question 65   Comparison of budgetary control and standard costing   Answer page 309

Budgetary Control and Standard Costing are both terms used commonly in Cost Accountancy.

You are required to compare these two approaches, showing clearly similarities and differences.

(Institute of Accounting Staff)

Question 66 Preparation of standard costs   Answer page 309

(a) What information is required when setting material and labour cost standards for a firm's products? How is such information obtained?
(b) 'Standards should be realistic'. Explain.

(Association of Certified Accountants)

Question 67 Variance analysis (material)   Answer page 310

(a) Compound XYZ is manufactured in batches of 100 cylinders, the standard input material per batch being 250 gallons of ABC at £1.20 per gallon.
During November, 30 batches of XYZ were produced from an input of 7,450 gallons of ABC which cost £9,076.

You are required to calculate the material price and usage variances and to show the relevant entries in the Work in Progress Account, assuming the materials are debited thereto at actual cost price.

(b) Discuss the limitations of material price and usage variances as instruments of management control, making reference, if you wish, to the variances you have calculated in (a).

(Association of Certified Accountants)

Question 68 Variance analysis (labour)   Answer page 310

The following information on three departments is available:

Department	A	B	C
Standard hours of production	8,200	7,600	4,200
Standard rate per hour	65p	55p	76p
Actual hours worked	8,740	7,220	4,290
Direct wages paid	£5,986	£3,682	£3,132

You are required to:
(a) calculate the labour variances and sub-variances on the above:
(b) indicate the areas of investigation which you would follow up after calculating the variances.

(Institute of Accounting Staff)

In a cost period, CD Ltd. sells 70 units of product E for £4,480.

Standards for one unit are:	£	£
Sale Price		64.00
Prime Cost		
Wages — 27 hours at £1.90 per hour	51.30	
Material — 13 gallons at 46p per gallon	5.98	
		57.28
Gross Profit		£6.72

The actual costs for the period were: wages £3,572 (1.841 hours);
material £563 (1,017 gallons) and sales income was £4,480.

You are required (a) to analyse the variances for labour and material
cost; (b) to indicate the use which should be made of this information.

(Institute of Accounting Staff)

SC Manufacturing Company Ltd. manufactures a uniform product and
operates a standard costing system.
Standard cost data are as follows:

From each ton of raw materials consumed it is planned that 40
units of product will be produced. The standard price per ton is
£100.
Twenty employees are engaged at a standard rate of £1.25 per
hour. A 40-hour week is in operation and there are 48 working
weeks per annum. The standard performance for the whole factory
is set at a total of 50 units per hour.
Budgeted production overhead for the year is £288,000.
Budgeted output for the year is 96,000 units.

Actual data for the first week in May were as follows:
Production was 2,020 units. Consumption of raw material was
52 tons at an actual price of £98 per ton.
Three employees were paid at £1.30 per hour, two were paid at
£1.20 per hour, and the remainder were paid at standard rate.
Actual production overhead incurred was £6,200.

You are required to calculate the following variances:
(a)   (i) direct material cost;
       (ii) direct material price;
       (iii) direct material usage;

(b) (i) direct wages cost;
(ii) direct wages rate;
(iii) direct labour efficiency;
(c) (i) production overhead cost;
(ii) production overhead expenditure;
(iii) production overhead volume.

(Institute of Cost & Management Accountants)

Question 71   Operating statements   Answer page 312

KC Chemicals Ltd. produce an industrial purifying agent known as Kleenchem, the budgeted weekly output/sales of which is 10,000 litres, the standard cost per 100 litres being:

Material   250 kg costing 50p per kg
Labour   4 hours at £1.25 per hour
Overhead   £5 (budgeted absorption of fixed cost)

The standard selling price if £1.50 per one-litre container.
During week ended 26 November the output of Kleenchem was 9,860 litres all of which was sold, the invoiced value being £14,750. The material input was 24,720 kg, which cost £12,300. Production employees booked 380 hours to the process and were paid £490. Overhea amounted to £525.

You are required to use the foregoing information to produce the operating statement for the week ended 26 November in standard costing format.

(Association of Certified Accountants)

Question 72   Variance analysis   Answer page 313

(a) Explain briefly:
(i) how standards are compiled for material and labour costs for a product;
(ii) the nature and purpose of material and labour variances.
(b) Calculate the material and labour variances from the data set out below and present your answers in the form of a statement for presentation to management.

	Standard
Weight to produce one unit	12 kilograms
Price, per kilogram	£9
Hours to produce one unit	10
Wages rate, per hour	£2

Actual production and costs for week ended 12th November 1977:

Units produced	240
Material used	2,640 kilograms
Material cost	£26,400
Hours worked	2,520
Wages paid	£5,544

(Institute of Cost & Management Accountants)

Answers

Answers for the examination practice questions have been carefully written to provide the student with clear answer guides and key facts that would be needed to pass professional accountancy examinations. Additional detail for a fully comprehensive answer is given in the relevant chapter.

Answer 1   Costing principles   **Question page 17**

(a) The main purpose of cost classification is to provide executives and managers with information that will assist them to manage effectively. Managers are concerned with the planning and control activities of the business, but to be able to perform these tasks adequately, they must be supplied with suitable data regarding the breakdown of the total costs of the business.
(b) Production, Marketing, Administration.
(c) By type of expenditure, e.g. advertising, consumable tools, hire of plant. By cost element, i.e. materials, wages, expense.

Answer 2   Costing principles   **Question page 1**

(a) Salaries - marketing manager, salesmen, sales office staff, drivers.
     Associated costs — company national insurance and pension fund contributions.
     Advertising and publicity.
     Salesmen's cars — depreciation, petrol, insurance, etc.
     Delivery vans — ditto.
     Market research.
     Travel and entertainment.
     Warehouse costs — rent, insurance, etc.
(b) By sales area, by product group, by method of distribution.
     The purpose of analysing costs is to assist management to plan and control the activities of the business. For example, the classification of marketing costs by sales area will enable management to assess the efficiency with which each area is operating. An analysis by product group would assist in the determination of the profitability of the various products.

(a) Differences between bin card balances and actual stores in hand may arise because of:

(i) clerical errors, e.g. making an incorrect entry on the bin card, calculating the balance in hand wrongly, entering details on the wrong bin card, omitting an entry altogether;

(ii) physical errors and losses, e.g. issuing errors, pilferage, evaporation, breaking of bulk;

(iii) issuing materials without a material requisition.

(b) Differences between the bin card and stores ledger account may occur because of:

(i) clerical errors on bin card and/or stores ledger account;

(ii) material requisitions being lost on their way to the cost office;

(iii) delay in making an entry in the stores ledger account.

Action to be taken to avoid such differences may take the form of:

(i) ensuring that material requisitions and goods received notes are made our legibly;

(ii) insisting that, without exception, materials will not be issued unless a properly authorised material requisition is presented to the storeman;

(iii) prohibiting access to the stores, the only exception being the storemen themselves;

(iv) serially numbering material requisitions and requesting the costing department to ensure that a check is kept on the receipt of all requisitions from stores;

(v) investigating the causes of differences and, if necessary, taking measures to dismiss or transfer employees who, repeatedly, make clerical errors.

FIFO

Date	Purchases Qty.	Price £	Amount £	Sales Qty	Price £	Amount £	Balance Qty.	Price £	Amount £
May 1	50	30	1,500				50	30	1,500
6				40	30	1,200	10	30	300
8	40	35	1,400				50	—	1,700
13				10	30	300			
				10	35	350	30	35	1,050
15	70	42	2,940				100	—	3,990
20				30	35	1,050			
				50	42	2,100	20	42	840
22	60	28	1,680				80	—	2,520
27				20	42	840			
				50	28	1,400	10	28	280
29	30	32	960				40	—	1,240

LIFO

Date	Purchases Qty.	Price £	Amount £	Sales Qty.	Price £	Amount £	Balance Qty.	Price £	Amount £
May 1	50	30	1,500				50	30	1,500
6				40	30	1,200	10	30	300
8	40	35	1,400				50	—	1,700
13				20	35	700	30	—	1,000
15	70	42	2,940				100	—	3,940
20				70	42	2,940			
				10	35	350	20	—	650
22	60	28	1,680				80	—	2,330
27				60	28	1,680			
				10	35	350	10	30	300
29	30	32	960				40	—	1,260

Weighted Average

Date	Purchases Qty.	Price £	Amount £	Sales Qty.	Price £	Amount £	Balance Qty.	Price £	Amount £
May 1	50	30	1,500				50	30	1,500
6				40	30	1,200	10	30	300
8	40	35	1,400				50	34	1,700
13				20	34	680	30	34	1,020
15	70	42	2,940				100	39.60	3,960
20				80	39.6	3,168	20	39.60	792
22	60	28	1,680				80	30.90	2,472
27				70	30.9	2,163	10	30.90	309
29	30	32	960				40	31.725	1,269

(a) Weighted Average

Date	Receipts Qty.	Receipts Price £	Receipts Amount £	Issues Qty.	Issues Price £	Issues Amount £	Balance Qty.	Balance Price £	Balance Amount £
1.1.78							60	15	900
January				50	15	750	10	15	150
31.1.78	80	15.50	1,240				90	15.444	1,390
February				60	15.444	927	30	15.444	463
28.2.78	50	15.75	787.50				80	15.631	1,250.50
March				60	15.631	938	20	15.631	312.50
31.3.78	100	15.50	1,550				120	15.521	1,862.50
April				90	15.521	1,397	30	15.521	465.50
30.4.78	60	15.25	915				90	15.339	1,380.50

(b) FIFO

Date	Receipts Qty.	Receipts Price £	Receipts Amount £	Issues Qty.	Issues Price £	Issues Amount £	Balance Qty.	Balance Price £	Balance Amount £
1.1.78							60	15	900
January				50	15	750	10	15	150
31.1.78	80	15.50	1,240				90	—	1,390
February				10	15	150	30	15.50	465
				50	15.50	775			
28.2.78	50	15.75	787.50				80	—	1,252.50
March				30	15.50	465	20	15.75	315
				30	15.75	472.50			
31.3.78	100	15.50	1,550				120	—	1,865
April				20	15.75	315	30	15.50	465
				70	15.50	1,085			
30.4.78	60	15.25	915				90	—	1,380

Answer 5 continued

(ii)   Using the first in, first out basis, the quantities in stock represent the latest purchases. Stock is therefore valued at current market prices, whereas with the weighted average method, the valuation of closing stock will be based on the average of a number of prices. In a period of rising prices, FIFO will produce a higher valuation than the weighted average method.

The reverse is true with regard to the cost of production. Under FIFO the issue price to production does not reflect current market conditions; in times of rising prices, production will be charged with an amount which is less than the current price. If the weighted average price is used the cost of production will tend to be higher when prices are rising, for this method smooths out any fluctuations in the issue price.

Answer 6   Valuation of stores issues   Question page 46

Section (c)

The difference of £450 is dealt with in the accounts thus:

> Dr. Materials price variance account
> Cr. Stores ledger control account

Note: The adverse materials price variance comprises —

100 units x £1	£100
75 units x £2	£150
40 units x £5	£200
	£450

Replacement cost

	£	£
(a) Cost of production:		
50 units x £43	2,150	
65 units x £44	2,860	
50 units x £46	2,300	
		7,310
(b) Value of closing stock: 50 units x £46		2,300
		9,610
(c) Purchase cost, as in (i)		9,050
		560

In the accounts the difference would be dealt with as follows:

> Dr. Stores ledger control account
> Cr. Stock revaluation reserve account.

Sections (a) and (b) overleaf

Weighted average price

Date	Receipts			Issues			Balance		
	Qty.	Price £	Amount £	Qty.	Price £	Amount £	Qty.	Price £	Amount £
May 1	100	41	4,100				100	41	4,100
10	75	42	3,150				175	41.429	7,250
15				50	41.429	2,071	125	41.429	5,179
20				65	41.429	2,693	60	41.429	2,486
23	40	45	1,800				100	42.860	4,286
30				50	42.860	2,143	50	42.860	2,143
			9,050			6,907			

(a) Cost of production   £6,907

(b) Value of closing stock   £2,143

(c) Purchase cost   £9,050 — there is no difference between purchase cost and the aggregate of (a) and (b)

Standard cost

(a) Cost of production, 165 units x £40   6,600

(b) Value of closing stock, 50 units x £40   2,000

   8,600

   9,050

   450

(c) Purchase cost is the same as for the weighted average method

(a)

Re-order level = Maximum usage x Maximum delivery period
              = 3,000 x 4 months
              = 12,000

Maximum level = Re-order level + Re-order quantity
              - (Minimum usage x Minimum re-order period)
              = 12.000 + 8,000 − (2,000 x 2)
              = 16,000

Minimum level = Re-order level − (Normal usage x Average re-order
                                                            period
              = 12,000 − (2,500 x 3)
              = 4,500

Average stock level = $\dfrac{\text{Maximum + Minimum stock levels}}{2}$

$$= \frac{16,000 + 4,500}{2}$$

$$= 10,250$$

(b) The optimum stock level will be one that takes into account the high cost of holding stocks whilst ensuring production is not hindered because of shortage of materials. The re-order level must be reviewed periodically; also, the rate at which material is being consumed. The availability of capital is a further consideration, as is the opportunity to take advantage of quantity discount. Consideration of all these points i necessary if FC Limited is to ensure that stocks are at an optimum level

(a)

FIFO

Date	Receipts Qty.	Price £	Amount £	Issues Qty.	Price £	Amount £	Balance Qty.	Price £	Amount £
April 30							100	-	3,900
May	100	41	4,100				200	-	8,000
June	200	50	10,000				400	-	18,000
July				100	-	3,900			
				100	40	4,100			
				50	50	2,500	150	50	7,500
August	400	51.875	20,750				550	-	28,250
Sept.				150	50	7,500			
				200	51.875	10,375	200	51.875	10,375
October				100	51.875	5187.5	100	51.875	5187.50

Weighted average

Date	Receipts Qty.	Price £	Amount £	Issues Qty.	Price £	Amount £	Balance Qty.	Price £	Amount £
April 30							100	39	3,900
May	100	41	4,100				200	40	8,000
June	200	50	10,000				400	45	18,000
July				250	45	11,250	150	45	6,750
August	400	51.875	20,750				550	50	27,500
Sept.				350	50	17,500	200	50	10,000
Oct.				100	50	5,000	100	50	5,000

Answer 8 continued

Date	Receipts Qty.	Receipts Price £	Receipts Amount £	Issues Qty.	Issues Price £	Issues Amount £	Balance Qty.	Balance Price £	Balance Amount £
April 30							100	-	3,900
May	100	41	4,100				200	-	8,000
June	200	50	10,000				400	-	18,000
July				200	50	10,000	150	-	5,950
				50	41	2,050			
August	400	51.875	20,750				550	-	26,700
Sept.				350	51.875	18,156	200	-	8,544
				50	51.875	2,594			
October				50	41	2,050	100	-	3,900

(b)

Trading Accounts
for six months ended 31st October

	Weighted Ave. £	FIFO £	LIFO £
Sales	47,900	47,900	47,900
Opening stock	3,900	3,900	3,900
Purchases	34,850	34,850	34,850
	38,750	38,750	38,750
Closing stock	5,000	5187.50	3,900
Cost of goods sold	33,750	33,562.50	34,850
Gross profit	14,150	14,337.50	13,050

(c) FIFO has the advantage of being realistic because it conforms to the physical method of issue. Furthermore, profits, although higher under FIFO, are not overstated, for it could be argued that, as the 400 bought in August were reduced by £6.125 per unit, the closing stock valuation is by no means exaggerated. The LIFO method is too conservative, especially in a period of rising prices. It will be noticed that the valuation of the 100 units has not increased over the six months.

	Skilled £	Unskilled £
Wages £1.20 x 40 x 52	2,496	
£0.80 x 40 x 52		1,664
Holiday bonus	30	-
Food allowance (49 weeks)	294	196
Lodging allowance (49 weeks)	441	294
Pension fund	123	-
	3,384	2,154
Total wages cost £3,384 x 2		6,768
£2,154 x 3		6,462
		13,230
Hours - 49 weeks x 40 hours		1,960
less Idle Time		196
		1,764
Total hours 1764 x 5		8,820

$$\text{Labour rate } \frac{13,230}{8,820} = £1.50 \text{ per hour (or £7.50 per group hour)}$$

Operation	Grade	Production per week	Workers needed	Weekly rate per worker £	Weekly cost £
1	A	180	48	18.00	864
2	B	108	80	19.80	1,584
3	C	72	120	21.60	2,592
4	D	216	40	25.20	1,008
5	E	144	60	28.80	1,728
			348		7,776

The involvement of the cost department in the timekeeping and payroll preparation of the manufacturing organisation would entail carrying out the following activities:

(a) Calculating the number of hours worked by each employee from the clock cards, making deductions for lateness and absenteeism, comput ing overtime and bonus, and ascertaining the gross pay. Overtime prem ium hours must be shown separately. For pieceworkers, the gross pay will be based on the quantity produced.

(b) Analysis of activity bookings, identifying direct labour hours and indirect hours, idle time being an example of the latter. The total of the activity bookings must reconcile to the total of attendance hours of dir ect workers. Any differences will need to be investigated.

(c) Preparation of the payroll, making the necessary deductions, and arriving at the net pay for each employee. Also, preparation of a cash analysis and the wage packets.

(d) Calculating the labour cost of jobs or products, also departments. Computing the cost of various items of overhead, e.g. Production Contro. Accounting, Idle Time, Supervision.

••

Answer 12   Employee remuneration calculations   Question page 74
••

(i)   Hourly rate -

Salmon	40 hours x £1.25	=	£50
Roach	38 hours x £1.05	=	£39.90
Pike	36 hours x £1.20	=	£43.20

Basic piece rate -

(ii)

Salmon	270 units x £0.20	=	£54
Roach	200 units x £0.25	=	£50
Pike	220 units x £0.24	=	£52.80

Individual bonus scheme

(iii)   Salmon $\dfrac{5}{45}$ x £50   =   £5.56 Remuneration = £55.56

Roach $\dfrac{12}{50}$ x £39.90   =   £9.58 Remuneration =£49.48

Pike $\dfrac{8}{44}$ x £43.20   =   £7.85 Remuneration =£51.05

Bonus workings:

	Time allowed Hours	Time taken Hours	Time saved Hours
Salmon	45	40	5
Roach	50	38	12
Pike	44	36	8

(b)   This method of remuneration can prove quite effective be cause there is an incentive for the employee to produce more and increase his earnings. The work force is therefore likely to be more contented. Supervision costs would probably be lower than under Time Rates, and the overhead can be spread over a greater number of units, thus reducing the unit cost.

However, the quality of the work may suffer as workers seek a high output. To counter this, more may need to be spent on inspection. A further disadvantage for the employer is the additional clerical costs involved in regularly calculating the bonus.

Premium bonus schemes do not reward industrious employees to the same extent as piece-rates. It is a feature of the former method that any savings made by the employee are shared with the employer. This is particularly beneficial to the employer as any errors made in setting the initial allowed times do not have such a crucial effect. For this reason, a premium bonus scheme may not be acceptable to some employees.

Answer 13   Labour incentive schemes   Question page 75

(a)   General principles which should be applied to incentive schemes. Answer should include:

(i)   Full discussions must take place between the employer and the representatives of the employees prior to the introduction of the scheme.

(ii)   The scheme must be capable of being understood by the employees.

(iii)   The amount of the bonus should be sufficient to stimulate the employees to greater effort.

(iv)   An adequate programme of inspection must be provided.

(v)   Workers should not be penalised if a situation arises which is beyond their control.

(vi)   The payment of the bonus should be made as soon as possible after the completion of the work.

(vii)   The scheme should provide the employer with a reduction in the cost per unit.

(b)   Advantages of 'high day rate'.

(i)   Simple to operate and easy to understand.

(ii)   Quality not sacrificed in effort to increase output.

(iii)   Reduction in clerical costs.

Disadvantages.

(i)   An increase in the cost of supervision would be expected.

(ii)   Withdrawal of incentive might result in lower output.

(iii)   Dissatisfaction on the part of workers whose output is high and who are not able to achieve significantly higher wages than the slower workers.

An individual bonus scheme is preferable to a group scheme where:

(a)   it is necessary to reward individual effort;
(b)   where the quantity produced can be measured for individual workers.
(c)   where it is difficult to find a suitable basis for dividing the bonus between the group.

Features of such schemes include: a reward for effort; the sacrifice of quality in some instances.

Effects include: increased output; a more contented labour force; the employer more able to retain his better workers; less supervision required; an increase in inspection costs; an increase in clerical costs.

Labour turnover is a term which signifies the extent to which employees leave an organisation. It can be measured by using the following formula:

$$\frac{\text{Number of employees leaving during a period}}{\text{Average number of employees}} \times 100$$

A high labour turnover rate would indicate that the numerator, i.e. the number of employees leaving during a period, was high in relation to the denominator, the average number of employees. A high rate will bring with it loss of output, lower morale and higher costs.

However, there may be instances when a high rate is acceptable. For example, there would be little value in retaining employees during a period when sales orders had fallen drastically, and when the organisation envisages a significantly lower level of activity for a considerable time. In such circumstances, there may be no other alternative to large-scale redundancies, and using the formula above would give rise to a high labour turnover rate.

One of the problems of calculating a labour turnover rate is to determine first of all the manner in which it is to be calculated. Some accountants would suggest that the numerator should state 'Number of employees leaving during a period who have to be replaced.' At a time of redundancies, this formula would be preferable, for the first formula's result would be somewhat distorted by an event which is out of the ordinary.

The labour turnover rate is important if costs are to be controlled effectively. Costs which are increased as a result of a high rate include advertising for personnel and interview expenses, training, scrap, machine breakdown and general administration.

The stores turnover rate is the rate at which stocks are consumed. Clearly, it is preferable to have a high turnover rate, thus holding stock for as lower period as possible. The quicker stocks can be turned into sales, the quicker an organisation can recoup the cost of materials and the labour expended in transforming the materials into finished goods. However, there are other factors to consider. In order to take advantage of a generous offer of quantity discount, the organisation might think it worthwhile to accept a higher stores turnover rate in the short term. Also in some companies, the consequences of being out of stock of an important item of material may be severe. A buffer stock, to avoid a 'stock-out' may be necessary.

The stores turnover rate, as an indicator of how well stock is being controlled, is an important statistic in controlling costs. The holding of stocks involves the employment of capital which could perhaps be used more profitably elsewhere in the business if it were not tied up in stocks. The level of stocks also has a bearing on storage costs, such as rent, lighting and insurance; and the risk of deterioration, evaporation or obsolescence increases with the level of stocks held.

Answer 16   Prevention of fraud and labour turnover   Question page 75

To: Board of Directors

Rise in Cost of Production

I have now completed my investigation into the significant increase in the cost of production. Two of the main reasons for the rise over the last year are: fraud in connection with wages; and labour turnover.

Fraud in connection with wages. I would recommend that the following steps are taken to minimise fraud.

(a)   Segregate the work of preparation and payment of wages so that individual clerks are responsible for completing one stage only. One clerk should be responsible for the calculation of gross pay, another for payroll preparation, a third for making up the wage packets, and yet another for issuing of the packets to employees. Periodically the clerks should move from their present tasks to another stage in the sequence.

(b)   Proper authorisation of overtime before it takes place, use being made of an overtime permit.

(c)   Supervision of the paying of wages, preferably by a person who can identify the recipient of the wage packet.

(d)   Ensure that unclaimed packets are signed for by the person collecting the money.

(e)   The personnel manager should periodically check the payroll to ensure that no fictitious persons appear thereon.

Labour turnover. A high labour turnover rate indicates that the number of employees leaving an organisation during a period is high in relation to the average number of employees employed during that period. A high rate is not desirable because it usually causes loss of output, a lowering of morale and higher costs.

Loss of output occurs because of the time taken to find a suitable re-placement; and even when the new recruit starts, he normally has to undergo a period of training before he is able to produce the same quantity of output as his predecessor. Furthermore, once an employee has han handed in his notice, he does not have the same incentive to work as hard as he once did; consequently, his output suffers.

Apart from loss of output, a high labour turnover rate brings with it additional costs, for example, recruitment expenses and training costs. Also, a new starter is likely to produce work of a lower standard, with a higher incidence of scrap. A perpetually high rate means the employ-ment of more staff in the personnel section.

It is the responsibility of the personnel manager to seek ways of keep-ing the labour turnover rate as low as possible.

Signed: ....

Cost Accountant

Answer 17   Overhead absorption   Question page 102

Direct labour hour rate $\dfrac{£30,000}{6,000}$ £5 per direct labour hour

Direct materials percentage rate $\dfrac{£30,000}{£12,000}$ x 100 250 per cent

Direct wages percentage rate $\dfrac{£30,000}{£8,000}$ x 100 375 per cent

Prime cost percentage rate $\dfrac{£30,000}{£20,000}$ x 100 150 per cent

(b) 1 unit of

	Gamma		Delta	
	Overhead	Total cost	Overhead	Total cost
	£	£	£	£
Direct labour hour rate	2,000	3.05	2.00	3.90
Direct materials percentage rate	1.875	2.925	2.25	4.15
Direct wages percentage rate	1.125	2.175	3.75	5.65
Prime cost percentage rate	1.575	2.625	2.85	4.75

	Manufacturing £	Assembly £	Finishing £	Power £	Administration. £
Balance per Departmental Distribution Summary	24,000	21,000	18,000	3,000	5,000
Power costs	1,200	750	450	-3,000	600
Administration costs	1,960	1,680	1,120	840	-5,600
Power	336	210	126	-840	168
Administration	59	50	34	25	-168
Power	10	6	4	-25	5
Administration	2	2	1	-	-5
	27,567	23,698	19,735		

Direct labour hour rate $\dfrac{£3,960}{8,250}$ = £0.48 per direct labour hour

Machine hour rate $\dfrac{£3,960}{11,000}$ = £0.36 per machine hour

Direct materials percentage rate $\dfrac{£3,960}{£6,600}$ x 100 = 60 per cent

Direct wages percentage rate $\dfrac{£3,960}{£9,900}$ x 100 = 40 per cent

Job 99

	Overhead absorbed	Total cost	Profit (50% of cost)	Selling price
	£	£	£	£
Direct labour hour rate	6.72	43.22	21.61	64.83
Machine hour rate	5.40	41.90	20.95	62.85
Direct materials percentage rate	8.70	45.20	22.60	67.80
Direct wages percentage rate	8.80	45.30	22.65	67.95

(b)   **Direct labour hour rate.** Most production overhead costs fluctuate with the amount of time spent producing the finished article. It is therefore appropriate to apportion production overhead on the basis of the length of time taken to produce each article. In this way, those articles which make most use of production facilities are charged with a higher proportion of the overhead.

Machine hour rate. This method of overhead absorption is particularly suitable for cost centres where production is largely mechanised, seeing that many of the overhead costs are caused by the use of plant and machinery, e.g. power, depreciation, maintenance and insurance.

Direct materials percentage rate. This method is only suitable where the cost of direct materials represents a very high proportion of prime cost; in other words, where the amount of labour involved in the product or service is insufficient to use it as a basis for absorbing the overhead.

Direct wages percentage rate. This method can be used instead of the direct labour hour method where only slight variations occur in the rates of pay of different grades of workers.

	X £	Y £
Depreciation	18,000	15,300
Central Admin.		
Expenses	1,530	1,530
Fuel	2,700	3,150
Servicing	2,160	3,240
Tyres	3,240	3,780
Drivers remuneration	7.200	7,200
Total cost per annum	34,830	34,200
Add profit margin of 20 per cent	6,966	6,840
	41,796	41,040
Hourly rate	£46.44	£45.60

Buy Y: the annual cost is lower, as is the initial capital outlay

Workings	Machining £	Finishing £	Maintenance £	Materials Handling £
Overhead - period VI	5,600	4,300	3,800	3,500
Maintenance	2,280	1,140	− 3,800	380
Materials handling	1,164	1,940	776	− 3,880
Maintenance	466	232	− 776	78
Materials handling	23	39	16	− 78
Maintenance	10	6	− 16	-
	9,543	7,657		

Predetermined overhead absorption rates:

Machinery dept. $\dfrac{£9,000}{300}$ = £30 per machine hour

Finishing dept. $\dfrac{£7,500}{3,000}$ = £2.50 per direct labour hour

Therefore, overhead absorbed during period VI:

| Machining dept. | 292 x £30 | = | £8,760 |
| Finishing dept. | 3,100 x £2.50 | = | £7,750 |

(a)

Machining dept. production overhead account

	£		£
Overhead incurred	9.543	Overhead absorbed	8,760
		Under absorbed	783
	9,543		9,543

Finishing dept. production overhead account

	£		£
Overhead incurred	7,657	Overhead absorbed	7,750
Over absorbed	93		
	7,750		7,750

(b) Factors which give rise to the under/over absorption:

Machining dept. - Over-expenditure of overhead, and machine hours less than budget

Finishing dept. Over-expenditure of overhead, and direct labour hours more than budget.

(c)

Machining dept.		Finishing dept.	
	£		£
Over expenditure of overhead	543	Direct labour hours above budget:	
Loss of machine hours		100 x £2.50	250
8 x £30	240	less over-expenditure of overhead	157
Under absorbed	783	Over-absorbed	93

....

Answer 22   Under/over absorption of overhead   Question page 10

....

	Machining	Assembly	Tooling	Maintenance
	£	£	£	£
Overhead absorbed	11,400	7,300	5,000	2,500
Tooling department	3,500	1,000	−5,000	500
Maintenance dept.	1,500	900	600	−3,000
Tooling	420	120	− 600	60
Maintenance	30	18	12	−60
Tooling	9	3	−12	-
	16,859	9,341	-	-

Predetermined overhead absorption rates:

Machining department $\dfrac{£16,000}{400}$ £40 per machine hour

Assembly department $\dfrac{£9,600}{2,400}$ £4 per direct labour hour

Overhead absorbed during May:

Machining department	415 x £40	£16,600
Assembly department	2,350 x £4	£9,400

(a)
Maching Department
Overhead Account

	£		£
Overhead incurred	16,859	Overhead absorbed	16,600
		Under absorbed	259
	16,859		16,859

Assembly Department
Overhead Account

	£		£
Overhead incurred	9,341		9,400
Over-absorbed	59		
	9,400		9,400

(b)

Machining department	£	Assembly department	£
Over-expenditure of overhead	859	Under-expenditure of overhead	259
Additional hours - 15 x £40	600	Shortage of hours 50 x £4	200
Under-absorbed	259	Over-absorbed	59

Answer 23   Direct and indirect costs   Question page 106

(a)   Direct costs are those costs which can be easily associated with a particular product, job, contract or salcablc scrvicc. In job costing, dircct materials are materials that can be identified with a single job, and direct wages consist of the remuneration paid to employees whose efforts and skills are applied to individual jobs. Overhead, however, cannot be identified with specific jobs and has to be shared.

(b)   By recording the job number on purchase orders, goods received notes, material requisitions, time sheets and job tickets, and by keeping a separate account for each job, the cost of direct materials and direct labour can be ascertained for each job.

(c)   It is necessary to distribute the production overhead in such a way as to ensure that each job receives an appropriate charge. This is done by the process of overhead absorption; overhead is allotted to jobs by calculating overhead rates, usually predetermined. In calculating an overhead rate, one has to decide upon a suitable base in order to divide the overhead equitably between the various jobs.

Overhead Absorption has been defined as 'the allotment of overhead to cost units by means of rates separately calculated for each cost centre.' The basic information required comprises (a) the predetermined overhead cost for each production centre, and (b) data to calculate a suitable base, e.g. direct labour hours.

The methods most commonly used are the direct labour hour method, machine hours, direct wages percentage rate, direct materials percentage rate, prime cost percentage rate, and the unit cost rate.

In practice, there is the problem of deciding on the method of overhead absorption to adopt; also, estimating the overhead to be incurred and the level of activity.

Overhead Absorption

The following report deals with various methods of absorbing production overhead. I have considered five methods, and the report discusses the relative advantages and disadvantages of each.

Direct labour hour rate. As most production overhead costs fluctuate with the amount of time spent in manufacturing the product, this method has much to commend it. Its use means that production overhead is apportioned on the basis of the length of time taken to manufacture each item. However, this method is not suitable in those departments where operations are largely carried out by using plant and machinery.

Machine hour rate. This is the method which should be employed where production is largely mechanised, for overhead costs such as power, depreciation, maintenance and insurance are influenced by the extent to which machinery is used. A disadvantage of adopting this method is that it will be necessary to record the number of machine hours used in the manufacture of each product.

Direct materials percentage rate. This rate might be appropriate in those departments which manufacture products where perhaps the prime cost is made up almost entirely of direct materials. In such circumstances, the employment of an overhead absorption rate based on labour hours or costs might lead to an unfair charge in respect of production overhead.

Direct wages percentage rate. This rate could be used instead of the direct labour hour rate; it has the advantage of not being dependent on records of hours worked. However, where rates of pay for different grades of workers vary significantly, the use of this method would result in an unfair distribution of overhead, especially where production overhead is related to the amount of time spent on the manufacture of each product.

Cost unit rate. Where the units passing through a cost centre are the same, this is the easiest method to employ. But it cannot be used if the products passing through the cost centre are in any way dissimilar.

Signed ....

Management Accountant

Answer 26   Overhead absorption   Question page 107

To: The Chairman

Production Overhead Absorption Rates

The absorption rate, using the direct wages percentage method, is calculated by dividing the budgeted direct wages cost into the budgeted production overheads, and expressing the result as a percentage The rate is then used by applying it to cost units. For example, if direct wages of £10 were to be expended on the manufacture of a product, then a charge of £20 (assuming a 200 per cent rate) would be made to the product to cover production overhead. Next year, the charge will be £30.

Put simply, two factors contribute to the increase; an increase in budgeted overhead and/or a reduction in direct wages. The latter can be caused by a reduction in activity due to loss of orders. If the bu budgeted overheads tend to be mainly fixed in nature, as opposed to variable, it would not be possible to reduce them to the same extent as the reduction in activity. Increased mechanisation could also be a factor. The acquisition of new plant and machinery would cause an increase in the amount for budgeted depreciation; at the same time, manual labour would probably be reduced.

In this last example, an increase in the rate might bring about a lower total cost figure. If, for example, the wages to be paid to produce product X are to be cut by 50 per cent because of a deliberate policy of mechanisation, then, although the overhead will be higher due to additional depreciation and maintenance expenditure, the higher overhead absorption rate will be applied to a much reduced direct labour charge.

Signed ....

Cost Accountant

	Mechanical £	Electric £
Sales	325,000	225,000
Direct materials	150,000	165,000
Direct labour	50,000	24,000
Prime cost	200,000	189,000
Factory overhead	17,250	22,750
Factory cost	217,250	211,750
Administration overhead	16,000	14,000
Marketing overhead	9,750	6,750
Total cost	243,000	232,500
Profit/(loss)	82,000	(7,500)

Unit cost and profit for each model:

	Mechanical	Electric
Number of models sold	5,000	3,000
	£	£
Direct materials	30	55
Direct labour	10	8
Prime cost	40	63
Factory overhead	3.45	7.58
Factory cost	43.45	70.58
Administration overhead	3.20	4.67
Marketing overhead	1.95	2.25
Total cost	48.60	77.50
Profit/(loss)	16.40	(2.50)
Sales	65.00	75.00

Comments:

1. A degree of caution is necessary when seeking to interpret the above figures; for example, the basis for apportioning overhead is often arbitrary.

2. Also, no analysis is provided of fixed and variable costs: the Electric may have made a valuable contribution to profit, although shown in the accounts as a loss.

Workings:

Direct materials -		£
	Opening stock	45,000
	Purchases	324,000
		369,000
	Closing stock	54,000
		315,000

Factory overhead

	Mechanical £	Electric £	Total £
Indirect labour	5,000	10,000	15,000
Power	3,900	2,600	6,500
Depreciation	5,400	7,200	12,600
Remainder	2,950	2,950	5,900
	17,250	22,750	40,000

Administration overhead

	Mechanical £	Electric £	Total £
Computer bureau's charge	6,500	4,500	11,000
Remainder	9,500	9,500	19,000
	16,000	14,000	30,000

Answer 28   Direct and indirect costs   Question page 108

	£	£
Direct materials cost 100 x £3.50		3,500
Direct wages cost 5 x 120 hours x £1.50	900	
Bonus - time saved:		
Yew 40 hours		
Elm 20 hours		
Fir 30 hours		
90 x £0.50	45	
		945
Special pack		250
Processing costs		850

Production overhead (Rate $= \dfrac{£19,200}{9,600} = £2$ per hour).

		£
600 hours x £2		1,200
		6,745

Selling price		10,000
less Quantity discount		1,500
		8,500
Profit		1,775

(b) Problems which company may experience if it receives a bulk order from the American department store:

    (i)   availability of materials, labour and working capital;
    (ii) the price to be negotiated;
    (iii) estimating the cost of material, labour and overhead in future periods.

Answer 29   **Overhead absorption**   **Question page 10⁹**

Current overhead absorption rate using direct wages percentage rate:

Budgeted overheads	£225,000
Budgeted direct wages	£150,000
Rate, therefore	150 per cent

(b) Production overhead charged to job 657:

150 per cent of £170   £255
Production cost, therefore:

	£
Direct materials	190
Direct wages	170
Production overhead	255
Production cost	615
Gross profit	205
	820

(c)(i)

Disadvantages of using blanket overhead rates.

Overheads absorbed by departments - job 657

	A	B	C	Total
Using blanket direct wages percentage rate	£150	£90	£15	£255
Using suggested departmental rates	£120	£24	£30	£174

Production overheads often vary between departments. For example, one department might employ expensive machinery, and the depreciation charged to that department may cause the overheads to be comparatively high. Cost units which pass through that department only, should be charged for the costly facilities they use.

    (ii) Departmental rates

Budget information	A	B	C
Production overheads	£120,000	£30,000	£75,000
Direct labour hours	-	50,000	25,000
Machine hours	40,000	-	-
Rates			
Direct labour hour rate	-	£0.60	£3.00
Machine hour rate	£3.00	-	-

(d)   Overhead absorbed by job 657

A £120, B £24, C £30, Total £174

(e)   Over/under absorption using Direct Wages Percentage Rate

Overhead absorbed = 150 per cent of £140,000 = £210,000
(A=£45,000,B=£120,000,
C=£45,000)

Overhead incurred = £130,000 − A
                   = £ 28,000 − B
                   = £ 80,000 − C

Therefore, under/over absorption =

A	£85,000	under
B	£92,000	over
C	£35,000	under
Total	£28,000	under-absorbed

Using suggested rates

	A £	B £	C £
Overhead absorbed	135,000	27,000	90,000
Overhead incurred	130,000	28,000	80,000
Under/over absorption	5,000	(1,000)	10,000

Total = £14,000 over absorbed

Answer 30   **Contract cost accounts**   Question page 141

B Construction Limited

Contract Accounts

£000		£000
Jan 3 Materials issued to site	161	Jan 3 Materials returned from site	14
Wages	68	Oct 31 Plant c.d.	86
Plant, at cost	96	Materials on site c.d.	24
Hire of plant and machinery	72	Cost to date c.d.	361
Supervisory staff:direct	11		
indirect	12		

	Head office charges	63		
Oct 31	Wages accrued c.d.	2		
		485		485

Oct 31	Cost to date b.d.	361	Oct 31	Value of work certified	400
	Profit and loss account	43		Cost of work not certified c.d.	40
	Profit in suspense c.d.	36			
		440			440
Nov 1	Cost of work not certified b.d.	40	Nov 1	Wages accrued b.d.	2
	Plant b.d.	86		Profit in suspense b.d.	36
	Materials on site b.d.	24			

(b) Profit based on formula:

$$\text{Notional estimated} \times \frac{2}{3} \times \frac{\text{cash received}}{\text{value of work certified}}$$

$$= \quad £79,000 \times \frac{2}{3} \times \frac{£330,000}{£400,000} = £43,450 \text{ (rounded to £43,000)}$$

Although it is normally imprudent to anticipate profit before the completion of a job, in contract costing some account must be taken of profit to date. Where contracts are uncompleted at the end of an accounting year, some estimate of the profit must be made and included in the annual accounts. In making an estimate, it must be borne in mind that, although the contract may appear to be proceeding according to plan, problems could occur in the future before the contract is finished.

It is necessary, therefore, to make a conservative estimate, taking into account the length of time before completion and the likelihood of defects occurring in the future. The formula used is thought to be an acceptable basis for arriving at the profit to date. Not only is the notional profit reduced by one-third, but a further reduction is made to take account of cash not yet received, i.e. money retained by the customer to protect him from faulty work which may not be apparent at the time.

(c)
Balance Sheet (extract)
As at 31st October 1978

	£000		£000	£000
Current Liabilities		Fixed Assets		
Wages accrued	2	Plant, at cost	96	
		Depreciation to date	10	
				86

Current Assets
Materials on site   24
Work in progress (361 less
progress payments of 330
plus profit of 43)   74
                                        98

Answer 31   **Process costing** Question page 142

Process Account

	lbs	£		lbs	£
Material A	400	500	Finished stock	3,000	7,500
Material B	3,000	1,200	Work in progress c.d.	400	800
Supervision		300			
Operators' wages		3,000			
Overhead		3,300			
	3,400	8,300		3,400	8,300

Equivalent production:

	Cost £	Equivalent production lbs	Cost per lb. £
Materials	1,700	3,400	0.50
Labour and overhead	6,600	3,300	2.00
			2.50

Work in progress:

		£
Materials	400 lbs x £0.50 per lb	200
Labour and overhead	300 lbs x £2.00 per lb	600
		800

Sections (a) and (b) on next page

Process 1 Account

	Units	Unit Cost £	Amount £		Units	Unit Cost £	Amount £
Raw material	5,000	1,50	7,500	Normal loss in process	750	1.00	750
Direct labour			8,525	Transferred to process 2	4,500	5.00	22,500
Direct expenses			5,975				
Abnormal gain	250	5.00	1,250				
	5,250		23,250		5,250		23,250

Process 2 Account

	Units	Unit Cost £	Amount £		Units	Unit Cost £	Amount £
Transferred from Process 1	4,500	5.00	22,500	Normal loss in process	450	1.50	675
Material			2,040	Transferred to finished stock	4,000	9.00	36,000
Direct labour			7,920	Abnormal loss	50	9.00	450
Direct expenses			4,665				
	4,500		37,125		4,500		37,125

Process accounts continued on next page

Normal Loss Account

	£		£
Process 1	750	Scrap sales	500
Process 2	675	Abnormal gain	250
		Scrap sales	675
	1,425		1,425

Abnormal Gain Account

	£		£
Normal loss	250	Process 1	1,250
Costing profit and loss	1,000		
	1,250		1,250

Abnormal Loss Account

	£		£
Process 2	450	Scrap sales	75
		Costing profit and loss	375
	450		450

Answer 33   Process costing   Question page 143

(a) Job costing has been defined as 'that form of specific order costing which applies where work is undertaken to customers'special requirements'. (I.C.M.A. Terminology) This method of costing is applicable where the business receives orders for work which is peculiar to the needs of individual customers: each job, therefore, is likely to be different from the next.

On the other hand, process costing is particularly suitable for the costing of standardised goods where individual orders cannot be related to the goods being produced. The cost of each unit is ascertained by averaging the total costs over the number of units produced. This method is used, for example, in industries which are engaged in the manufacture of chemicals and paper, and in oil refining.

Process accounts continued on next page

Process 1 Account

	Kg.	Cost per kg. £	Amount £		Kg.	Cost per kg. £	Amount £
Materials	10,000	0.70	7,000	Normal loss in process	500	0.16	80
Mixing labour			860	Output transferred to Process 2	9,200	1.00	9,200
Overhead			1,720	Abnormal Scrap	300	1.00	300
	10,000		9,580		10,000		9,580

Process 2 Account

	Kg.	Cost per kg. £	Amount £		Kg.	Cost per kg. £	Amount £
Transferred from Process 1	9,200	1.00	9,200	Normal loss in process	1,000	-	-
Materials	10,800		11,700	Output - Packing Dept.	18,000	1.22	21,960
Mixing labour			740	Work in process	1,000	1.16	1,160
Overhead			1,480				
	20,000		23,120		20,000		23,120

	Cost £	Equivalent production	Cost per kg. £
Input from Process 1, plus materials	20,900	19,000	1.10
Mixing labour and overhead	2,220	18,500	0.12

Therefore, output cost equals:

	£
Input from process 1 plus materials, 18,000 x £1.10	19,800
Labour and overhead, 18,000 x £0.12	2,160
	21,960

Work in process: Input plus material, 1,000 x £1.10	1,100
Labour and overhead, 500 x £0.12	60
	1,160

Abnormal Scrap Account

	£		£
Process 1	300	Scrap sales - 300 x £0.16	48
		Costing Profit and Loss	252
	300		300

Packing Dept. Account

	£
Output transferred from Process 2	21,960

Process A Account

	Kg.	Cost per kg. £	Amount £		Kg.	Cost per kg. £	Amount £
Material X	40,000	0.20	8,000	Normal loss	10,000	0.15	1,500
Labour			258	Transferred to pro.B	29,600	0.25	7,400
Overhead			742	Abnormal loss	400	0.25	100
	40,000		9,000		40,000		9,000

Process B Account

	Kg	Cost per kg. £	Amount £		Kg.	Cost per kg. £	Amount £
Transferred from pro.A	29,600	0.25	7,400	Normal loss	3,960	0.15	594
Material Y	10,000	0.50	5,000	Finished stock	36,000	0.35	12,600
Labour			128				
Overhead			540				
Abnormal gain	360	0.35	126				
	39,960		13,194		39,960		13,194

Normal Loss Account

	£		£
Process A	1,500	Scrap sales	1,500
Process B	594	Scrap sales	540
		Abnormal gain	54
	2,094		2,094

Abnormal Loss Account

	£		£
Process A	100	Scrap sales	60
		Costing profit and loss	40
	100		100

Abnormal Gain Account

	£		£
Normal loss	54	Process B	126
Costing profit ans loss	72		
	126		126

Answer 35   Process costing   Question page 145

Process 1

	Units	Cost per unit £	Amount £		Units	Cost per unit £	Amount £
Raw material	10,000	0.60	6,000	Normal loss	1,000	0.20	200
Direct materials			8,500	Output transferred to Process **2**	9,200	2.50	23,000
Direct wages			4,000				
Direct expenses			1,200				
Production overhead (75%)			3,000				
Abnormal gain	200	2.50	500				
	10,200		23,200		10,200		23,200

Answer 35 continued

Process 2

	Units	Cost per unit £	Amount £		Units	Cost per unit £	Amount £
Output transferred from Process 1	9, 200	2.50	23,000	Normal loss	460	0.50	230
Direct materials			9,500	Output transferred to Process 3	8,700	5.00	43,500
Direct wages			6,000	Abnormal loss	40	5.00	200
Direct expenses			930				
Production overheads			4,500				
	9,200		43,930		9,200		43,930

Process 3

	Units	Cost per unit £	Amount £		Units	Cost per unit £	Amount £
Output transferred from Process 2	8,700	5.00	43,500	Normal loss	870	1.00	870
Direct materials			5,500	Finished goods	7,900	9.00	71,100
Direct wages			12,000				
Direct expenses			1,340				
Production overhead			9,000				
Abnormal gain	70	9.00	630				
	8,770		71,970		8,770		71,970

Answer 35 continued

Abnormal Loss

Process 2	£		£
	200	Scrap sales	20
		Costing profit and loss	180
	200		200

Abnormal Gain

	£		£
Normal loss - process 1	40	Process 1	500
Normal loss - process 2	70	Process 3	630
Costing profit and loss	1,020		
	1,130		1,130

(b) (i) Normal loss. This is the loss likely to occur under normal conditions. It is often estimated on the basis of past results and expressed as a percentage of the input to the process.

(ii) Abnormal loss. A loss which exceeds the normal loss and which is transferred to Costing Profit and Loss Account.

(iii) Abnormal gain. This is where the loss in process is less than expected. This gain, like the abnormal loss, is transferred to Costing Profit and Loss Account.

(iv) Scrap. Discarded material, having some recovery value, which is usually either disposed of without further treatment or re-introduced into the production process in place of raw material.

(v) Waste. Discarded substances having no value.

Process Account

	Kg.	Cost per kg. £	Amount £		Kg	Cost per kg. £	Amount £
Material	8,000	0.80	6,400	Normal loss	1,200	0.50	600
Wages			1,200	Finished stock	7,000	1.10	7,700
Overhead			480				
Abnormal gain	200	1.10	220				
	8,200		8,300		8,200		8,300

Normal Loss Account

	£		£
Process account	600	Scrap sales	500
		Abnormal gain	100
	600		600

Abnormal Gain Account

	£		£
Normal loss	100	Process account	220
Costing profit and loss	120		
	220		220

Answer 30 continued

Process 2 Account

	Units	£		Units	£
Work in progress b.d.	8,000	96,000	Transferred to process 3	7,200	147,600
Refining material		31,594	Work in process c.d.	800	13,510
Wages		23,940			
Overhead		9,576			
	8,000	161,110		8,000	161,110

Equivalent units:

	Cost £	Equivalent units	Cost per unit £
Opening work in process	96,000	8,000	12.00
Refining material, wages and overhead	65,110	7,600	8.50
			20.50

Work in process:

	£
Refining material, wages and overhead 460 x £8.50 per unit	3,910
Opening work in process 800 units x £12 per unit	9,600
	13,510

(a)   A by-product is a product which is recovered incidentally from the material used in the manufacture of main products. After further processing, the by-product can be sold to earn additional revenue; alternatively, it can be used again in the manufacturing process instead of purchasing new material. The value of a by-product would be small in relation to the value of main products.

A joint product, on the other hand, is not produced merely by the way, but, like other main products, it comes into being because it is the deliberate intention of management to produce it.

(b)

Product	Production (tonnes)	Selling price per tonne £	Sales value of production £000	Process costs £000	Cost per tonne £	Closing stock tonnes	Closing stock amount £000
J	5,000	100	500	300	60	1,000	60
K	8,000	125	1,000	600	75	2,000	150
L	5,000	80	400	240	48	500	24
M	3,000	200	600	360	120	300	36
			2,500	1,500		3,800	270

The costs have been apportioned using Sales Value of Production and it is assumed that this represents a reasonable basis. If, for example, one or two products have to undergo further processing after the point of separation, this method of apportionment would be unsuitable as it would produce an inequitable distribution of costs.

Workings

Calculation of absorption rates :	X	Y	Z
Works overhead	£5,000	£7,200	£9,600
Direct labour hours	12,500	36,000	64,000
Works overhead rate per direct labour hour	£0.40	£0.20	£0.15
Administration overhead	£2,870	£14,686	£8,978
Works cost	£20,500	£41,960	£89,780
Administration overhead as percentage of works cost	14	35	10

Cost Ledger Sheet   Job 707

	X £	Y £	Z £	Total £
Direct materials	650	940	230	1,820
Direct wages	800	300	665	1,765
Works overhead	400	80	105	585
Works cost	1,850	1,320	1,000	4,170
Administration overhead	259	462	100	821
Total cost	2,109	1,782	1,100	4,991
Profit, 20 per cent of total cost				998.20
Selling price				5,989.20

Workings

Calculation of overhead absorption rate: $\dfrac{£10,000}{17,500}$ = £0.60 per direct labour hour

Calculation of overhead absorbed:

	Job 1	Job 2	Job 3
Direct wages	£528	£451	£308
Direct hours (divided by £1.10)	480	410	280
Overhead absorbed (multiply by £0.60)	£288	£246	£168

(a) (i)   Cost Accounts

	Job 1 £	Job 2 £	Job 3 £
Purchases	215	- -	46
Stores issues	2,752	2,341	1,473
	2,967	2,341	1,519
Returns to stores	71	-	-
Cost of materials	2,896	2,341	1,519
Direct wages	528	451	308
Overhead absorbed	288	246	168
	3,712	3,038	1,995
Sales	4,500		
Profit	788		

Overhead Control Account

	£		£
Overhead incurred	800	Overhead absorbed	702
		Overhead under-absorbed -	
		transferred to Costing	
		Profit and Loss	98
	800		800

Work in Progress Control Account

	£		£
Purchases	261	Returns to Stores	71
Stores Issues	6,566	Transferred to Costing	
Direct Wages	1,287	P. & L. - Job No.1	3,712
Overhead Absorbed	702	Balance c.d.	5,033
	8,816		8,816
Balance b.d.	5,033		

(iii)

Costing Profit and Loss Account

	£		£
Cost of Sales	3,712	Sales	4,500
Overhead under-			
absorbed	98		
Net profit	690		
	4,500		4,500

(b) Estimated cost of job No.1   3,675
     Actual cost   3,712

     Adverse variance   37

Explanation of variance:

Materials	46 A
Direct wages - rate variance 480 x 5p	24 A
- less hours, 20 x £1.05	21 F
Overhead - less hours 20 x £0.60	12 F
	37 A

Possible causes:

Materials variance - higher consumption than planned
 - higher price than estimated
Wages variance - higher rate negotiated by employees
 - higher productivity

Answer 40   Cost accounts Question page 162

Raw Materials Stock

	£		£
Balance b.d.	146,138	Factory overhead	10,680
Cost Ledger Contra	85,440	W.I.P. - Materials	106,800
		Balance c.d.	114,098
	231,578		231,578

Work in Progress - Materials

	£		£
Balance b.d.	28,480	Finished Goods Stock	113,920
Raw Materials Stock	106,800	Balance c.d.	21,360
	135,280		135,280

W.I.P.- Labour

	£		£
Balance b.d.	44,500	Finished Goods Stock	144,180
Cost Ledger Contra	149,520	Balance c.d.	49,840
	194,020		194,020

W.I.P. - Factory Overhead

	£		£
Balance b.d.	11,125	Finished Goods Stock	36,045
Factory overhead	37,380	Balance c.d.	12,460
	48,505		48,505

Finished Goods Stock

	£		£
Balance b.d.	7,298	Cost of Goods Sold	284,711
W.I.P. - Materials	113,920	Balance c.d.	16,732
- Labour	144,180		
- Factory Over-			
head	36.045		
	301,443		301,443

Cost of Goods Sold

	£		£
Finished Goods Stock	284,711		

•••

Answer 41   Cost accounts   Question page 163

•••

(a)   Work in Progress

	£		£
Balance b.d.	9,600	Finished Stock	19,680
Direct labour	3,600	Balance c.d.	7,200
Production overhead			
absorbed	2,880		
Raw materials	10,800		
	26,880		26,880

Finished Stock

	£		£
Balance b.d.	12,000	Cost of Sales	23,760
Work in progress	19,680	Balance c.d.	7,920
	31,680		31,680

Raw Materials Stock

	£		£
Balance b.d.	14,400	Work in Progress	10,800
Creditors	8,400	Balance c.d.	12,000
	22,800		22,800

Workings

Debtors

	£		£
Balance b.d.	8,400	Bank	28,800
Sales	29,700	Balance c.d.	9,300
	38,100		38,100

Creditors

	£		£
Bank	7,200	Balance b.d.	6,400
Balance c.d.	7,600	Raw Materials	8,400
	14,800		14,800

Bank

	£		£
Balance b.d.	2,000	Direct labour	3,600
Debtors	28,800	Creditors	7,200
		Production overhead	3,200
		Marketing overhead	1,200
		Admin. overhead	800
		Balance c.d.	14,800
	30,800		30,800

(b)

Profit and Loss Account
for the month of October 1978

	£		£
Cost of Sales	23,760	Sales	29,700
Production overhead under-absorbed (£3,200 − £2,880)	320		
Marketing overhead	1,200		
Administration overhead	800		
Net Profit	3,620		
	29,700		29,700

Balance Sheet
As at 31st October 1978

	£		£	£
Capital	45,000	Fixed Assets		5,000
Net Profit for month	3,620	Stocks:		
	48,620	Raw materials	12,000	
		Work in progress	7,200	
Creditors	7,600	Finished stock	7,920	
				27,120
		Debtors		9,300
		Bank		14,800
	56,220			56,220

$$= 9,600$$

Journal

		Dr. £	Cr. £
Oct 8	Stores ledger	1,900	
	Cost ledger contra		1,900
9	Work in progress	1,000	
	Stores ledger		950
	Materials price variance		50
10	Cost ledger contra	95	
	Stores ledger		95
13	Production overhead	200	
	Stores ledger		190
	Materials price variance		10
16	Work in progress	700	
	Stores ledger		665
	Materials price variance		35
16	Work in progress	100	
	Production overhead		100
17	Stores ledger	950	
	Cost ledger contra		950
20	Production overhead	100	
	Stores ledger		95
	Materials price variance		5
21	Work in progress	600	
	Stores ledger		570
	Materials price variance		30
24	Cost ledger contra	190	
	Stores ledger		190
28	Stores ledger	95	
	Materials price variance	5	
	Work in progress		100
31	Stock adjustment	40	
	Stores ledger		38
	Materials price variance		2

(a)	£000	£000
Profit per financial accounts		57
Add Debenture interest	2	
Discount allowed	8	
Administration overhead over absorbed	10	

Selling and distribution overhead over-absorbed	14	
		34
		91
Less Interest received	1	
Discount received	3	
Interest on capital	30	
Notional rent	20	
Production overhead under-absorbed	15	
Difference in stock valuation	21	
Profit per cost accounts		90
		1

(b) Although interest on capital is a financial item, some cost accountants choose to include it in the cost centre accounts. They charge a notional amount to each cost centre based on the amount of capital employed in the cost centre. It is argued that if, for instance, one department requires a lot of plant and machinery, that department is consuming a high proportion of the company's capital, and capital has to be paid for in terms of interest and dividends.

Furthermore, where premises are owned by a business, there is no cost incurred in renting property. But some cost accountants are of the opinion that a notional charge for rent should be made to cost centres for the use of buildings that they occupy.

Answer 44 **Break even calculations** Question page 192

	£
Previous year: Sales 13,000 x £5	65,000
Variable cost 13,000 x £4	52,000
Contribution	13,000
Fixed costs	18,000
Profit/(loss)	(5,000)
Current year: Fixed costs	21,000

Selling price £6

First 10,000 units will provide a contribution of £5,000 (10,000 x £0.50 per unit)

Therefore a contribution of £16,000 still required to cover fixed costs of £21,000

Contribution per unit, above 10,000, equals £1 per unit.

A further 16,000 units, in addition to 10,000 units, must be sold.

Sales at BEP, then, equals 26,000 x £6, £156,000

(b) Contribution on additional 4,000 units = £4,000. Therefore, profit on sale of 30,000 units is £4,000.

••

Answer 45   Break even calculations   Question page 19:

••

(a) Cost of additional 2,000 units:

	£	Cost per unit (£)
Material	6,000	3.00
Labour	4,000	2.00
Overhead	3,000	1.50
	13,000	6.50

Therefore, variable cost of 6,000 units:

	£
Material	18,000
Labour	12,000
Overhead	9,000

Fixed cost, therefore:

	£
Labour	3,000
Overhead	2,700
	5,700

(b)
$$BEP = \frac{Fixed\ cost}{Contribution\ per\ unit} = \frac{£5,700}{£1.50} = 3,800\ units$$
(sales = £30,400)

••

Answer 46   Cost plus pricing calculations   Question page 193

••

		£	£
Materials -	Heywood	2.30	
-	Helix	0.35	
-	Packing	0.75	
-	Container	0.60	
			4.00
Labour -	Fitters	0.45	
-	Polishers	0.05	
			0.50
Variable overhead - 0.6 hours x £0.90			0.54
Fixed overhead - 0.6 hours x £1.50			0.90
Cost			5.94

Profit ($33\frac{1}{3}$ per cent on sale price is equivalent
to 50 per cent on cost)   2.97

Selling price (for 10)   8.91

Selling price (for 1)   =   £0.89 or £0.90

Workings: Budgeted hours   =   40 x 48 x 5   9,600

$$\text{Variable overhead rate} = \frac{£8,640}{9,600} = £0.90 \text{ per hour}$$

$$\text{Fixed overhead rate} = \frac{£14,400}{9,600} = £1.50 \text{ per hour}$$

Answer 47   **Marginal costing and decision-making**   **Question page 193**

Profit and Loss Budget

	Edinburgh £000	York £000	Gloucester £000	Total £000
Sales	440	400	700	1,540
Contribution- 25 per cent	110	100	175	385
Branch expenses	60	61	83	204
Central office costs	44	40	70	154
Total costs	104	101	153	358
Profit/(loss)	6	(1)	22	27

York branch provides a contribution of £100,000, The closure of the branch would save £91,000. Therefore, York factory should remain open.

Answer 48   **Break even calculations**   **Question page 194**

Contribution per unit = £9.80 − £9 − £0.80

$$BEP = \frac{\text{Fixed cost}}{\text{Contribution per unit}} = \frac{£12,600}{£0.80} = 15,750 \text{ units} (£154,350)$$

(b)   Contribution per unit = £9.80 − £8.40 = £1.40

$$BEP = \frac{£22,400}{£1.40} = 16,000 \text{ units } (£156,800)$$

(c)   in (a) the margin of safety is 18,000−15,750 units i.e. 2,250 (£22.050)

in (b) the margin of safety is 18,000−16,000 units,i.e. 2,000 (£19.600)

(a)   'Cost behaviour' relates to the manner in which costs respond to movements in the level of production or sales. Variable costs, in total, tend to vary in direct proportion to changes in the volume of production or sales, whereas fixed costs are relatively unaffected by such changes. However, there is a point when even fixed costs become variable. If production increases substantially, additional facilities may be required, for example, extra floor space. Furthermore, inflation affects both fixed costs and variable costs.

The efficiency of management's decisions will often depend on the extent to which cost behaviour is understood. The fixing of selling prices, and decisions on the nature and quantity of products to be sold must take into account the fact that fixed costs are relatively unaffected by movements in the volume of production or sales.

(b)   Firstly, reduce the costs of periods 2, 3 and 4 to period 1 levels

$$\text{Period 2} - £3,256 \times \frac{100}{110} = £2,960$$

$$\text{Period 3} - £4,560 \times \frac{100}{120} = £3,800$$

$$\text{Period 4} - £5,800 \times \frac{100}{125} = £4,640$$

The differences in units and costs between periods 1 and 2 are:

300 units costing £3,600   = £1.20 per unit

Variable costs, therefore, at period 1 cost levels are
Period 1 — 1,500 x £1.20 = £1,800
    2 — 1,800 x £1.20 = £2.160
    3 — 2,500 x £1.20 = £3,000
    4 — 3,200 x £1.20 = £3,840

Fixed costs are therefore £800, e.g. period 1, £2,600 − £1,800
In period 5 the estimated variable cost is:

$$4,000 \times £1.20 \times \frac{135}{100} = £6,480$$

Fixed cost will be £800 x $\dfrac{135}{100}$ =   £1,080

Total cost   £7,560

Period 1

	Marginal £000	Absorption £000
Sales	64	64
Direct costs	40	40
Fixed overhead	20	20
	60	60

less closing stock:
2,000 x variable cost of £4 per
unit ... 8

$£60,000 \ x \cdot \dfrac{2,000}{10,000}$ ... 12

Cost of Sales	52	48
Profit	12	16

Period 2

Sales	96	96
Opening stock	8	12
Direct costs	40	40
Fixed overhead	20	20
	68	72
Profit	28	24

(b)   Under marginal costing, only variable costs are charged to cost units. Fixed costs are written off against the sales of the period in which they occur; consequently, they are not included in closing stock. In absorption costing, fixed and variable costs are absorbed at the point of manufacture, and a proportion of all costs, including fixed, will be included in the valuation of closing stock.

As a lower stock valuation produces a lower profit figure, the use of marginal costing will give lower profits on an operating statement in those periods when production exceeds sales. However, when the sales during a costing period exceeds production, as in period 2, marginal costing will show a higher profit figure.

	Factory £	Stores £	Office £
Selling price	1.75	1.86	1.90
Marginal cost	1.12	1.25	1.30
Contribution per unit	0.63	0.61	0.60

Mild steel required: 2,000 x 0.84 = 1,680 square metres
                        2,400 x 0.78 = 1,872 square metres
                        1,600 x 0.75 = 1,200 square metres
                                       4,752 square metres

Contribution per square metre of limiting factor, i.e. mild steel:

Factory $\dfrac{£0.63}{£0.84}$ = £0.75

Stores $\dfrac{£0.61}{£0.78}$ = £0.782

Office $\dfrac{£0.60}{£0.75}$ = £0.80

Therefore, concentrate production on Office, then Stores.

Office   1,200 sq.metres used to provide contribution of
          1,600 x £0.60   = £960

Stores   1,300 sq.metres used to provide contribution of

$$2,400 \times £0.61 \times \frac{1,300}{1,872} = £1,017$$

Total contribution   = £960 + £1,017   = £1,977

(b) However, before management decides to adopt the above production pattern, it must consider whether there is an outstanding commitment to supply Factory shelving during the month. Furthermore, would long term sales of Factory shelving be jeopardised by failing to produce that product for an entire month?

Management must also consider whether an alternative source of supply exists, elsewhere in Europe perhaps.

It should be noted that in the calculations above, direct labour is considered a variable cost. But what will the direct labour force do during this period of reduced production? The shortage of steel is not within their control, and if the industrial dispute is likely to be settled quickly, then presumably the machinists and sprayers will be paid for idle time and not laid off. One would therefore need to investigate the composition of direct labour pay to ascertain whether it is strictly variable.

••

Answer 52   Margin of safety and contribution   Question page 196

••

(a) (i)   The contribution/sales ratio is contribution expressed as a percentage of sales, e.g.

	£
Selling price per unit	2.00
Marginal cost	1.20
Contribution	0.80

$$\text{Contribution/sales ratio} = \frac{\text{Contribution}}{\text{Sales}} \times 100$$

$$= \frac{£0.80}{£2.00} \times 100$$

$$= 40 \text{ per cent}$$

(ii)   The margin of safety is the excess of normal or actual sales over sales at break-even point. The excess sales is usually expressed as a percentage of either normal sales or actual sales. Using the above figures, let it also be assumed that fixed costs are £9,000 per annum and normal sales are 15,000 units per annum.

$$\text{BEP} = \frac{\text{Fixed costs}}{\text{Contribution per unit}} = \frac{£9,000}{£0.80} = 11,250 \text{ units} \atop (£22,500 \text{ sales value})$$

Excess of normal sales over sales at break-even point
$$= 15,000 - 11,250$$
$$= 3,750 \text{ units}$$

Margin of safety, therefore is $\dfrac{3,750}{15,000} \times 100 = 25$ per cent

(b)   Contribution/sales ratio is 40 per cent, margin of safety is 25 per cent. The profit/sales ratio is found by applying the contribution /sales ratio to the margin of safety, thus: 40 per cent of 25 per cent = 10 per cent. This can be verified as follows:

Sales   = 15,000 x £2 = £30,000
Profit = Contribution less fixed costs
        = (15,000 x £0.80) − £9,000
        = £12,000 − £9,000
        = £ 3,000, i.e. 10 per cent of sales.

(c)   The percentage margin of safety indicates whether the business is susceptible to a drop in the volume of sales. A narrow margin of safety would mean that a slight decline in volume might have a significant effect on profits.

(d)   Current year: Variable costs £80, contribution £40, Contribution /sales ratio $33\frac{1}{3}$ per cent.

Forthcoming year : Material £66, labour £20, variable overhead £6, variable cost £92. Selling price therefore = £92 x $\dfrac{100}{66\frac{2}{3}}$ = £138

Percentage increase required = 15 per cent

Answer 53   Marginal costing and eecision-making   Question page 196

(a) Contribution   = fixed cost + profit
                    = £275,000 + £85,000
                    = £360,000
     Contribution per unit = £6
     Therefore, expected sales = 60,000 units

Strategy	Selling price per unit £	Contribution per unit £	Estimated sales	Total contribution £
1	9.50	5.50	66,000	363,000
2	9.30	5.30	72,000	381,600
3	9.00	5.00	75,000	375,000

Strategy number 2 is the most profitable.
(b) Management would have to consider the degree of risk involved in each of the strategies; for example, the second and third strategies rely heavily on increased volume and if this is not forthcoming, there is every chance that even the original contribution would not be achieved. Management should also consider the availability of materials, labour and working capital.

Answer 54   Marginal costing   Question page 197

1975 Sales at 1974 price levels   = $\dfrac{720}{1.2}$ = 600

(a) Marginal cost of sales on 600, based on 1974 ratios, should be:
     $600 \times \dfrac{390}{650}$ = 360

     Actual is 340, therefore *saving of £20,000*
(b) 720 − 600; therefore *saving of £120,000*
(c) Reduction in sales volume: 650 − 600

     Contribution lost = $50 \times \dfrac{260}{650}$ = £20,000 *reduction of profit*

(d) Fixed costs have increased by £20,000. Therefore *reduction of £20,000 profit.*

Summary (a) = £20,000
        (b) = £120,000
        (c) = (£20,000)
        (d) = (£20,000)
             £100,000

Answer 55   Marginal costing   Question page 197

Original Budget

	X	Y	Z	Total
Selling price	£40	£50	£60	
Marginal cost	£30	£30	£32	
Contribution per unit	£10	£20	£28	
Sales (units)	8,000	6,000	10,000	24,000
Total contribution	£80,000	£120,000	£280,000	£480,000

Fixed cost £12 x 8,000 = £96,000
         £15 x 6,000 = £90,000
         £18 x10,000 = £180,000

		£366,000
Profit		£114,000

(ii)   Budget at Maximum Sales Demand

	X	Y	Z	Total
Contribution per unit (as above)	£10	£20	£28	
Sales (units)	10,000	7,500	12,500	30,000
Total contribution	£100,000	£150,000	£350,000	£600,000
Fixed cost (as above)				£366,000
Profit				£234,000

Answer 56   Marginal costing   Question page 198

D Limited
Profit Forecast
for year ending 30th June 1979

	£000	£000
Sales (150,000 jars)		450
Material cost	71.25	
Direct wages cost	135.30	
Variable overhead:		
Production	41.25	

Selling	22.50	
Distribution	29.70	
Variable cost		300
Contribution		150
Fixed cost		126
Profit		24

(b) The increase in volume of 50 per cent does not compensate for the reduction in selling price from £4 to £3. It is more profitable therefore to maintain selling price and volume at existing levels.

(c)

Profit Statement

	£000	£000
Sales (100,000 jars)		440
Material cost	50	
Direct wages cost	90.2	
Variable overhead:		
Production	27.5	
Selling	22	
Distribution	19.8	
Variable cost		209.5
Contribution		230.5
Fixed cost		126
Profit		104.5

	£
(d) Profit	110,000
Fixed cost	126,000
Contribution	236,000
Variable cost	209,500
Sales	445,500

Selling price per jar £4.45½
Price increase = £0.45½, 11.375 per cent on £4.00

••

Answer 57   Marginal and absorption costing   Question page 199
••

(a) Marginal

	March		April	
	£000	£000	£000	£000
Sales		500		600
Variable production				
costs	250		300	
Variable selling costs	50		60	
		300		360
Contribution		200		240

	March		April	
Fixed costs	139		139	
Profit	61		101	

Stock valuation at end of March is 2,000 units x £25 = £50,000

(b) Absorption

	March		April	
	£000	£000	£000	£000
Sales		500		600
Opening stock	-		66.5	
Cost of production	399		349	
Less Closing stock				
$399 \times \frac{2}{12}$	66.5		–	
		332.5		415.5
		167.5		184.5
less selling expenses	64		74	
less administration expenses	26		26	
		90		100
Profit		77.5		84.5

To: Managing Director,

Effect of increases in Direct Wages

I have shown below the two alternatives being considered regarding the current pay claim, namely, (a) an increase in the hourly rate for all direct workers of 10 per cent, and (b) the introduction of a productivity deal with a bonus of £0.08 for every unit produced.

	Existing budget £000	£000	Alternative (a) £000	£000	Alternative (b) £000	£000
Sales		2,400		2,400		2,565
Direct Materials	480		480		540	
Direct wages	720		792		828	
Variable production overhead	108		108		121.5	
Variable selling overhead	120		120		128.25	
Variable distribution overhead	96		96		108	
		1,524		1,596		1,725.75
Contribution		876		804		839.25
Fixed cost		556		556		556
Profit		320		248		283.25

It is recommended that the Bonus alternative is pursued. However, three uncertain factors should be taken into consideration; union reaction, the likelihood of achieving the volume of sales predicted and whether the estimate of Work Study relating to production will be achieved.

A direct cost is a cost which can be easily identified with a particular product or saleable service, e.g. wages paid to workers who transform raw material and components into a finished product.

(b)   An indirect cost cannot be identified with a particular product or service; an element of sharing is involved, and there is therefore a need to apportion the costs between two or more products. Examples include rent, rates, electricity, office salaries.

(c)   An overhead absorption rate is a rate calculated in order to allot overhead to cost centres, i.e. to products or saleable services. The direct labour rate is an example; this is calculated by dividing the estimated overhead cost attributable to a cost centre by the appropriate number of direct labour hours.

(d)   The budget period for which the budget is prepared and used This is usually a year and coincides with the organisation's financial year.

	A	B	C
Budgeted sales (units	20,000	15,000	8,000
Contribution per unit	£5	£8	£10
Therefore, contribution	£100,000	£120,000	£80,000

	£
Total contribution	300,000
Fixed labour costs	110,000
Budgeted profit	190,000

Recommendations:
(a)   Increase in contribution = 25 per cent

of £300,000	75,000
Advertising campaign	65,000
Increase in budgeted profit	10,000
Therefore, budgeted profit	200,000

(b)   Elimination of fixed labour costs   110,000
Increase in variable labour costs:

Product A	£40,000
B	£15,000
C	£40,000
	95.000

| Increase in budgeted profit | 15,000 |
| Therefore, budgeted profit | 205,000 |

(c) Budgeted sales x contribution per unit

A	30,000 x £3	90.000
B	22,500 x £6	135,000
C	12,000 x £8	96,000
		321,000
	Fixed costs	110,000
	Budgeted profit	211,000

Option (c) is to be recommended because it gives the highest budgeted profit.

Answer 61   Budgeting and marginal costing   Question page 218

	A	B	C	D
Contribution per unit	£4	£6	£8	£9
Contribution per £1 of material	£0.44	£0.50	£0.47	£0.45

	Units	Contribution per unit £	Contribution £	Material £
Manufacture product B	5,000	6	30,000	60,000
C	5,000	8	40,000	85,000
D	2,750	9	24,750	55,000
			94,750	200,000
Fixed costs			80,000	
Profit			14,750	

Answer 62   Cash budgets   Question page 218

Workings

Material used - July £30,000.   Stock level at end of month-£66,000
Aug. £31,500   £70,500
Sept £34,500   £75,000
Oct. £36,000   £72,000
Nov. £39,000
Dec. £33,000

Purchases - July = £30,000 less stock reduction of £6,000 = £24,000
Aug = £31,500 plus stock increase of £4,500 = £36,000
Sept = £34,500 plus stock increase of £4,500 = £39,000

Cash Budget

	July £	Aug. £	Sept £	July - Sept. £
Balance at start of month	10,000	(5,100)	(600)	10,000
Receipts: Cash Sales	4,000	4,200	4,600	12,800
Debtors(2/3)	17,400	24,000	25,200	66,600
Debtors(1/3)	8,200	8,700	12,000	28,900
	29,600	36,900	41,800	108,300
Payments: Creditors	36,000	24,000	36,000	96,000
Rent	1,500	1,500	1,500	4,500
Salaries,wages and commision.	4,800	5,100	5,000	15,400
Rates	800			800
Other expenses	1,600	1,800	2,000	5,400
	44,700	32,400	45,000	122,100
Balance at end of month	(5,100)	(600)	(3,800)	(3,800)

Answer 63 **Subsidiary budgets**

Question page 219

Workings

		A £	B £
Direct materials cost	M1	5	2
	M2	5	6
Direct wages cost	W1	12	15
	W2	12	5
Fixed production overhead,£0.80 per hour		16	12
Cost of production		50	40
Admin.selling and distribution costs		10	8
Total cost		60	48
Profit- 25 per cent of cost		15	12
Selling price		75	60

Production budget

	Units	Units
Sales	50,000	80,000
Increase in finished goods stock	10,000	10,000
Production	60,000	90,000

Direct materials cost budget

Material M1 - Product A	60,000 units x 10 kilos	600,000 kilos
B	90,000 units x 4 kilos	360,000 kilos
		960,000 kilos

@ £0.50 = £480,000

Material M2 - Product A	60,000 units x 5 kilos	300,000 kilos
B	90,000 units x 6 kilos	540,000 kilos
		840,000 kilos

@ £1 = £840,000

Purchases budget
M.1. £480,000—£80,000 decrease in stock = £400,000 = 800,000 kgs
M.2. £840,000— £60,000 increase in stock = £900,000 = 900,000 kgs

Direct wages budget
W.1 Product A 60,000 hours x 8 hours = 480,000 hours
   B 90,000 hours x 10 hours = 900,000 hours

1,380,000 hours @ £1.50 = £2,070,000

W.2 Product A 60,000 hours x 12 hours = 720,000 hours
   B 90,000 hours x 5 hours = 450,000 hours

1,170,000 hours @ £1.00 £1,170,000

Answer 64   Budgetary control   Question page 22

(a) (i) Quarterly budgets should take account of the additional activity during the summer months.

(ii) A more detailed approach to budgeting is required. To add 16 per cent across the board produces meaningless targets. Costs are influenced by price and usage.

(iii) To divide by 4 means that price movements throughout the year are ignored. If the annual increase in wages occurs half way through the year, this should be reflected in the budget for wages in the latter six months.

(b) Comparison of actual results against fixed budget. Reasons for variances. Analysis of variances by cause.
(c) During preparation of budget, segregate fixed and variable costs. Provide monthly reports, so that prompt corrective action can be taken. Three months is usually too long to wait in order to see whether the budget is being attained.

Answer 65 Comparison of budgetary control and standard costing Question page 243

Both techniques involve accounting for variances between actual results and a predetermined plan. In both cases, variances are investigated and corrective action taken. Standard costing involves estimating the costs of products and services. Budgetary control, on the othet hand, is concerned with estimating the costs of all areas of the business, including overhead expenditure and capital expenditure. Another difference is the amount of detail involved in the preparation of predetermined costs. In standard costing, the process of predetermining costs is more exact than in budgetary control. A standard is calculated for each operation that makes up the manufacture of each individual product.

Answer 66 Preparation of standard costs Question page 244

(a) The standard cost of direct materials is made up of two separate components, namely, price and usage. With regard to usage, an allowance will have to be made for unavoidable losses, such as wastage during the production process. The technical specification, or bill of materials, will provide details of quantity, quality, dimensions,part numbers, sizes and description of material.
The purchasing department will supply material prices, which should allow for expected movements in price levels during the budget period.
The technical specification, or operations list, provides the information to enable labour standards to be set. Against the description of each operation should be noted the machine to be used to fulfil the task and the category of labour employed on the task. The setting of standards for labour is closely related to the technique of work study.
The estimated rate of pay will depend on existing wage rates and expected future settlements during the budget period.
(b) Expected standards, as opposed to ideal standards, recognise that some wastage in manufacture is unavoidable. Consequently, targets will take this fact into account, but, at the same time, will seek to minimise the extent of inefficient operating. Such realistic standards are more likely to produce a response from the work force.

Ideal standards, on the other hand, assume the absence of spoiled work, breakdown of plant and machinery, faulty materials, etc. Management and workers are likely to become dispirited because of their inability to achieve such unrealistic targets.

Answer 67 Variance analysis (material) Question page 244

Standard cost of actual production 30 x 250 x £1.20		£9,000
Actual quantity x standard price 7,450 x £1.20		£8,940
Actual cost		£9,076
Usage variance £9,000 − £8,940		£60F
Price variance £ £8,940 − £9,076		£136 A
Total variance		£76A

Work in Process Account

	£		£
Materials	9,076	Price variance	136
Usage variance	60		

(b) Limitations:
The causes of the variances have still to be established.
The variances cannot always be related to individual responsibility.

Answer 68 Variance analysis (labour) Question page 244

	A £	B £	C £
Standard cost	5,330	4,180	3,192
Actual hours x standard rate	5,681	3,971	3,260
Actual cost	5,986	3,682	3,132
Efficiency variance	351A	209F	68A
Rate variance	305A	289F	128F
Total labour variance	656A	498F	60F

(b)
Rate variances. Investigate grades of workers used and compare with technical specification; also, level and timing of wage settlements compared with standards. Efficiency variations. Investigate current methods of production, machines used, extent of machine breakdown and spoiled work, availability of materials, operator efficiency.

Material variances

	£
Standard cost 70 x £5.98	418.60
Actual quantity x standard rate 1,017 x £0.46	467.82
Actual cost	563.00
Usage variance	49.22 A
Price variance	95.18 A
Total material cost variance	144.40 A

Labour variances

	£
Standard cost 70 x £51.30	3,591.00
Actual hours x standard rate 1,841 x £1.90	3,497.90
Actual cost	3,572.00
Efficiency variance	93.10 F
Rate variance	74.10 A
Total labour cost variance	19.00 F

(b) These variances will be a starting point for further investigation. If possible, they should be further analysed and related to individual responsibility.

Materials

	£
Standard cost of actual production $\dfrac{2,020}{40}$ X £100	5,050
Actual quantity x standard price 52 x £100	5,200
Actual cost	5,096
Usage variance	150 A
Price variance	104 F
Total material cost variance	46 A

Labour

	£
Standard cost of actual production $\dfrac{2,020}{50}$ x 20 x £1.25	1,010
Actual hours x standard rate 40 x 20 x £1.25	1,000
Actual cost 3 x £1.30 x 40 = £156	
2 x £1.20 x 40 = £ 96	
15 x £1.25 x 40 = £750	1,002
Efficiency variance	10 F
Rate variance	2 A
Total wages cost variance	8 F

$$\text{Overhead - Absorption rate} = \frac{£288,000}{96,000} = £3 \text{ per unit}$$

Overhead absorbed 3,020 x £3	6,060
Budgeted overhead $\dfrac{£288,000}{48}$	6,000
Actual overhead	6,200
Volume variance	60 F
Expenditure variance	200 A
Overhead cost variance	140 A

Answer 71   Operating statements   Question page 246

Workings

Materials	£	
Standard cost of actual production 9,860 x £1.25	12,325	
Actual quantity x standard price 24,720 x £0.50	12,360	
Actual cost	12,300	
Usage variance	35	A
Price variance	60	F

Wages		
Standard cost of actual production 9,860 x 5p	493	
Actual hours x standard rate 380 x £1.25	475	
Actual cost	490	
Efficiency variance	18	F
Rate variance	15	A

Fixed overhead		
Fixed overhead absorbed 98.6 x £5	493	
Budgeted overhead 100 x £5	500	
Actual overhead	525	
Volume variance	7	A
Expenditure variance	25	A

Sales		
Actual quantity x Standard selling price 9,860 x £1.50	14,790	
Actual sales	14,750	
Price variance	40	A
Difference in quantity x standard contribution 140 x £0.15		
Volume variance	21	A

Operating Statement
for week ended 26th November 1976

	£	£
Budgeted profit		1,500
Add favourable variances		
Materials price	60	
Labour efficiency	18	
		78
Less Adverse variance		1,578
Materials usage	35	
Wage rate	15	
Overhead volume	7	
Overhead efficiency	25	
Selling price	40	
Sales volume	21	
		143
Actual profit		1,435

Answer 72   Variance analysis   Question page 246

(i) The standard cost of direct materials comprises two separate components: price and usage. With regard to usage, the technical specification, or bill of materials, will provide the details of the description of materials, the dimensions, part numbers, quantities and quality. The purchasing department will supply details of prices, but these must take into account price rises that are likely to occur during the period in which the standards are to be used.

The technical specification, or operations list, will indicate the various operations required in order to manufacture each product. Against the description of each operation will be noted the machines to be used to fulfil each task, the department in which the manufacturing process is to be carried out and the category of labour to be employed. The grade of worker to be used on each operation will have to be decided and his anticipated rate of pay during the period in question.

(ii) The direct materials cost variance is the difference between the standard cost of direct materials specified for the production achieved and the actual cost of direct materials used. The variance can be broken down into two sub-variances: price and usage. The direct wages cost variance is the difference between the standard direct wages specified for the production achieved and the actual direct wages incurred. This variance can also be further analysed: efficiency and rate variances are its two components.

The purpose of variance analysis is to compare actual performance with the predetermined standard cost so that deviations from plan can be investigated and corrected.

(b) **Workings**

Materials £

	£
Standard cost of actual production 240 x £108	25,920
Actual quantity x standard price 2,640 x £9	23,760
Actual cost	26,400
Usage variance	2,160 F
Price variance	2,640 A
Materials cost variance	480 A

Labour £

	£
Standard cost of actual production 240 x £20	4,800
Actual hours x standard rate 2,520 x £2	5,040
Actual cost	5,544
Efficiency variance	240 A
Rate variance	504 A
Wages cost variance	744 A

Statement of material and labour variances
Week ended 12th November 1977

	£	£
Standard cost of actual production (240 units)		30,720
Add Adverse variances:		
Materials price	2,640	
Labour efficiency	240	
Wages rate	504	
		3,384
		34,104
Less Favourable variance:		
Materials usage		2,160
Actual cost		31,944

Index